PERSPECTIVES ON EGYPT, ISLAM, AND THE DARK ERA OF TRUMP

Dr. Yassin El-Ayouty, Esq.

Copyright © 2019 Dr. Yassin El-Ayouty, Esq.

All rights reserved.

ISBN: 9781795000963

TABLE OF CONTENTS

FOREWORD ....

Not by Walls But by Integration - Canada Builds a Strong Nation 1

Ask Not What's Wrong With Islam - Ask What's Wrong With Its Understanding!! 5

The Goring of America's Governance By Trump's Bullying Arrogance!! ...11

Where Has the Majesty of Law Gone? Contributing To the Pain of Nine-Eleven By Abra-Cadabra Legislation!! 21

In Trumpism I Can't See The Face of The United States 27

Viewing the U.N. And Its Charter From the Perspective of Realism 33

With the Fall of 2012, Legitimacy of the Muslim Brotherhood Had Collapsed!! 39

In The Nile Valley, Two Heroes of Unity: One, Since 3100 B.C., Is Celebrated; The Other, Since 1954 A.D., Is Ignored. 45

"Not My President!!" Screamed The Millions Against Trump!! So Do I!! ...51

Egyptian Mythology Regarding America's Love for the Muslim Brotherhood 59

Launched By Trump, A War of Cultures Has Begun!! 67

Under Trump, The Arrival of A Chaotic "American Spring!!" 77

Uncanny Similarity Between Donald Trump and Deposed Egyptian President Mohamed Morsi 81

Fake News About Truth and Victory, Across Pages of Modern History 85

Striking Syria Is a Legal Strike For Humanity!! 89

Do Not Blame Instability on Foreign Conspiracies - Blame It on Marginalizing Minorities 95

Series of Failed Mischief By the Muslim Brotherhood In Egypt and Abroad!! 99

The New American Rebellion: Cities and States Against Trump 105

The Imperial Presidency of Donald The Mindless 109

The Fiftieth Anniversary of the Arab Calamity Caused by Nasser 117

Peering Through Middle Eastern Fog: Wahhabism Receding, Ottomanism Rising 123

The Ottoman Evil Spirit In Trump's White House 127

Judging By His UN Speech, Trump Should Be Certified "Insane"!! 131

A Foolish American Interpretation of Egyptian-Russian Relations 137

A Rare Arab Occurence: Judging Leaders By Their Peformance 143

With Trump As Captain, The Ship of State Is Sinking 149

Getting to Know the State of Kuwait 155

Absolute Justice For All: The Islamic Judicial Magna Carta Of Omar, In the 7th Century AD 159

Guantanamo Bay? Human Rights Laws Have Never Lived There!! 165

The Historic Abandonment: The Present US Department of Justice Neither Defends Nor Enforces Civil Rights 171

By Invitation: In January, the Rabbi Was Unable To Go To Al-Azhar, But In May, Al-Azhar Was Able To Go To the Rabbi 179

Why is America's War In Afghanistan Another Endless Vietnam!! Unwinnable!! 183

From the Abbasids (656-1258 AD) To the Muslim Brotherhood (1928-2013 AD): The Abuse of Islam As a Political Power Tool 187

Like a Piece of Swiss Cheese: American Democracy Has Many Holes In It!! 191

65 Years Ago, My Professor at Rutgers University Predicted the Emergence of an American Dictator! 195

The Ugly Faces of Foreign Intervention In Internal Affairs 199

When Journalism Becomes a Tool For American Imperialism 205

Mr. Attorney General Sessions: Why Did You Deport Due Process - The Pillar of Justice? 209

The Genius of the Prophet Muhammad: From the Desert, Laying the Foundation of A Mighty Muslim Nation 215

From a Mayor and a Prosecutor to a Huckster and an Imposter: The Rise and Fall of Rudolph Giuliani 221

We Shall Need MAGA After the EXIT of President Gaga!! 225

Since 1882, The Rise of Egyptian Democracy Found Its Main Protector: The Egyptian Armed Forces 231

A SUNSGLOW Occasion Enriching the Global Debate on Immigration 237

What A Bad Day for America At the UN!! An Avalanche of Contradictions By Donald Trump and of Laughter At Him 241

What a Shame!! The U.S. Supreme Court Is No Longer "Supreme" 245

The American President Is "Analfabeto" (In Spanish: "Illiterate") 249

To Achieve Ordered Liberty, Governance and Religion Have to be Kept Apart 253

Adopting a Muslim Brotherhood Refrain: Brainless Trump Calls El-Sisi "A F... Killer!!" 257

The Rule of Law vs. The Rule of Trump!! 263

Below the Mason-Dixon Line There Is Another America With a Mind of Its Own 269

ABOUT THE AUTHOR 273

FOREWORD

As a blogger, my focus has been in three directions: Egypt after Mubarak; the New Islamic Religious Revolution; and America's attitudes towards both Egypt and the Islamic Revolution by which terrorism is being fought.

This volume is a continuum of earlier volumes on the same topics. The only difference is the time span –from 2016 to 2018. No more volumes may be expected thereafter, as I transit, under urging by my wife, Grace, and our son, Joseph to write my autobiography. I am in the process of heeding that call.

The title chosen for this book, "Perspectives on Egypt, Islam, and the Dark Era of Trump" encapsulates the subject matter. This is although the issues are underpinned by international law and international organization.

This and prior volumes were produced with the superb technical help of our webmaster, Mr. Raymond Chan.

The encouragement of both Grace El-Ayouty and our son Joseph has played a large part in my going forward with my ever present passion for writing analytically and otherwise.

Perspectives on Egypt, Islam and the Dark Era of Trump

NOT BY WALLS BUT BY INTEGRATION - CANADA BUILDS A STRONG NATION

Friday, September 2, 2016

These are reflections on my 64th annual anniversary. It was on August 27, 1952 that I sailed from Alexandria, Egypt, as a Fulbright scholar to New York City, my first journey outside of the land of the Nile. A journey by sea of 21 days aboard the Ex Cambion of the then famed American Lines.

Born to an Islamic scholar, and a mother who traced her lineage to Imam Al-Hassan Ibn Imam Ali, the cousin of the prophet Muhammad, I turned to my turbaned father seeking one last advice before boarding that beautiful vessel. In his ear, I whispered: **"How should I live in America, and how to maintain my classic Arabic language?"**

His answer was: **"Live as they live."** As to classic Arabic, I shall mail to you a copy of the speeches of Imam Ali Ibn Abi-Taleb. Entitled **"The Path To Eloquence."** It is, after the Quran, the highest form of the Arabic language.

That fatherly counsel held me in good stead for 64 years in North America. It liberated me from the strictures of my life in Egypt, and opened the door to my initial UN employment- chief of the Arabic Language Section, UN radio. I married a Catholic wife, still my beloved spouse for 46 years, and became an honorary member, since 1974, of a Jewish reform temple, in Great Neck, Long Island. And after early retirement from the UN, I now, aside from law practice, teach **"Islamic Law and Global Security"** at Fordham University. A Jesuit institution, I am also adjunct professor at St. Francis College.

Thus, in America, I kept on observing my Azhari father's advice: **"live as they live"** a part of the American model of **"the melting pot,"** the fusion of several cultures within the pot of Americanism. Not a bad model for a nation of immigrants to whose flag I swore allegiance. This is although it does not recognize my duality of citizenship, both Egyptian and American. To me, no conflict. You can be a brother and a cousin at the same time.

Yet, my abhorrence of the alarming statements of an ignoramus like Donald Trump calling for a Muslim ban and a wall against Latin immigration, inspired me to look at the Canadian model of **"integration,"** not of **" fusion."** A model akin to the UN system which allows all employees to travel to their countries of origin. The rationale is simple: observe the UN Charter through service to the entire membership, but keep your civilisation roots intact. Put in other words, integrate your culture within the broader context of multiplicity.

This is the essence of Canadian nation-building. Not by walls and nativism/chauvinism. But by the creation of a two-way cultural highway: from the country of origin to Canada, and from Canada, the values of harmonious diversity.

These are not mere empty words about the higher-value Canadian model. It is a model reflected fully in government deeds and the public square realities. Both fitting neatly the alphabet of globalization in this puzzling age of rage. No dysfunctional Trumpist ideology of faith tests, Nazi-like reliance on vigilantism, no cozying up to strong-arm dictatorships.

Just witness Canada's welcome of new comers from areas like Syria and Iraq. Witness Prime Minister Justin Trudeau at Canadian airports. Putting warm jackets on the backs of immigrant children. Watch him dance at a Philippino cultural festival. On August 20, that young and photogenic P.M.. whose father I served at the UN, being enthusiastically welcomed in Toronto at the **"Taste of Manila."** The Toronto Star reported on the chants of onlookers **"Justin, Justin."** Declared the PM that differences were a source of strength that makes communities stronger.

Or watch the arrivals at the Lester Pearson airport in Toronto, standing by the curbside at Terminial One of Air Canada. And observe the greeters and the greeted: Somalis, Syrian, Bangladeshis and others. A tower of Babylon, speaking happily in a multitude of languages, hugging each other outwardly, and hugging the Canadian model of integration under their colorful shirts, Sikh turbans, or Muslim veils.

Or observe the provincial and federal support of non-governmental organizations engaged in the on-going Canadian enterprise of integration at all levels. Bolstored by free education, health insurance, and freedom of expression.

And when a cultural hurdle arises, the Canadians have no hesitation to seek advice. Such as when some Syrian refugees balked at eating Canadian food. Reason: an ill-placed fear that utensils were used in eating pork products, a culinary prohibition in Islam. So I was asked to provide an opinion (a fatwa-like explanation). In response, I wrote that water was a purifier. Washing those utensils made them wholesome. Veracious eating began in earnest. The Canadian model of nation-building through integration also has a substantial security side-effect. It is countering the lunatic ideology of Jihadisim. Confronting, and eventually decimating the likes of ISIS and Boko Haram, are not by the force of arms alone. Ideology is an in dispensable supportive weapon. For Islamic Law (Sharia) properly defines **"Allahu Akbar"** not as a battle cry. Its legal meaning is **"all humans are equal before God, regardless of faith."**

A true reflection of the Canadian model in an all-encompassing secular sense!! It is not by walls but by integration, Canada builds a strong nation.

DR. YASSIN EL-AYOUTY, ESQ.

ASK NOT WHAT'S WRONG WITH ISLAM - ASK WHAT'S WRONG WITH ITS UNDERSTANDING!!

Friday, September 9, 2016

Bernard Lowis was dead wrong by asking: **"What Went Wrong With Islam."** So was his disciple, the Somali Ayaan Hirsi Ali, an Islamophobe whose last of four books is entitled: **"Why Islam Needs a Reformation Now."** Both of them, in my view as a specialist in Islam, have missed a central fact. Islam, as a faith, is constantly self-renewing through interpretation.

This is called **"The Tafseer (interpretation) Jurisdiction."** Thus between the two unalterable bases for Islamic Law (Sharia), namely the **Quran, and the Hadith** (the latter for the ascertainable utterances and conduct of the Prophet Muhammad), stands Tafseer.

In other words, Tafseer, otherwise meaning **ijtihad** (the application of common sense to the text) is akin to the soft tissue between the vertebrae of Islam's backbone. That soft tissue prevents the pain of one bone colliding with another.

Tafseer, an element in the formulation of **fatwas** (a non-binding opinion on a matter of religion), functions also if there is no text. It is called **"The Non-Text Jurisdiction."** It is an extrapolation of a rule from precedent.

To illustrate: If I am asked: **"What would a Muslim astronaut in outer space face while praying?"** My response would be **"His Mecca is where his capsule rotates."** Now where do I base my fatwa on? **Outer space is its own universe.** Not unlike the vast desert of the **Empty Quarter in southern Arabia,** on a cloudy day, with no compass to point to

Mecca. That astronaut, let us call him **Ali (meaning the ever-high)** and his co-religious **Ahmed (another name for Muhammad)** stand in the same footing. With no shoes, but with faith.

Understanding Islam should begin by the realization of the following facts about Islamic practice: Islam equates between all faiths; no one has the authority to call another **"an apostate;"** gender equality is ensured; the law of inheritance is supplemented by legislation; ritual and human transactions are separate one from another; **"modesty"** in female appearance does not necessarily mean a **"niqab"**

It also calls for the realization that: **jihad** is self-defense and self-policing against debased urges; and the **Caliphates ended 1400 years ago** with the bloody termination of the reign of **Ali Ibn Abi Taleb, Muhammad's cousin.**

As to the vocabulary of Islam and its law (Sharia), the following words and terms do not even exist: **"sword;" "holy war."** The word **"Muslim"** does not refer only to adherents of Islam. It denotes any human being who submits his/her will to that of the Creator. And **"Allahu Akbar,"** is not a battle cry. It means **"all humans are equal before the One Creator."**

In Islam, **judges** are to be defendant-oriented; **adultery** is made impossible to prove. (It requires four witnesses to be present); and **women** have the same rights and obligations as those for men. **Self-sacrifice** is abhorred; **all places of worship** are to be protected and revered; **dictatorships** should be toppled; and **worship should be made easier, not an oppression chore.**

Above all, **intent** is a basic determinant of culpability; **corruption** is to be tackled by both law and improved life conditions; and **dialogue** is a means to clearing up misunderstandings.

There is no Sunni Islam and Shii Islam. There is one faith, with a variety of contrasting practices; **the State authority** should be respected; and **local laws** should be the norm for regulating the conduct of Muslims and non-Muslims alike.

Contrast the above list which I have kept to bare essentials with the following **modes of departure** by Muslims. And of **incomprehension** by non-Muslims:

Does jihad mean the killing of the innocent or of the non-Muslim? **Of** course not.

Are these crimes against humanity to be funded by the so-called charitable foundations in the Muslim world? **No!!** Aiding and abetting the commission of a crime makes the supporter complicit in perpetrating those heinous crimes.

Doesn't the Quran state in Chapter V/32: **"We prescribed to the children of Israel that whoever kills a soul, unless it be for retaliation or because of spreading corruption on earth, it would be as if he had killed all mankind ...?"** It does.
Is retaliation or evaluation of corruption a justification for any Muslim to take the law in his/her hand for the purpose of injuring another? **No.** This is called **"self-help,"** not sanctioned by any law unless the person is cornered at their home and has no duty to retreat.

Is murderous jihadism justified by past colonial maladministration? **No.** Decolonization, UN membership, and bilateral treaties have all put an end to the prolongation of these past grievances. And acceptance of foreign aid puts an end to the myth that there is no statute of limitations to those past misdeeds.

In light of the above, there is no **"collective punishment"** in Islam as a faith, or in Sharia (Islamic Law) as a legal system. Back to the Quran: **"God does not impose on any soul a burden greater than it can bear; it receives every good that it earns, and it suffers every evil that it earns..."** (Chapter II/286).

More on point: **"While He is the Lord of all things, every soul is accountable for itself; no bearer of burdens bears the burden of another..."** (Chapter VI/164).

There is an urgent need to reform the thinking of Muslims about their own faith. Anecdotal evidence shows that the majority of Muslims have not read the **114 Chapters (Suras) of the Quran.** I am not boasting, but I am stating a personal fact. I have read those chapters nineteen times. I am now on reading number 20. **The more you read, the more you discover.** And this discovery is aided by the vast spectrum of interpretations.

But the context of my readings is already framed by one Islamic adage: **"God desires ease for you and not hardship."** (Chapter II/185) The theme of **"ease"** is repeated in the Quran **39 times. No mention of** theocracy. **No mention of a caliphate** -a human invention, not a religiously mandated system of governance.

In the Quran, I found no **reference to virgins awaiting in heaven those who kill themselves**
or others. Found **no** reference **to proselytization.** But found the need for explanation **(DAWA).** DAWA for harmonious interaction among all humans. So is it by sword that some marauding Muslims advocate for their faith? Here I let the Quran answer those misguided thugs: **"Call mankind to the way of your Lord with wisdom and sound advice..."** (Chapter XVI/125).

Even Muhammad was admonished in the Quran to steer away from arrogance in his call for faith. The Quran asserts as follows: **"It was by God's Mercy that you were kind to them; had you been harsh and hard of heart, they would have dispersed from around you... And consult them in the matter, and when you reach a decision, place your trust in God..."** (Chapter III/159).

On the other hand, **the non-Muslim world should also reform its outlook on Islam and Sharia. It takes two to tango!!** Unwittingly, that sector of humanity has unwittingly adopted the jihadi interpretation of Islam and its values as mouthed by the enemies of humanity. Evidence here abounds. Examples:
    that Islam is a faith of the sword;
    that the war on terror should be waged by a ban on Muslim immigrants;
    that the niqab is mandated by the Islamic faith;
    that the stoning for adultery, and the beheadings, and the severence of limbs, are all within the judicial sentencing mandated by Islam;
    that Muslims understand only force to cause them to submit;
    that dictatorship is the way of Islamic governance;
    that Sharia is meant to be spread world-wide to replace legislation;
    that Islamization is a global blueprint;
    that the Muslim world supports, outwardly or inwardly terrorism; and
    that western knowledge and teaching are non-Islamic.

All of the above is utter nonsense. Islamophobia is caused by both ignorant Muslims and ignorant non-Muslims. The two sides seem to be spoiling for endless war. It is not going to happen. But anxiety about it have caused 38 States of the 50 American States either to **ban Sharia or its mention in their courts.**

Books authored by ex-Muslims, like Ayaan Hirsi Ali, stand for those nonsensical misconceptions. On the dust jacket of her book **"Heretic,"** she posits provocative questions, basically of the red herring type. She says **"When a Muslim see you reading this book and says, 'I am offended, my feelings are hurt,' your reply should be: 'What matters more? Your sacred text? Or the life of this book's author?'"**

Ayaan: **those who threaten you for your book have not read their book (the Qura). Neither have you,** as you selectively picked certain verses from the Quran. Selections which have not been encapsulated into legislation. Except in retrograde theocracies, or in your unhappy land where Somali tribal experiences are the norm. Like genital mutilation which you suffered.

Sharia does not enter that dark realm of genital mutilation. And modern legislation in countries like **Egypt, Tunisia, Lebanon, Turkey,** has criminalized it. A prime example of correcting by man-made law the tribal seepage in monotheism. In your country of birth, women enslavement is common. But you have found undeserved fame for falsely claiming that the face of the Muslim world can only be seen through one narrow and ancient window. That of Somalia which is now a horribly failed State.

In the social sciences, including law, we always say that **faith is non-negotiable.** But Hirsi does not seem to comprehend that basic axiom. One of her calls is **for the need to re-write the Quran!!** Well, Ayaan, were you to ever fathom the meaning of faith, you might realize that **Islam's dogma is premised upon one central belief: The Quran is the word of God.** Therefore you need, if you ever could, to ask God (in Arabic, Allah) to produce your desired **"amendments."** If you succeed, give me a call!!

My dwelling on the perception gap between the Muslim and the non-Muslim worlds does not encompass the entire problem. **For perceptions are expressed in words in various languages.**

Here we have a real dilemma. The Muslim world at the mass level does not converse or read or write in **Chinese, English, French, Russian, or Spanish.** These, in addition to Arabic, are the UN-official languages. The reverse is true regarding non-Muslims in regard to Arabic.

Closing the gap needs a global linguistic remedy. 9/11 was hugely condemned by the Muslim world. Yet that condemnation did not register. On the contrary, it was misconstrued. Considered silence translated into a quiet approval.

All the above is not an advocacy for Islam. It is an advocacy for overcoming the ills of this age of rage, symbolized by Trumpism, and by its reaction to jihadism through a redirection of the global conversation regarding faith and governance.

Mixing faith with governance has proved to be a combustible mix. *Each of them should be observed as separate. With governance looking upon faith as a system of values, not a blue print for regulating human affairs.*

The hereafter should be left to the hereafter. Meaning: live and let live. And if you can't, then "Get a Life!!"

THE GORING OF AMERICA'S GOVERNANCE BY TRUMP'S BULLYING ARROGANCE!!

Friday, September 23, 2016

What a super weird phenomenon. That out of control bully called Donald J. Trump!! The more he lies, the more he is believed by his public which glorifies under-education. And the greater the manifestations of his shallowness in all matters, domestic or foreign, the louder he shouts **"Make America Great Again."**

Trump has positions on every issue. But what he adopts today, he changes tomorrow. When called on the flip flops, he assures his audiences that the reporting is to blame. Or he hires voices, civil and military, to explain the absence of coherence. They call such hired guns surrogates. **A surrogate is a substitute, a deputy.** Originally referring to the grantor of a marriage license. But that surrogateship is subject to unpredictable firing. So the surrogates, when boxed in by a media question, have found a firewall. They respond: **"Ask him."**

Donald Trump's vocabulary is rotative. His verbiage galaxy gravitates to a non-changing vocabulary. The words **"disaster," "terrible," "stupid," "crooked," "dishonest," "liar," "hell," "trust me," "sit down," "get him out," "phony,"** and **"loser,"** gush out constantly from his mouth. With lips pierced forward, and hands gesturing, and a face dripping of bullying arrogance.

His journey of 16 months in presidential politics has proved disastrous for this only super power, called the United States. Like a raging bull charging in all directions, he has gored both the union and the concept of **"State."** A practiced con man for two decades as a real estate tycoon turned entertainer, he has sensed an opening for coveting the **"oval office."** To Trump, governing and deal-making have the same modus operandi. So he proclaims to rapturous applause that **"no body can make deals like Trump."**

But America has a complex system. Many governments, from a municipal water authority to the state legislature, in every one of the fifty states. With a federal government of limited and enumerated powers. And with delicate checks and balances prescribed in the Constitution. And with an electoral system where voting for a president does not automatically elect that president. **There is an electoral college, changing demographics, varying state rules for validating the right to vote, and a competition limited largely to the Democratic Party and the Republican Party.**

Yes there is a durable Constitution which has survived unscathed for 240 years, which a defined yet overlapping jurisdictions for the three branches of government -Congress, the Executive, and the Judiciary. But the definition of **"a person"** has now been enlarged by a Supreme Court decision (in the case of **Citizens United**) to consider money as also endowed with a voice. Under the elastic theory of the freedom of expression. Thus donations to candidates for office are regarded, by that unhappy decision, as a variant of **"freedom of expression."** On top of all of that, **the Second Amendment to the Constitution grants everyone the right to bear arms.**

Yet America's governance is not akin to a Trump deal for running a casino or building a **"Trump Tower."** The Donald does not see it that way.

For him **"Make America Great Again"** is like another project where success depends on being a super-tough negotiator. **Ready to bamboozle the other side by either staring them down, walking out of the room, or offering enticements which may not be kept.**

This Trumpism has created a cancerous lack of trust by the average citizen in how America is run. An issue which I now predict, whether Trump wins or loses the presidency, shall contaminate faith in America's institutions. **The bond of trust between the government and the governed has been impaired.** Not necessarily for all time. That instinctive faith in America's exceptionalism, equality before the law, and the generational advancement towards a continuum of improvement, is fading.

Born to wealth, **Trump has been a life-long practitioner of using others as temporary tools.** His upbringing has never led to feeling the pain of the downtrodden. His real estate dealings, largely **dependent on gaming the system of taxation and finance,** are not conductive to giving. But to taking, under the guise of giving. His chances for military service, community service, volunteering for involvement with society for uplifting purposes, **were either avoided or evaded. Not thought of as worthy of his time.**

Trump's time has come to ride a wave of American unease about globalization, immigration, job outsourcing out of America, and the shrinkage of the whites demographics. **By 2030, the whites shall be 45% of the entire population.** Having a black president in the White House forced the racial issue to the surface. Or to the belief that if a black man can be president, **"so can I,"** a wealthy white deal-maker.

"I alone can fix it" is a Trump campaign slogan. Not conducive to learning from the experts. In fact, intended to downgrade experience in favor of **"gut feeling."** Politicians embedded in Congress, practicing the art of political longevity, gave a bad name to **"politician," "political correctness," "the ways of Washington,"** and **"business as usual."** A circular argument: **"If I am not doing well, the government is responsible."** So shrinking government, while despising it, has become the lifeblood of the Trump corpus of non-ideas for combative conservatism.

Topping all of this, is the fear from jihadism, which has splintered. Causing the conventional ways of defense and offense to become irrelevant. One single terrorist act anywhere stokes **the fires of rage, helplessness, and the need for brutalizing responses.**

So for month after month after month, Trump has been at it. **Goring the American system to satisfy the political circus.** A circus which he has been found to respond to his need for self-adoration **-narcissism. Thus arose the populist call for change -any change.** Trump's disconnected thoughts have been broadcast nearly constantly. Had Trump been forced to pay for that free publicity, **the cost would have been $2 Billions.**

The truth of the matter is that there is no end to the range of the Trumpist rage. He strikes in every direction. Here follow selections. **Limited here to the Executive,** described by Trump's wayward movement as rigged and broken.
- **About President Obama as a citizen:** He is illegitimate. **Why Donald?** He is probably born out of the U.S. Trump has thus acknowledged to be the profane author of **"the Birther Movement."** In

spite of his recent admission to the contrary as a price for gaining Afro-American support.

• **About Obama's professional credentials:** Trump claims that Obama's education at Harvard may be untrue.

• **About Obama's record as President:** "Weak;" "the worst President in the history of America."

• **About Hillary Clinton as Secretary of State:** "If elected to the presidency, she will be the continuation of the disastrous Obama years."

• **On Hillary's fitness for the Oval Office:** "She has a poor judgment;" "influenced by donations by the millions of dollars to the Clinton Foundation;" "a liar;" "exposed our national security to danger through her emails on a personal server." For Trump, it is always "Crooked Hillary."

• **On Hillary's advisors:** "She brought in Huma Abidin, possibly a member of the Muslim Brotherhood, to guide her decision-making."

• **On Founding ISIS:** "Obama and Hillary founded ISIS."

• **How about Secretary of State, John Kerry?:** Donald claims that he would make better deals than John Kerry. **"Kerry left the negotiations room where the Iran nuclear deal was being negotiated to ride a bicycle."** A characterization by a lunatic with zero experience in foreign affairs.

• **On foreign affairs:** "Wouldn't be nice to bring Russia in with us to fight ISIS?;" "Putin of Russia is a better president than Obama. He is strong; ours is indecisive." "I'll nullify the Iran nuclear deal on day one of my presidency."

• **On military matters:** Donald would replace the present generals by "my own generals;" "I'll make our military so strong that nobody would dare mess with us;" "Why do we have nuclear arms if we don't use them?;" "NATO is obsolete."

• **On terrorism:** Trump arrogantly claims to know more about ISIS **"than the Generals."** He claims to have a secret plan to deal with ISIS. A charlatan who avoided by subterfuge any form of military service, or for this matter, any national service.

And on and on, Trump projects **"the tough guy"** image. Without the benefit of any facts. Yet his blatant racism regarding blacks, Muslims, Latino has gone on for a year and a half unchecked. **Nicholas Kristof,** in a column in the **New York Times** of September 8, 2016, sums up the idiocy of Trumpism. Such an **admirable summation is difficult to ignore quoting from** with elaboration:

- **"Whether in his youth, in his business career or in his personal life, Trump's story is that of a shallow egoist who uses those around him;"**
- **"He made a mess of his personal life and has been repeatedly accused of racism, of cheating people, of lying, of stiffing charities;"**
- **"His life is a vacuum of principle, and he never seems to have stood up for anything larger than himself;"** and
- **"Over seven decades, there's one continuing theme to his life story: This is a narcissist who has no core. The lights are on, but no one's home."**

The Republican party, the party of Lincoln, has largely been hijacked by **that con man, Donald J. Trump.** What remains has been badly splintered. **This election for US president is undoubtedly the most important in our lifetime.**

Those in America who feel either angry, left behind, or disadvantaged, are flocking to the banner of Trumpism. If elected to the Oval office, the consequences for America and the world cannot be predicted. The only prediction is that the trust between the citizen in the US and his or her government is, as of now, shaken to its roots. **"The system must be changed"** has been a Trump advocacy. **"Trust Me,"** Trump keeps on repeating. Though his whole history is a tattered record of lying and cheating.

Serious damage has also been visited upon the quality of political discourse. Expletives have been liberally used. Incitement to violence by Trump against his detractors has become common place.

We now have a debased language, expressing misfacts, **propagated through his Nazi-like rallies, proclaiming the end of the American orderly system of governance.** A reminder of the pre-Nazi Weimar Republic. In favor of **"America First,"** dressed up in a racist vestments, brandishing the fear of **"soon we shall have no country."**

In all certainty, **that bully, win or lose, shall benefit.** If he loses, as I pray he would, Trump will relaunch his biggest **"reality show."** Blaming that loss on conspiracies. And if he wins, **the consequences cannot be but ominous.**

Mr. Trump: Here are reasons for my assessment: Your lying about your contacts with Russia for personal gain; **your appearance on the Kremlin TV to denigrate Obama, and American foreign policy;** your threat to nullify American defense commitments and trade agreements; your boasting about readiness to use nuclear arms against European allies; and your insane claim to single-handedly **"Make America Great Again."**

Furthermore, you have:

- Called for packing the U.S. Supreme Court with judges who will tilt that institution further to the right;
- Mocked the disabled, **falsely claimed seeing Muslims celebrating in New Jersey the criminal destruction of the World Trade Center;** denigrated women for their menstrual period;
- Attacked the media for fact-checking, and for calling you on your barrage of lies;
- Tweeted obscenities and was convulsively rattled for getting opposing tweets in return;
- Fabricated your health record by claiming that you are the healthiest person who have ever run for office; though refusing to divulge a credible health record;
- Insinuated that **those with guns might remove Hillary from the scene;**
- **Thought that Saddam and Qaddafi should have stayed in place to fight terrorism;**
- Continuously calling for an **American grab of Arab oil fields by the force of arms;**

- Called for punishing women for seeking abortion;
- Declared as a policy priority the deportation of eleven million undocumented immigrants now living in the U.S.;
- **Called for arming Japan, Saudi Arabia and South Korea with nuclear weapons;**
- Advocated the legality of water boarding as a means of extracting confessions from terrorist suspects;
- Insisted on calling criminal jihadists **"Islamic terrorists,"** though they, by their crimes, have opted out of Islam. Even when such criminal acts are committed by American citizens who happen to claim being Muslims;
- Kept on calling or insinuating that President Obama is **"a closet Muslim."** Which is patently an Islamophobic lie. Mr. Trump: **Islam is a faith not a disease.** What drips from your mouth in regard to Islam is what ISIS loves to exploit.

It was a Muslim immigrant **(Mr. Khizr Khan)** who had lost his son, a US army officer killed in a battle in Iraq, who publicly impugned your credentials as a patriot. On national TV, he challenged you on two main fronts: **Your knowledge deficit regarding the U.S. Constitution, and your moral deficit regarding sacrificing for your country.**

Holding aloft a copy of the U.S. Constitution, Mr. Khan intoned: **"Have you even read the U.S. Constitution?"** Then slammed you down on your narcissism, saying **"Have you ever sacrificed anything or anyone?"**

Your retort manifested your ignorance of the meaning of sacrifice. For you responded by parading **your record as a builder.** Khan meant nation-building. You, being alien to community giving, thought of hiring labor to construct **"Trump Towers"** as sacrifice for your nation. What an imbecile!!

Khan lost his son in the war on Iraq. Your sons from 3 marriages stand safe in shiny suits, **ready to inherit your ill-gotten gains.** Reason to support the return by America to compulsory military service. Might be a factor in slowing down congressional penchant for endless wars.

You are still adamantly refusing to divulge your tax returns, raising suspicions about whether you have even paid any taxes since 2008. Justifiable suspicions as you bragged about gaming the system and exploiting loopholes.

Your so-called charitable foundation is a means of enriching your **"deplorable"** self, causing the New York Attorney General to begin investigating it. And the case against the fraud called **"Trump University"** is going forward. Regardless of your racist attacks on the federal judge who presides over it. Calling that judge biased because of **"his Mexican ancestry."**

Sir, how can you expect this electorate to believe in your oft-repeated call on the public **"Believe Me."** It is a steep climb for anyone, but your own core crowd of **"America Firsters,"** to believe in you as a possible occupant of the Oval office.

You, Donald Trump, has received last week a dishonorable mention on the world stage. It was issued by none other than the **U.N. High Commissioner for Human Rights, Prince Zeid Raad Al-Hussein of Jordan. He slammed you down as among the politicians who "peddle fear to exploit economic hardship and social tension."**

Another deeply negative assessment of you, Mr. Trump, was voiced **in emails by General Colin Powell** of the U.S. Without mincing his words, he described you as "a national disgrace and an international pariah."

In the same vein, the US Congressional Black Caucus (CBC) responded to Trump's racism. Honoring in Washington, D.C. both Obama and Hillary Clinton on September 17, the CBC spokesmen let loose on Trump all kinds of epithets. Called him **"a racist," "a bigot,"** a **"fraud."** It was payback time for Trump's constant humiliation of America's first black president.

At that ceremony telecast on CNN internationally, Obama urged black voters to give him a befitting send-off. **"Vote for the continuation of my legacy,"** he urged his audience -meaning voting for Hillary. The symbiotic relationship between Trump and the **"Alt Right"** (extreme right) would undoubtedly, in a Trump presidency, destroy the Obama legacy.

That call for American **"national action now"** (Obama's words at that farewell ceremony) reverberated south of the border, and north of the border.

In Mexico, Trump's call for a wall along the southern border was met with derision. In his lunatic characterization of the Mexicans as **"rapists"** and **"drug dealers,"** he was advocating an ideology of hate **"of the other."** That Trump wall **"should be paid for by Mexico,"** he hallucinated publicly. The proud Mexicans poured on their president torrents of criticism for inviting Donald to Mexico City. Combining those attacks with laughter as they called on crazy Trump to **"Come and Get it!!"**

In Canada, while I was in Toronto this past August, I raised this question at formal dinners. **"What would Canada do if Trump occupied the Oval Office?"** Their confident answer was: **"We shall welcome American immigrants into our midst to help Canada keep on building!!"**

Mr. Trump: Calling you "unfit for the presidency" is an understatement. You, a prospective war criminal and a war lord, pose a clear and present danger to America and the world; might ignite either endless wars or a civil war in this great land; and make America not **"Great Again,"** but an America ruled by a **gun-toting mobocracy.**

Concluding by a statement unambiguously disqualifying Trump from the occupancy of the Oval Office. Uttered by Jennifer Granholm, the former Governor of the State of Michigan. Said she: "Trump is a con man. Completely unacceptable. Trying now to con America into believing that he can be President!!"

WHERE HAS THE MAJESTY OF LAW GONE? CONTRIBUTING TO THE PAIN OF NINE-ELEVEN BY ABRA-CADABRA LEGISLATION!!

Friday, September 30, 2016

This measure, JASTA, which caused Obama to veto, and caused Congress to over-ride it, is **practically a legal hoax!!** We are talking law, not politics. Defending the majesty of law. Not the criminality of 9/11 by 19 crazy jihadis of whom 15 claimed to hold Saudi passports. Led by an Egyptian who drank vodka before guiding his band of misfits into the killing of 3000 innocent civilians. **Including 600 Muslims.**

A hoax (from hocus) is to trick others into believing or accepting as genuine something false and preposterous. **That act of Congress, now law, fits that criteria,** but with dangerous global ramifications. This **abra-cadabra measure** demeans not only the term law, but also the U.S. Senate. Why? **Totally unenforceable.** Any suit based on it, if ever, shall automatically fall in the category of vexatious litigation.

As an international lawyer who has no business relationship with the Government of Saudi Arabia, I have never accepted to litigate a case in which I cannot find my way to a probative proof. The law of evidence, as well as criminal law, require a nexus, a causality, between the accused and the criminalized act. In this regard, how can that requisite be satisfied?

Where is the magic which can link between the Government of Saudi Arabia and a specific and proven instruction or direction to that band of crazies? Telling them **"Go and attack America!!"** Even if by some magic, a litigant, in this case a family member who lost his/her beloved on that horrible day could find a member of the Saudi governmental hierarchy who is implicated, the corporation or authority, namely the Government, cannot be proven liable.

And suppose an American litigant might claim someday that funding of terrorism have at times been **traced to a charitable foundation in Saudi Arabia.** You still, as an attorney for the American plaintiff, have to prove in an American court that that foundation is a government front.

And let us say that you are able to prove that with documentation whose veracity and authenticity can be established (the **foundation is acting on behalf of the Government**). How are you going to serve process on such a presumed defendant, and haul them from Saudi Arabia to an American court of law with appropriate jurisdiction. **Kidnap them?**

In addition, **how can the rightful claims of the Saudi Government that its sovereign land has also been attacked by the same maniacal ideology, be handheld?** Is the American plaintiff's attorney going to say: **"We are only concerned about America's victims of terror?"** The argument that terror is a global phenomenon, and that America and Saudi Arabia are **partners in fighting** it would be enough to debunk the plaintiff's argument establishing a credible cause of action.

This is a sad day for US Congress as it legislates, not only for a patently magical (thus losing) case. But also for its **ultimate effect on the respect of the Rule of Law.** As well as of the respect owed by Congress to the Executive in matters of foreign affairs.

This is politics at its worst, painting America, once again, into a corner. Especially when **Guantanamo is still open with Muslim detainees** who, since 2002, have been neither charged nor released. Except for Khalid Sheikh Mohamed. **Only one!!**

With terrorism becoming a global phenomenon, so is the growth of **the concept of universal jurisdiction.** A judge in Spain (Judge Jarson) was able to subpoena **Pinochet,** a former president of Chile, for human rights abuses affecting Spanish citizens. But Pinochet at the time of that action was **no longer head of State. Was a mere senator,** seeking medical attention in London.

The **International Criminal Court (ICC),** established on the basis of the Rome Charter of 1998, has become the image of ineffectiveness. That is although it acts on the same principle: **universal jurisdiction.** Its woes stem from its complicated procedures; the lack of an agreement between it and the U.N. Security Council; the inclination to focus more on African officials than on others.

To all of this mix, add the fact that the **U.S. has not yet become a member of the ICC.** Here again the law against Saudi official culpability in terrorism is **weakened by the U.S. non-ICC status.**

And since the U.S. is committed to the principle that no outside authority could legislate for the U.S., so **is the position of all sovereign States around the world.** State sovereignty remains supreme.

Along the same line of legal reasoning, the **doctrine of foreign sovereign immunity shields sovereigns from the reach of foreign courts.** You cannot impel a foreign sovereign to appear before a court unless that sovereign agrees to waive that immunity. Such a waiver happens once in a while in cases of diplomats committing an unlawful act while in foreign jurisdictions. Even in such cases, the **capital of that erring diplomat could bring him home because the offended government would exercise the right to have him/her recalled.**

No Saudi Government shall ever surrender that principle of international law, particularly when it is wrongly targeted for what is clearly an offense in which **it has no role.**

In fact the **late King Fahd** rebuffed the efforts of **Osama Bin Laden in 1990** when that Saudi national offered to defend the Kingdom from the aggressive moves of Saddam against Kuwait and Saudi Arabia.

It is ironic that it was Chief Justice John Marshall, of the US Supreme Court who, in 1812, was the first to authoritatively render the doctrine of foreign sovereign immunity. (The Case of The Schooner Exchange v. McFaddon).

Note that foreign sovereign immunity does not deny plaintiffs all relief. It only shuts them out of their own national courts. The families of the victims of 9/11 may legally **avail themselves of the Saudi judicial or diplomatic channels.** A decidedly non-promising prospect.

The American law now known as **"The Justice Against Sponsors of Terrorism Act (JASTA)"** unhappily, **shall not help the families of the 9/11 victims to find either solace or closure.** Congressional machinations in this troublesome presidential election year could only advance the search by those legislators to keep their congressional seats.

Any attorney representing the Saudi Government could find **plenty of ammunition in the report of the independent American commission which found no evidence of Saudi Government involvement of any kind or form.** Obviously any Saudi holder of American assets or accounts shall have to consider the danger of an illegal seizure of such accounts.

With this law, the US global presences (military, diplomatic, intelligence, economic, educational..etc) are now in danger of counter litigation all over the world. **The European Union has warned that if JASTA is passed, other countries could adopt similar legislation defining their own exemptions to sovereign immunity.**

As a starter, Riyadh has not only vehemently denied any involvement in 9/11. It has threatened to take counter-measures of various kinds.

The fabric of international law, **especially in the area of sovereign immunity,** the corner stone of the **law of treaties,** is now being subjected to wear and tear. Even US laws, such as the **Foreign Sovereign Immunities Act of 1976 (FSIA)** needs now to be revisited.

The cautionary approach taken by the co-sponsors of that impossible to enforce act, **(Senator Schumer of New York and Senator Corker of Tennessee),** shall effect no damage containment.

Said Corker: **"I do want to say I don't think the Senate nor House has functioned in an appropriate manner as it relates to a very important piece of legislation... I have tremendous concerns about the sovereign immunity procedures that would be set in place by the countries as a result of this vote."**

So, I ask Senator Corker in his capacity as Chairman of the Senate Foreign Relations Committee: **"Sir!! Then why co-sponsor it and vote for it?"** It was President Jackson who hailed from Tennessee who objected to a ruling by Chief Justice Marshall. Jackson uttered an objection which we, as students of American constitutional law, memorized. He in effect said: **"John Marshall made his ruling. Let him enforce it."** Senator Corker: What cannot be enforced, should not be legislated.

9/11, for Saudi Arabia and the whole world was no **"Act of State."** So **"the effect principle"** (the effect of a sovereign act on another sovereignty) has no place here. JASTA is nothing more than the politicization of law. This is why I can't find any majesty in that legal hoax.

Hitting Saudi Arabia, while seeking its cooperation in anti-jihadism, and at Obama, by rendering his veto ineffective, and at the entire fabric of the principle of friendly relations among nations, are nothing but **legitimating the charge against America of becoming a super power with an ineffective rudder to its ship of State.** JASTA is born with a boomerang destined to hurt these United States.

The Romans, through Latin, were way ahead of the U.S. Congress. They bequeathed to us, lawyers, an exit from bad laws. Phrased it in these words: **"Modus et conventio vincunt legem." (Custom and agreement overrule the law.)**

Sadly, the exit here is to ignore that silly JASTA. A law which tantalizes but shall not deliver. Which prompted the Saudi Crown Prince to declare in Ankara, Turkey, on September 29: "Our Lands are being targeted. Up with our defenses."

DR. YASSIN EL-AYOUTY, ESQ.

IN TRUMPISM I CAN'T SEE THE FACE OF THE UNITED STATES

Friday, October 7, 2016

The more outrageous Trump becomes, the bigger and louder his rallies become. **Like a train hurtling over a weak bridge toward a wreck, with the passengers elated by the inevitable catastrophe.** These are largely white men, mostly with no more education than what they got in high school. Dismissive of the rules and values of a constitutional system of 240 years on which they have turned their backs as **"politics as usual."**

Donald has tapped into this lode of rage **against globalization, immigration, foreign alliances, freedom of trade, foreign sovereign immunities, and international organizations.** The internal governance system, he claims, **is rigged.** So are the media, the political parties, the judiciary, the Obama presidency. And even the microphones through which he extols the dark face of the United States. As for the military, Trump says that he, as president, **shall select his own generals.** The prospect of a private Trump militia.

A thug who proclaims the greatness of Putin as compared to **"the worst President in the history of the U.S. - Barack Obama."** A con who is suspected of having **paid no taxes for nearly two decades** (because **"I am smart"**).

A war horse who threatens to wage war on Iran, usurp the right of the Arabs to their oil, spread nuclear weapons world-wide, bomb the families of suspected ISIS terrorists, and condone Russia's territorial grab in the Ukraine and its **cyber intervention in the U.S. elections.**

What he says today, he denies the following day. His anti-minorities and

Islamophobic utterances are depicted by his surrogates **(Governor Christie of New Jersey and former New York City Mayor, Rudy Giuliani)** as **"misunderstood."** Why? **"He is not a politician!!"** So why is he in the game in national politics? **"Because he is an agent of change who shall make America Great Again!!"** How crazier could this get?

Here follows a horrific panorama of that dark side of America, as could be seen in Trumpism on and off the stage of presidential debates:

- Amid national uncertainty and fear arose Trump. **So did Hitler in Germany of the early 1930s.** You don't have to take my word for it. Read the book by the latest biographer of Hitler. The historian **Volker Ulrich** in his amazingly detailed book entitled **"Hitler: Ascent, 1889-1939."** Ulrich focused on Hitler as a politician who rose to power through **demagoguery, showmanship and nativist appeals to the masses.** In all of this, Trump is a replica.

- **Donald is all about Donald. Not about America.** The earth spins on an axis called Trump. One can see that love of self in Trump's performance, a losing one, in his **first debate with Hillary Clinton.** To hell with politics and the issues, he had insinuated. Described by **Frank Bruni of the New York Times** of September 28, in these words: **"He just pumped air into his hair and more air into his head and sauntered into action as if the sheer, inimitable wonder of his presense would be enough."** Thus the Donald interrupted Hillary **51 times** in the space of 90 minutes.

- A Republican woman of 51 confessed her dislike for Hillary. But she noted that Trump's answers during that first debate lacked details of substance. **"I don't think he has the experience...His behavior is unpresidential, unkind, un-everything."**

- Others who remain sympathetic to Trump attacked his questioning whether Obama was born in America. **"The Birther movement."** A woman texted her husband that Trump had lost her when he dodged responsibility for stoking the birther movement.

- When it comes to being Commander in Chief, Trump, believing that he could outsmart the whole world, espouses the concept of **"strategic ambiguity."** Meaning that he never wants to show America's hand to its adversaries. But during his debate with Hillary, that tough looking guy appeared utterly confused. For when asked about **"the first strike option,"** he deflected the moderator's question. **"I think that once the nuclear alternative happens, it's over."** Yet Trump is not reluctant to build nuclear weapons and have others acquire them.

- Trump keeps on repeating that he was against the war on Iraq. A blatant lie!! **Trump is on record as supporting that losing war which**

has cost trillions of dollars and much blood-letting. Donald has supported that disastrous war in September 2002. That is when Congress was still debating whether to authorize military action.

• And when Obama failed to get Iraqi approval to keep sizable American forces after 2011, Trump has continued to castigate the President and Hillary for that failure. From there, he stupidly jumps to insanely charging both of being **founders of ISIS.**

• His racism is like neon signs in Times Square. From **the ban on Muslims from coming to the U.S., to his description of Mexicans as rapists and drug dealers, to his denigrating not only Afro-Americans, but also the historic symbol of Afro-American achievement, namely electing Obama** not once but twice.

• While the polls show that Trump is winning virtually no support from Afro-Americans, he full-throatedly propagandizes a proven lie. **"You see what's happening with my poll numbers with Afro-Americans. They're going, like, high!!"**

• More of the dark side of America is Trump's big lie about the economic and social status of the Afro-Americans who make up 15% of America's demographics. **"Our African-American communities are absolutely in the worst shape that they've ever been in before -ever, ever, ever."**

• No quantifiable measurement supports that characterization of black America. But the record shows that Trump and his father had in the 1970's and the 1980's forbidden renting apartments to people of color in Trump buildings in New York City.

• In the State of Pennsylvania, a woman in West Chester voiced an opinion prevalent among women in America whose support for Trump is pivotal for winning the presidency. She said: **"I truly want to like him. I keep looking for something in him. But I can't have my children grow up and look at him as someone to respect."** She faulted him for refusing to release his taxes, for his shallowness, and his unwillingness to learn from experts. **He claims that he knows it all.**

• **The Trump Foundation** has been ordered by the New York State Attorney to **"cease and desist"** from raising money in the State; the Trump University has been found to be a big fraud; and **the money claimed to have been raised by Trump for American veterans seems to have been a pie in the sky.**

• Is it any wonder that the **Wall Street Journal** has recently reported that not one chief executive among the **"Fortune 100"** has donated money to Trump's campaign? Many companies won't do business with him either. This robs Donald of his claim that **his alleged success in business, in** spite of three bankruptcies, qualifies him to lead America into a new gilded age.

- Commented the **New York Times of September 27** on Trump's performance in the first presidential debate watched by nearly 100 million Americans: **"It's absurd that the fate of the race, and the future of the nation, might carom this way or that based on a 90-minute television ritual so dominated by fear and falsehood."**

- This evaluation came after that paper's editorial lamented: **"There was a fundamental emptiness to the ritual (the debate), because of the awful truth that one participant (Trump) had nothing truthful to offer."**

- His anti-feminism has become the talk of America on the eve of the second Clinton vs. Trump debate. A tape has been discovered demonstrating his infidelity to Melania, his present wife (and third spouse). The tape heard over and over again on public media as of October 6 had Trump describe his sexual advances towards a married woman. Including **"You can do anything to women when you are famous."** Causing a Republican Senator to describe that presidential candidate **"a malignant clown."**

The tragedy of a possible Trump presidency lies in **denying the healing power of compromise.** In any system of governance, the settlement of disputes by mutual concession is a powerful elixir. It is the very opposite of the adversarial system of producing winners and losers. Half of the loaf is better than none. Trumpism is so polarizing that it **looks as the very face of paralysis.**

When you add the compromise deficiency element in Trumpism, to the damage already inflicted on the trust in the system of governance, you **will find an America which is hardly recognizable as a robust democracy.** For the U.S. Constitution itself has been the product of compromises. Thus enshrined as a resilient document of 240 years!!

In this age of rage, the most outrageous prospect is to imagine that megalomaniac, Donald J. Trump standing on **January 20, 2017, taking the oath of the office as the 45th President of the U.S.**

**"I Donald J. Trump, do so solemnly swear... that I will faithfully execute the Office of President of the United States, and will do to the best of my ability, preserve, protect and defend the Constitution of the United States."

May we never hear the air waves carry these words stipulated by the U.S. Constitution.

An oath is a formal calling upon God to witness to the truth of what one says or to witness that one sincerely intends to do what one says.

For how can Trump, if elected, take that oath? **Throughout his entire life of 70 years, he has not kept any promise, or stayed the course of what he promised to do.**

His own cult of personality makes him think that when he builds a tower, he is building a bridge. Reason why I can't see in Trumpism the face of the United States which proclaims "In God we Trust." Fortunately for America, and the world, Trump is not a God.

DR. YASSIN EL-AYOUTY, ESQ.

VIEWING THE U.N. AND ITS CHARTER FROM THE PERSPECTIVE OF REALISM

Friday, October 14, 2016

Not by lamentations, but by congratulations, should a former UN staffer like me, greet the appointment of the new Secretary-General. I have served under four of his predecessors: **Dag Hammarskjold, U Thant, Kurt Waldheim, and Javier Perez de Cuellar.**

Antonio Guterres, now the 8th Secretary-General, deserves to succeed. He, a former Prime Minister of Portugal, and a former UN High Commissioner for Refugees, has the right tools for UN leadership. However I am not questioning the worthiness of the new captain of the UN ship. **I am not sure whether the ship itself is still sea-worthy.**

Born in 1945, the UN is governed by a charter born out of the smoldering ruins of the Second World War. Its elements were taking form as early as 1942, following the entry of the US in that war. **A war whose human casualties are estimated at 40 millions.** Its founding members numbered, in San Francisco, 51 States. **That number has now grown to 193.**

Over the past 71 years, the world has changed several times over. Issues of war, peace, and development are no longer the same. Even pen and paper, except for old hands like mine, are no more. **The State is now competing with the non-State actor for hegemony.** Even globalization has lost its luster. Digitization has become the medium, and landing on the moon might soon be eclipsed by landing and living on Mars.

Yet the Charter remained the same. Not because of its resilience and relevance to the vastly changing circumstances. But because it is nearly impossible to revise. **Article 109 provides for that remote possibility.** That possibility cannot become a reality due to two impossibilities: **unanimity amongst the Big Five Powers** in the Security Council (U.S./U.K./France/Russia/China); and the **super-majority of two-thirds approval** by the entire membership.

So the U.N. is blanketed by too much ice to make it a sea-worthy ship for **its new captain, Antonio Guterres.** And there is hardly anything that he could do about it. That is although the UN Secretary-General is, under the Charter, **two in one: Chief Administrative Officer (Article 98), and, at his discretion, a political entity (Article 99).**

Here are selective lamentations in regard to the shackles built into the Charter:

- To begin with, let us overlook the anomaly of calling the organization, "the United Nations." Nations? **The membership is made up of States, not nations,** immersed in the daily struggle for upholding their sovereignty.
- In fact, once in a while, we get the entertaining spectacle of two delegations, each claiming representation of the State. **The Dominican Republic, China, Mali, and Tshad** are examples.
- The right of States to **self-defense is relegated to Article 51;**
- That basic sovereign right is expressed at the **end of Chapter VII,** the main tool of the Big Five hegemony expressed as sanctions against other States.
- The preamble of the Charter in regard to the **fundamental right of every individual to dignity, and to gender equality** is vague and exhortatory. It took 3 years for the General Assembly to amplify those rights in the **Universal Declaration of Human Rights (1948).**
- The rights of civilians for protection from war-faring combatants found their way to expression in 1949. In the **Geneva Conventions of 1949 and the International Convention on Civil and Political Rights (1966).** Genocide, that mass murder for any reason, was a later invention of the early 1950s.
- **Article 2, paragraph 7 forbids the intervention by States in the internal affairs of other States.** Great!! But that basic principle of sovereignty is made subsidiary to Chapter VII in sanctions where the Big Five (the permanent members of the Security Council) hold sway.
- **It is in the General Assembly (GA) where that equality of sovereignty is expressed.** The GA is considered the Parliament of

Man/Woman. Yet nearly all its resolutions are non-enforceable. They are a wish list of **"please, would you be so kind as to...!!"**

- The **only exception to the above is the budget.** But the arrears have for far too long overwhelmed payment of assessments on time. One country once paid $40 to avoid voting deprivation. Just to remain a hair-breadth under the arrears accumulated over 2 years.

- As to the Security Council, which has **"the primary"** (not the exclusive) **responsibility for the maintenance of peace and security,** well..? We have the veto power in the hands of 5 States from among 15 States, 10 of which are non-permanent members. The latter category **satisfies the scenery of geographic representation by regions (by caucuses),** but with hardly any impact on the decisions of war and peace. Only the resolutions of that body are enforceable.

- With decolonization virtually accomplished, one of the 6 main organs of the UN, namely the Trusteeship Council, has no job. Its ornate hall at UN Headquarters serves as a meeting space. Attempts to rename that Council **"The Human Rights Council"** have failed.

The above is beginning to **look like the Martin Luther list of grievances pinned to the door of that church in Gutenberg, Germany,** in the 16th Century. So we shall stop here to turn our lamentations towards the misperceived concepts and the cancerous impediments to the growth of that universal organization:

- Where is the UN today in the **global problems of terrorism, safe havens for internally-displaced persons, and genocidal wars** waged by leaders internally? Not to mention the horrors of Syria, Iraq, Yemen, Libya and of death by drowning of immigrants young and old.

- **"Internal affairs"** are to be designated and protected from outside interference by the State itself. The UN is shut out, unless through resort to the recently developed **laws of human rights and of humanitarian intervention.**

- That UN absence is now filled by States, or by regional defense arrangements. Bringing these issues to the UN Security Council is akin to the fig leaf of legitimating what sovereign powers have already decided to do outside of the UN.

- The term **"peace-keeping"** does not exist in the UN Charter. It was a Hammarskjold invention which was embarked upon in regard to the first Suez War of 1956. OK. We shall take whatever we get to help our troubled world through our only universal organization -the UN.

- But the **national contingents volunteered by States at their own volition, need two main strategic elements:** freedom of movement (which can only be granted by the States on whose soil the peace-keepers are stationed). **And prior training in joint exercises to at least learn the communication code of that array of multi-national forces.**

• That pre-training does not exist. Except in two or three of the Scandinavian States. For how can the UN membership agree on planning for peace-keeping, say, in the Philippines? The Philippines would be the first to angrily object saying: **"Who is the UN to anticipate a crisis in our country? This is nothing but fomenting a crisis. In any case, we shall not sign a status of forces agreement (SOFA)."** And the matter dies.

• In that regard the UN, being an inter-State system, has **no role to play in civil wars.** It was not designed for that purpose.

• **From where did the UN Security Council get its legal authority to ban individual citizens of sovereign States from travel** out of their localities? That Council is not a court of law; the banned persons are not put on advance notice; when I represented a travel banned victim, I discovered that the UN investigators used as evidence irrelevant indicators; and the expert reports on the need to end that system of **"you are guilty until you prove yourself innocent"** went nowhere.

Add to the above selected list that up to now there are **terms which lack precise** definition through international inter-State consensus. Terms like **"democracy,"** and **"aggression."**

So **Secretary-General Guterres, we wish you well.** You shall have your hands full. But you still have at your disposal tools which have proven their functional effectiveness.

Primary among these are the 30 specialized agencies and programs within **"the UN Family of Organizations."** Including, of course, your old office, **"The UN High Commissioner For Refugees."**

There are also the **more than 2000 non-governmental organizations around the world.** Representing what is referred to in the Charter by **"We the People."** Above all, **you are perceived worldwide as endowed by an unarticulated moral authority of the rare type -its neutrality.**

Let us not forget the central role of one of the 6 principal organs of the UN itself. **Namely, the UN Secretariat.** Under Article 98, you are the decider over that main organ which is in session 24/7. You, or your representative, hire and fire. Through this vast bureaucracy, the **entire equivalents within the Family of the UN Organizations are also influenced.**

In 1960, Hammarskjold has planted the flag of **"the independence of the international civil service."** His clarion call, which rattled the Soviets and troubled the British, was broadcast **through his Oxford University speech of that year.** Written for him by my late friend, the legal mind of the UN at the time, **Professor Oscar Schachter.**

On the other hand, **your powers under Article 99 are discretionary.** That article separates your capacity of executive from that of being empowered to raise issues of war and peace. Issues **you can submit to either the Security Council or the General Assembly for their consideration.**

Thus it is an illusive power on which decisions are not within your hands. Nonetheless it is a recognizable moral authority which may have consequences. **In this regard, even symbolism can be a factor for good.**

You also have on your side the Charter interpretation in ways never expected before. In the absence of revision, broad interpretation has **accelerated decolonization.** It also **gave birth to imaginative ways to leapfrog over the veto power.** An example on this is **"the presidential statement"** on behalf of the Security Council.

As an engineer and a mathematician, you, Secretary-General Guterres may, in spite of the assessment above, be able to navigate this unwieldy UN ship through these troubled waters towards harbors of safety. Your Portuguese ancestors, in the 17th & 18th Centuries, proved themselves as experienced mariners!!

DR. YASSIN EL-AYOUTY, ESQ.

Perspectives on Egypt, Islam and the Dark Era of Trump

WITH THE FALL OF 2012, LEGITIMACY OF THE MUSLIM BROTHERHOOD HAD COLLAPSED!!

Friday, October 21, 2016

In the New Egypt, the legitimacy of the Muslim Brotherhood had fallen within only six months of their assumption of the presidency. **Morsi came to power in June 2012 through popular elections.** The Muslim Brotherhood, for whom I had in error voted. Soon the Brotherhoodization of post-Mubarak Egypt began in earnest.

But out of illegitimate over-reach, their legitimacy through the ballot box, even if verifiable, was gone with the wind. **Within only 6 months!! Their collapse had nothing to do with El-Sisi.** It had to do with structural and ideological defects which brought their reign, in June 2013, to ultimate ruin.

Here is how!!
- Having joined the January 2011 Revolution late, **a lateness due to their fear of an ultimate Mubarak triumph,** the Muslim Brotherhood **(MB)** made a premature announcement. **"The MB will not field any candidate for the Office of President."**
- But later **"the Guidance Bureau" (Maktab Al-Irshad),** their politburo, changed course. Their Deputy Supreme Guide, moneybags **Khairat Al-Shatter** was to compete for that highest office **against General Shafik.**
- A quirk, or a quibble, or a twist in Egyptian electoral law, affecting the qualification of a presidential candidate, **disqualified Al-Shatter.** Constitutionally, the candidate for that post must be **"an Egyptian born to Egyptian parents, none of whom nor the candidate have the nationality of another State."** El-Shatter's mother had held an American citizenship, hence the disqualification of her son.

- The near equivalence of this Egyptian constitutional provision is to be found in the American Constitution. **Its Article II, Section 1, paragraph 5** begins as follows:

"**No person except a natural born citizen, or a citizen of the United States, at the time of the Adoption of this Constitution, shall be eligible to the Office of President.**" A provision which prompted crazy **Donald J. Trump,** the Republican Party presidential candidate to try to delegitimize the Obama presidency. By the nefarious efforts of **"the Birther Movement"** which claimed that Obama was born outside the U.S.

- So the MB in Egypt, searching for a replacement for the disqualified El-Shatter, found in **Mohamed Morsi** the person who would lead the New Egypt through the elections of June 2012. **And Morsi won.** End of the story of legitimacy of the headship of the New Egypt? No!! In fact that beginning was woefully defective. **President Morsi was elected while the new Constitution was still being drafted.** The cart was thus placed before the horse. With **Al-Itihadiyah Palace** (equivalent to the American White House) now occupied by a leader of the MB, the Brotherhood's appetite for garnering more power through accretion became insatiable. Inordinately greedy!!

Fancying Egypt, at that point, an Islamic Emirate in the making(Supreme Guide Mahdi Akef said **"To Hell with Egypt (Tuz I'i Masr),"** the constituent assembly began to frame an Islamic Constitution. What began as a group, on whose membership were all shades of post-Mubarak political thinking, soon turned into an **Ikhwan rubber stamp of the Bureau of Guidance.** The MB, with Morsi ensconced at Al-Itihadiya Palace, saw to it that **liberals, Copts, women, and any secular thinking individuals** were impediments to their long march to the **Islamic Emirate of Egypt.**

And with the non-MB elements abandoning the efforts of keeping Egypt a secular habitat, the **Islamic Constitution was readied for a plebiscite a few days before that vote in December 2012.** No national debate; no transparency; no voicing of any opposition to that illegal take-over by the Brotherhood under the guise of Islamism. The battle cry of **"Islam Is the Solution"** became the entire ideology of a movement. A movement which felt emboldened by one important fact: **The Armed Forces, as seen as of January 25, 2011, shall not intervene.**

In spite of the MB confidence in the ultimate success of their coup **(from the ballot box to an Islamic dictatorship),** Morsi declared himself in November 2012 that he was immune from any accountability before the law. His move, **reminiscent of Hitler becoming Germany's Fuhrer, as an epitaph of the Weimar Republic,** was not contested by even the moderate elements of the Muslim Brotherhood.

Not even the judiciary, a venerable institution with a glorious tradition based on a sophisticated fusion **between Islamic law (Sharia) and the Napoleonic code.** That institution was smitten into submission by the instrumentality of hordes encouraged to, among other things, besiege the Supreme Constitutional Court.

That Court had committed an act unforgiven by the resurrected Islamists: **the nullification of the legitimacy of one third of the Egyptian parliament,** convened as a vehicle for the recalibration of Egypt to fit in the Brotherhood mold.

By the time the Islamic constitution, which had no provision for the eventuality of recall of the President, was rushed for approval, other moves have been put in place by the Muslim Brotherhood:

• The de facto **lease of eastern Sinai to Hamas** which, through tunnels as well as porous borders, had begun to shift its armed confrontation with Israel to Egypt;

• The borrowing of the Iranian pattern of the **Revolutionary Guard** to create an Egyptian military institution as a parallel to the regular army;

• The increasing hostility towards the **Copts and the Shiis,** which expressed itself in attacks and hooliganism;

• The **changing pattern of Egypt's foreign relations in the Middle East** through enhanced amity towards Ordogan's Turkey, and Pakistan which was being increasingly Talibanised **(apostasy laws; harsh treatment of women; and anti-minorities practises);**

• Threat of military intervention in Ethiopia for its plan to build **Al-Nahdha Dam on the Blue Nile;**

• The **downgrading of Al-Azhar as the historic citadel of Islamic learning** framed into the ideology of tolerance, inclusiveness, and outreach to other faiths and creeds;

- Declaring **Egypt's historic monuments as un-Islamic idols** which cannot be tolerated by an Islamic State; and
- The systematic weeding out of Egyptian diplomats and consular officials for being **"insufficiently Islamic;"**
- Tourism was discouraged;
- The arts, the film industry; the vibrant music, the theater were looked upon as suspect cultural deviations.

Against this background, whereby Egypt of 7000 years was being turned on its head, **35 million Egyptians** rose as a human wave of protest. The motto of the June 30, 2013 revolution was: **"Go!!"** (IRHAL).

But the Brotherhood had a different perspective: **legitimacy (Shariyah) was being challenged, and its claimed majority among Egypt's nearly 100 million was the nuclear option to be used against the crowds in Tahrir and all over Egypt.**

By this calculation, the Brotherhood wrote its own phasing out certificate:
- **Morsi refused the entreaties of El-Sisi,** the Defense Minister, to accord Egypt a new start: **A new plebiscite on the presidency;** rejoining the broad national secular forces to avert the horrible spector of civil war; and the avoidance of military intervention to keep the peace, especially that the Police forces have been maligned by the Morsi regime;
- A Road-Map aiming at having all sectors and ideologies in Egypt come together, had to be put in place **even with the Brotherhood** opting to stay outside the broad national consensus;
- The **launching of a transitional government,** headed by the jurist **Adly Mansour, President of the Egyptian Supreme Constitutional Court.** This was met by the launching by the Brotherhood of the occupation of two main public squares in the heart of Cairo: Rabaa and Al-Nahdha. Those locations were declared by the Brotherhood **"mini-emirates;"**
- For 6 weeks (from July 3 to August 14, 2013), the appeals by the new transitional authorities for the sit-in participants to peacefully disband went unheeded.
- In both Rabba and Al-Nahdha, crimes were committed, weapons were stored and at times used, **foreign intervention was invited,** and the banner of **"Shariiyah (legitimacy),"** though false, was unfurled.

Finally the new authorities had to move on these two locations, where exits of safe passage were repeatedly declared. Those defensive security measures were manipulated by the Brotherhood in its deceptive cry of victimhood.

The battle lines have thus changed as of August 14, 2013. **Terrorism in Sinai, Cairo, and the western desert began in earnest.** Yet the secular Constitution was enacted in 2014 followed by presidential elections which produced a winner: El-Sisi.

Facts are facts, hard to ignore, and impossible to contest. The Secular Constitution of 2014 provides in its Article 5 that: **"The political system is based upon political and parties membership diversity, the peaceful transfer of power, separation of powers with checks and balances, the authority as based upon accountability, and respect of human rights and freedoms as provided in the Constitution."**

None of these provisions has equivalents in the Islamic Constitution. The only provision stressed by the Muslim Brotherhood was: **An emblem of two swords framing the Quran.** With the words **"Get Ready"** at its base. Get ready for what? For so-called Islamic rule which limits the freedom of expression and the practice of faith to only Brotherhood adherents?

Egyptian laws and regulations whereby the Brotherhood was banned and declared a terror organization were enacted. But only after that organization had decided to take matters in its own hands. Regardless of the popular will, manifested massively from June 30 to July 4, 2013. Prior to those fatal dates, **the Muslim Brotherhood** stubbornly refused to join the process of Egypt's rebirth after 60 years of military rule.

Nothing can ring more hollow than the claim that **"legitimacy"** resided only in an Islamist dictatorial rule. A rule raising false facades, impugning the legitimacy of the New Egypt which had brought peace to the Egyptian street, and a new sense of urgency to make up for lost time.

It is not by the constant repetition by media that the present Egyptian government is the outcome of a putsch. **It is the result of the vanquishing of a putsch by the Brotherhood in whose terrorist revanchist face one could only see an ISIS affiliate.**

The Muslim Brotherhood has no claim to legitimacy in Egypt as of the Fall of 2012. That is when it first put Morsi, its symbols, its ethos above the law. Such collapse is nearly impossible to repair. For it goes to the real core, beyond the facade of the mere use of faith for sordid ends of power.

IN THE NILE VALLEY, TWO HEROES OF UNITY: ONE, SINCE 3100 B.C., IS CELEBRATED; THE OTHER, SINCE 1954 A.D., IS IGNORED.

Friday, October 28, 2016

History can be kind to some great leaders, yet unkind to other similarly great leaders.

In Egypt, there was **Pharaoh Narmer (Mina) who united the two geographical parts of Egypt: the Delta, in the north, and the Valley in the south.** Around 3100 B.C., Narmer, not only established the First Egyptian Dynasty. He also brought Egypt, both Upper (meaning South), and Lower (meaning North) under one crown **-His!!**

The Narmer tablets, depicting that historic and enduring unity, are well known to Egyptians, especially those who, like myself, **taught the History of Egypt in Cairo.**

Our late Egyptology professor, **Dr. Ahmed Badawi,** drilled in our heads the name Narmer, at the University of Heliopolis. He even exhorted us to stop by the historic hotel called **Mina** House, located till today at the foot of the Giza Pyramids.

What Narmer accomplished for Egypt in regard to that geographic unity, **the British, during their heinous occupation (1882 - 1954) could not undo.** Trying to create North Egypt and South Egypt (Divide and Rule), they utterly failed. **Unity,** one could assuredly say, **is in Egypt's DNA.**

From Narmer, a celebrated unity hero for the past 6000 years, to **another**

Egyptian hero, Muhammad Naguib, first President of Egypt (1953 - 1954) who, until now is totally ignored. His dream of unity, though not attained, would have brought the Nile Valley, from the **Mediterranean to Uganda** into one proud entity, with the great Nile as its spinal cord.

Naguib's failure in accomplishing that breath-taking mission was not for lack of trying. It, as **could be seen from his memoirs, was due to the Nasser coup of 1952,** with its participants turning against one another. It boiled down to Naguib, whose mother was Sudanese, and Nasser, whose family hailed from Upper Egypt. **Near South versus Deep South.** A historic catastrophe which changed the entire history of the modern Middle East.

The **Naguib vs. Nasser split** had to do with different outlooks, personal, political and geostrategic. **Naguib, the fatherly face of the Nasser Coup,** was in favor of democracy in Egypt and of Egyptian/Sudanese unity. But Nasser, the young photogenic face of the army rebellion against the monarchy of King Farouk, guiding Egypt east (*Nach Ost* -as they say in German) for leadership of the Arab World.

The result: expulsion and imprisonment of General Naguib; the declaration by the Sudan of its independence in 1956; thrusting of Egypt in non-winnable Middle Eastern wars; the destruction of Egyptian democratic institutions until the revolutions of 2011 and 2013; and the unintended consequences of the growth of Islamism in Egypt, especially under President Sadat.

Returning now to the question which should haunt, if not all Egyptians, at least those who care about the full projection of Egyptian history and politics. Thus I turn to the memories of Muhammad Naguib, published in Arabic under the title of **"I was President of Egypt" (Konto Raiisan Li Misr).**

For fairness, **I have no means of verification of what Naguib argues in those memoirs.** Except for two circumstantial pieces of evidence: **The outcome of the Nasser/Naguib conflict; plus my personal knowledge of President Naguib when he was alive.**

I was his son's teacher in the early 1950s at the **Model School of Al-Naqrashi Pasha at Qubba Gardens, Cairo.** His character was stellar; spoke modestly and sincerely; and was attentive to the quality of education in post-war Egypt. He was also loved by his troops forming the **Frontiers Battalions (Selah Al-Hodood).**

These were reasons why the **Free Officers, led by Nasser** in that historic coup against monarchical Egypt in 1952, chose him to front that rebellion.

Without summarizing those 420 pages, published in various editions from 1984 to 2003, my focus in this blog posting is the junctures of that rift whose consequences are still present. Even within the scope of that limited material, I shall focus on the **manifestations of that rift as they impacted the destruction of the Naguib dream of unity between Egypt and the Sudan.**

As an army officer and a patriot who participated in the Egyptian uprising of 1919 against British occupation, Naguib, throughout his life, called himself **"Son of the Nile."**

His maternal grandfather, **Muhammad Othman Bek,** was a senior Army officer stationed in Khartoum., the Sudan. The Mehdi rebels in the Sudan in the late 1880s spared his life in recognition of Othman's **commitment to Nile Valley amity.**

Naguib's entire family lived in the **"Anglo-Egyptian Sudan,"** named as such by **the diktat of the British occupiers** of Egypt. A major stratagem of Great Britain in the Nile Valley was of dual nature. **To separate Egypt from the Sudan, and to separate the Sudanese north from the Sudanese south.**

That divide and rule approach was premised on ethnic and religious lines: North of Malakal was **"Arab and Muslim;"** south of that point was **"Negroid, and either Christian or animist."**

Following on his father's footsteps, **Naguib graduated from the Cairo Military Academy in 1918.** As with his father, his **early service was in the Sudan.** That is where some members of his family still live, and where his father was buried. Fondly, **Naguib recalls his childhood in the Sudan,** his camaraderie with the Sudanese, and his mother being Sudanese.

A total immersion which **provided Naguib with a purely Nilotic outlook which did not recognize the line of demarcation between Egypt and the Sudan.**

Such outlook was **deepened by Naguib's early education in the Sudan.** **From Wad Madani,** south of Khartoum, to Wadi Halfa, south of the Egyptian border. His icons were Sudanese officers and educators looking for British departure and for unity with Egypt.

So were Naguib's experiences in the Upper Nile region (south Sudan) as he had to travel with his family to wherever his father was transferred throughout the huge expanse called the Sudan.

At that time, the **Sudan was geographically the largest African country,** endowed with unlimited resources: water, land, diversified agriculture, huge animal resources, and a population full of pride and passion for being Sudanese.

Orphaned at the age of 13, following his father's death at the age of 43 in Khartoum, Naguib, though impoverished, was **admitted into Khartoum's Gordon College.** That was an exception, as the British occupation prevented Egyptians in the Sudan from applying for admission. But Naguib's father, though an Egyptian, was a senior officer in the service of **"the Government of the Sudan."**

His studenthood at Gordon was marred by his loyalty to Egypt. The sovereign in Cairo was **"The King of Egypt and the Sudan."** Not the British, a foreign occupier who saw to it that even the railroad from Cairo to Aswan would not be connected to the railroad in the Sudan **-a few miles from that connection.**

While being a student at Gordon College, Naguib's loyalty to that natural and historic unity caused him trouble. He refused to take down a text dictated by a British professor. In part, the text said that **"Egypt was ruled by the British."**

Standing in protest, Naguib was defiant: **"Sir!! Britain is only an occupier of Egypt. Egypt is internally self-ruled, but is a part of the Ottoman Empire."** His punishment was **10 lashes administered to his back. "I submitted to that degrading punishment, without even opening my mouth out of personal pride."**

Naguib was in fact an Egyptian Sudanese, not fitting in the mold of Nasser whose gaze was not South, but East. His fronting the Nasser coup and becoming Egypt's first president **proved to be a painful ordeal.**
- He felt that the Free Officers caused more harm to the cause of democracy and party politics than those opposed to the coup;
- He posited that **"We dismissed King Farouk but replaced him with 13 other kings;**

- He bemoaned his inability to stand up to **"the increasing Nasser dictatorship;"**
- Out of disgust with the direction of the Nasser's coup, **Naguib submitted his resignation** to the **"Revolutionary Command Council,"** made up of members of the Free Officers who submitted to Nasser's authoritarianism.
- Before submitting that resignation on **February 22, 1954,** he confronted the entire Command Council accusing them of **influence peddling, financial corruption, and other deviations,** such as the establishment of **"an Egypt as a State ruled by central intelligence."**
- His options were: **either to exercise his authority as president, or to resign and let Nasser have his way.** One of Naguib's central complaints was that he was forced to sign off on decisions by the high military command which were issued and then brought to him afterwards for a **pro forma** endorsement.
- **As to the Sudan,** Naguib who felt the inner pulse of the Sudanese more than any other member on the Revolutionary Command Council, saw that the complaints voiced by the Sudanese were on the upswing. Especially after the plebiscite on unity with Egypt, where the **vote was seven for unity, and one for independence.**
- Naguib was convinced that Nasser felt that **"the Sudan was a burden on Egypt, and should be jettisoned."** One of Nasser's side kicks was **Salah Salem** who advocated that **"the Sudan was definitely lost;"** a shock for Naguib!!
- Naguib's bottom line was that the Revolutionary Command Council **sacrificed the unity of the Nile Valley,** and acted accordingly, causing protests in Khartoum where the crowds chanted **"Sudan is for the Sudanese."**

Imprisoned till his death, Naguib bemoaned that his **name was expunged from schoolbooks in Egypt;** that he was beaten and insulted by officers who were encouraged to disregard his prior status as a patriot, and his having been the **first president of Egypt.**

In his memoirs, he expresses his deep pain for **the rising Nasser dictatorship, the loss of the unity of the Nile Valley, and the conversion by Nasser of Al-Azhar to a mere department for religious affairs.**

Naguib's championed the unity of the Nile Valley. To him, it was a means of bolstering the backbone of the Arab homeland through the creation of a strong State at the Arab geographic midpoint. He is more than deserving rehabilitation, though posthumously. That would be a means of rectification of that gap in the history of modern Egypt.

If Narmer is celebrated as the unifier of Egypt after 6000 years of his rule, so should Naguib who, in the early 1950s, saw in Egypt a fulcrum for a larger unity.

When I was sent as legal counsel to Darfour, the Sudan, in 2006 by the UN Security Council, I experienced sudden pain for what had been lost by the destruction of that unity. It was as if Naguib, from his grave, was whispering: **"See what has become of this beautiful land once that unity vanished."**

"NOT MY PRESIDENT!!" SCREAMED THE MILLIONS AGAINST TRUMP!! SO DO I!!

Friday, November 11, 2016

What the founders of America feared, has now happened. **Those greats, 240 years ago, all aristocrats and educated elite, have feared mob rule.** So they, in the Constitution, built a firewall to prevent that. **Called the Electoral College,** it is intended to filter the popular vote.

Though with an attractive name, **"representative democracy"** is no guarantee that the winner of the popular vote in a presidential election, does necessarily win the Oval Office. What counts here, by today's calculation, is **the winner of at least 270 electoral votes.** In recent history, it happened in 2000, in **Bush v. Gore.** Despite losing the popular vote, Bush became President. And now in 2016, **Hillary Clinton won the popular vote. But Trump is now the President-elect.**

On November 8, I voted for Hillary. But this, **in America's representative democracy,** the candidate whom I opposed, Donald Trump, cancelled my vote out. By comparison, when I, as a dual citizen (Egyptian American), voted for El-Sisi in 2014, my vote was tallied for the Egyptian presidential candidate of my choice. That is because in a country, like Egypt, you have **"popular,"** not **"representative"** democracy.

With Donald J. Trump expected to be sworn in on January 20, 2017, as **the 45th President of the U.S.,** America is a land of anxiety. Why?
- **He has never held public office before.** That is where a holder would normally get to such a position. Through the grueling practice of politics. And **"politics"** is essentially the art of compromise. **Donald has never practised that art;**

- Trump has worked assiduously, through his own voice magnified by his troupe of surrogates, to inject **doubt about the conventions of government.** He has weakened the trust in a sitting President, in the legislative and the judicial branches, and in the political parties, including his own party;
- Even before the results of this nasty campaign, he inveighed against the electoral system. Calling it **"rigged,"** is not reflecting the popular will, **needs to be closely monitored by his supporters,** and is driven by faulty polls and **"corrupt media;"**
- Donald has used, for his political advocacy, **the weapons of insults, smears, innuendoes, and cruel sarcasm,** against anyone who dared to disagree with him. An expert in TV showmanship, he **put fabrications ahead of facts, fear mongering ahead of "trust in America,"** violence ahead of conciliation, and bluster ahead of cool-headedness;
- He repeatedly declared **"I love wars;"** showed more **respect for Vladamir Putin** than he exhibited towards his own President; threatened to **wall off America against immigration; manifested outright Islamophobia;** and promised to undo America's alliances and treaty obligations;
- Trump, by his own declarations, has a **manifest disconnect with the global fight against terrorism.** His claim about his possession of a secret plan to fight **DAESH (ISIS)** is laughable. And his assertions that he knows about strategy **"more than the generals"** is lunacy. Especially that he has evaded serving in any military role or capacity;
- **He regarded tax evasion and avoidance as adeptness** at using the law as a vehicle for manipulation.

Keeping all the above in mind, to which we should add **his disdain for women, his uncontrolled propensity for unwanted and offensive sexual advances,** and his refusal to pay those who work for him, in violation of his contracts, **how can Trump lead America of the 21st Century?**

The danger of a mobocracy which produced a Trump presidency cannot be over-stated. He can have his way for **"America First."** But how can **he be trusted with the nuclear code,** with treating his political adversaries with respect, with the issues of climate change, the sanctity of treaties, free trade, and bolstering international institutions such as the United Nations family of organizations, about all of which he invented stupid accusations?

"**Making American Great Again,**" his battle cry, implies that America has been **on a slippery slope due to a dysfunctional system.** Any system of governance is always in need of change, because circumstances keep on changing. But how can President-elect Trump walk back from an ideology of **"making America hate again?"**

His unpredicted and unmerited victory has been due to an electoral system in which he does not believe. It was also due to the rise of the poorly educated white population in the industrial belt who **blamed economic unequality on the wrong party -the immigrant. The browning of America (by the year 2030, the white demography shall be at 45%).** The culture of fear was Trump's daily tool which was allowed a cost free microphone 24/7. And the length of the Clintons exposure on the American stage for 3 decades entailed the **negative cost of over exposure.**

An era of American history has just ended on November 8, 2016. And an uncertain era of anxiety has just begun. The writing is on the wall:

- Through gerrymandering, the Republican Party, the party of war and foreign interventions, has built institutions at the state level. The result: **38 out of 50 state governors are Republican;** both houses of Congress have Republican majorities sent through State elections;

- Since the passing of Justice Scalia, the US Supreme Court has been functioning without its full complement of nine justices. Votes of 4 to 4 means non-revision of the judgments of lower courts. **A defacto nullification of the Supreme Court's role of judicial review.** Now a Republican President, with expected support from a Republican majority in the Senate, can name and appoint conservative justices. Thus tilting the highest court of the land further to the right;

- Undoing the historic Obama signature legislative achievement, **"The Affordable Care Act."** Providing health insurance so far to nearly half of the 40 millions Americans who cannot afford health insurance;

- Cutting income taxes for the **top 1% of Americans (the billionaire class);**

- Threatening to deport en masse **11 million undocumented immigrants,** before **"allowing them to re-enter America legally."** Thus tearing the fragile fabric of poor families whose adults have invested their energies in jobs not preferred by American citizens;

- **Supporting the National Rifle Association (NRA),** under the deceptive mask of supporting the **2nd Amendment of the U.S. Constitution. There are 350 million guns in the hands of 9 million Americans.** Annually causing 30,000 deaths by gun violence all over America;
- **Pretending to be charitable to worthy causes,** such as the American veterans, when in fact hardly any contributions were made; and
- **Threatening to sue all women** (so far the total of 12) who have come forward accusing him of criminally assaulting them sexually.

Trump has called President Obama **"a traitor;"** threatened to institute criminal prosecution against Secretary of State Hillary Clinton for what he has fabricated as her **"gross negligence"** in Benghazi. That is where the U.S. Ambassador and 4 other Americans were killed by marauding Libyan militias. **It was the Republican's** in Congress who had refused to fund diplomatic security arrangements abroad. And the unfortunate death of that Ambassador was due to his decision to **travel from Tripoli to Benghazi where no security at that US facility was up to par.**

Trump's presidency **shall undoubtedly reflect the deep chasms in American society;** the decline of conventional norms of governance in Washington, D.C.; **the absence of the citizen's trust in law and order measures and institutions,** including the FBI as a neutral investigative arm of the Department of Justice; **the resurgence of torture of individuals suspected of terrorism.** Thus upending the legal principle of **"you are innocent until proven guilty by court of law."**

Even the appointment of top experts to make up for the inexpertise of Trump in governance, shall prove to be a futile remedy. The Donald's span of attention is very short; he digresses instinctively; he failed 3 times in debating Hillary; he gets bored with details; **and he has repeatedly declared that he relies only on his gut feelings.**

Snakes have the natural capacity of changing their skin. But not their nature. "Healing wounds," declared by Trump upon securing 278 electoral votes (for Hillary's 208 votes), shall be an impossibility for Trump, a racist who has befriended the stalwarts of the Klu Klux Klan.

Even Trump's battle cry **"Make America Great Again"** is plagiarized. Its **original author is James Fallon, national reporter of The Atlantic magazine.** That is the title of his book published in 1989.

Yet there may still be a ray of hope of this USA **-United States of Anxiety.** In the Senate, the Republicans have 54 seats, not the majority of 60 needed to overturn important items of Obama's legacy. Neither the so-called Obama Care, nor the right to abortion **(Trump has threatened women seeking abortion with punishment),** nor existing treaties which are already the law of the land since 1832.

In her concession speech, Hillary Clinton urged her supporters to **"continue to fight for what is right."** She added **"we must defend the American dream which is big enough for everyone."** So the battle for the soul of America is not an end.

But the message of Trump's victory to the outside world is that as **America has turned to the right and inward.** So should other States, looking for an American global role, seek their salvation from within. **"The Strong State" is the logical answer to the Trump so-called movement.**

It is catastrophic to see Obama, **a professor of constitutional law,** be replaced by someone who was **publicly challenged by a gold star father, Khizer Khan, a Muslim whose son, an American army officer was killed in Iraq.** His words addressed to Trump shall live on for a long time: **"Have You Even Read the U.S. Constitution!!"**

Trump's elevation to the presidency of America is akin to the **peasant rebellions of medieval Europe.** The periphery, for long neglected, rising, avenging their neglect from the center.

In multiple cities, anti-Trump demonstrations broke out. By the thousands, they marched through the streets from coast to coast. Their slogan was **"Not My President."** This is a reverse echo of the chants by what **those who could not accept a black man, Obama, to be their president.** An early sign of a deeply divided nation.

Calls are now filling the air. Calling on the Democratic leadership to step aside. Its ineptness in ignoring the backwoods where **"the forgotten"** either voted for Trump or stayed home on election day, shall undoubtedly be punished. This now looks like a form of an **"American Spring"** where the Millennials, the minorities, the women, and the blacks are lashing at both Trumpism and the old guard of the Democratic party.

What makes America America are not only the Declaration of Independence, and the Constitution. To these, one should add underlying but vibrant concepts. These are freedom of speech, freedom of assembly, equality before the law, no formal State religion, no formal language, no king, freedom of movement, openness to immigration, civilian control over the military, freedom of the press, freedom of choice, an independent judiciary, and enforced respect for privacy. Above all, **a peaceful and orderly transfer of power.**

This entire fabric of what makes the U.S. an attractive place to live and prosper shall be **severely tested by Trump -a racist and a xenophobe.** An unqualified, narcissistic, lying bully, against whom a popular majority has voted on November 8, **shall be sworn in on January 20, 2017 as the 45th President of the United States.** A magnification of the failures of democracy -**a term which has no precise definition in any legal dictionary.**

November 8, 2016 marks a huge turning point in American history.

- It shall be the date on which **a con man, a charlatan, was made President-elect;**
- His elevation to lead this great and powerful country was not through a popular vote. It was **through a dysfunctional system which delegates my vote to electors who can direct it to their choice, not mine;**
- **His victory is a defeat for an inclusive America, a post-racial America,** and America which by its own constitution must separate between religion and the State, **an America whose strength has been partly due to immigration, and partly through innovation;**
- Regardless of present feverish attempts to make him act presidential, he shall always be what he has been for his whole 70 years of life -**a rich man with no social conscience.** You cannot make a pig attractive by applying lipstick to its mouth.

So, **America, from now on, you have no claim to advise the world as to what democracy is, or how human rights might be observed;** or how to run their national life.

The News Desk of the **New Yorker** magazine wrote: **"The rest of the world is now at leisure to stand back and ponder the astounding dereliction of the American Presidential election."**

Mr. Trump: Like all the millions of Americans now planning to demonstrate against your presidency on January 20, 2017, I shall chant: **You Are Not My President:**

- **For you have no faith in the principles under-girding the U.S. Constitution;**
- **Your presidency has happened through deceptive promises to masses which fear the future;** and
- Your gutter language about **"a rigged system"** has made the teaching of national civics and respect for the law a real challenge. **For it was an idiocyncratic system which made of you, a crooked billionaire who defied every norm, a president-elect.**

The America which I have inhabited for 64 years has never elected for the presidency as vile a person as Trump. This shocking development has come about for a host of complex reasons. Not the least of these is that **Obama soaring favorability could not be transferred to Hillary Clinton. The Latino-Black coalition exists in name only.** One third of the Latin vote went to Trump, for the alluring promise of jobs. The threat of a wall on the Mexican border did not scare them off. And sizable numbers of the blacks did not vote. **A non-vote, in effect, was a vote for Trump.**

Now the only ray of hope for the de-Trumpization of America is in Trump's impeachment for any illegal act by him as President. Or in his voluntary resignation. Trump's removal, if it happens, would come at a much cheaper cost to America than threat of possibility of civil war.

EGYPTIAN MYTHOLOGY REGARDING AMERICA'S LOVE FOR THE MUSLIM BROTHERHOOD

Friday, November 18, 2016

Following Trump's non-merited victory in the presidential elections, there was elation in the Egyptian media. **A non-merited political victory in America causing euphoria in the Egyptian media.** Caused by the faulty assumption that Trump's victory shall diminish the Brotherhood sway in Washington, D.C.

This Egyptian mythology becomes more intriguing as some Egyptian opinion-makers claim that Hillary and Obama **"conspired with the Brothers against Egypt."** This is a direct quote from a message from a senior former Egyptian Ambassador.

I cannot falsely claim that I am neutral in my assessment of **Trump as a post-modern thug, or of the Brotherhood, as a dangerous vehicle of terrorism in the name of Islam.** Neutrality in either case would constitute, for me at least, giving my brain and my reasoning a holiday.

Having dealt in my previous blog postings with fascist Donald, my focus in this writing is on **the fraudulent assumptions that the Brotherhood had so far held sway in official Washington, D.C.** This myth of affinity is nothing more than **Brotherhood's propaganda** which the unwary Egyptian media and thinkers have come to take seriously.

Never wishing to lecture, except in my classrooms in New York City, as this would be a false self-elevation. I only wish here to share thoughts and observations gained from **my close proximity to the American political** environment. This proximity is continually enriched by my daily research and writing, as well as by my interactions with **a steady stream of thought updating from my own students and interns.**

New knowledge is my daily business. Old assumptions are my daily feeding of the trash bins. This has been impressed upon me since my senior year in **my beloved high school in Egypt (Zagazig High School)** where, in the science section, I nationally competed for the prize in the **Darwin theory of evolution. Evolve or perish.** I choose the former.

This month of **November 2016 marks the fourth abysmal anniversary of former Egyptian President, Mohamed Morsi,** declaring himself to be above the law. That declaration of November 2012 **marked the rise of Brotherhood fascism subverting the democratic goals** of post-Mubarak Egypt.

It also mercifully marked **the beginning of the end of Islamist rule in the country of 100 million Arabs,** nearly one third of the Arab nation. The demise of that dark rule was also by a popular uprising in June 2013 whose **success had to be guaranteed by the might of the Egyptian armed forces.** Case closed!!

America's grumbling about those developments, ignorantly calling the June 30 Revolution a military coup, was **never due to the influence of the Brotherhood in America.** It was due to America's sticking to the false measurement of **"every opposition is a form of democratic expression."** Not so!!

For the **"right to self-determination,"** a right derived from sovereignty which resides in the populace, **implies the right to determine what form of democracy it chooses.** There is no global consensus as to what democracy is, or how it should be practiced.

Case in point: Has the choice of Trump as President-elect come about through what should be considered **"democracy?" No!! It is a result of the Electoral College,** an anachronism in the US Constitution **intended to keep the mobs away** from having their votes directly counted. My vote for Hillary who got the majority of popular votes (63 million to 58 million) did not register. Swallowed in the bowels of a perennial quirk in American democracy.

There is another **anomaly in America's early support for the Brotherhood in Egypt.** That support, **now vanished,** was manifested by

Perspectives on Egypt, Islam and the Dark Era of Trump

Secretary of State Hillary Clinton meeting in Cairo and elsewhere with Brotherhood representatives. That was not to assist in the political aggrandizement of **the Brotherhood's Guidance Bureau** in Egypt. **It was to serve national American interests** in the largest Arab country.

Those American efforts are **legitimate pursuit of national American interests.** This is what national sovereignty is all about. **There is no love or hate in international relations. There are only national interests.** When they converge with foreign national interest, we call this convergence **"alliance."**

Alliances are not marriages. They are temporary liaison affairs which may sour at any moment. That notion is perennial, the relations with other nations are changeable. **The lessons of Darwinian evolution.**

This is why **outside intervention in national affairs is the riskiest form of relationship. Good fences (they are called borders) make for good neighbors.** And that good neighbor might be far away, but brought closer by mutual interests. Another reason why the Brotherhood had failed in Egypt, and ended up marked as **"terrorist."** In its terrorist acts in Egypt, it kept on **looking for support from beyond** national borders.

An organization which calls for foreign intervention through diplomacy, arms, funds, or propaganda, **is a traitor organization.** That is why the **most odious and stupid charge that Trump addressed to Obama was to call him "traitor."** There has never been any scintilla of proof on that. On the reverse side, it was billionaire **Trump who openly encouraged Russia to intervene in the American elections.** Through hacking into the emails of the Democratic National Convention.
Now **Trump (the traitor by these obvious measurements)** shall become President over the nation which he had deceived.

Add to **the falsehood of the Brotherhood claims of amity with the Democratic party,** and its treacherous attempt to subvert Egyptian sovereignty through soliciting foreign intervention, another dangerous falsehood. That is the unfounded claims by the same Egyptian source or sources that **"the lady (meaning Hillary) is the worst."** And that she and Obama **"conspired ...against Egypt and other Arab countries."** Mere words without the requisite backing of proof.

My disparaging such reasoning is not based on my being an attorney - searching for proof before I open my mouth. Attorneys do not have that dangerous luxury. It is based on my having taught political science before I taught law.

And my political science background has kept me a willing ally of national sovereignty. **Our world is made up of the nation-States. The United Nations** is an inter-state system, **not an inter-nation system.** Even in Islamic jurisprudence, I teach that Islam did not create a State. It created an **"Umma"** (a community). **What holds a State together is its internal strength.**

Thus a State that complains of **"conspiracy"** is in fact a weak State that **blames its misfortunes on others. Competition about national interests is not conspiracy.** So when my Egyptian respondents cry about what they erroneously see as an Obama/Clinton conspiracy on Egypt, **they in fact convey lack of awareness that the New Egypt is no longer buffeted by outside conspiracies.** Not even in its anti-terrorist struggle against the Sinai hit and run criminal marauders.

Where is my proof? Egypt of the present is rapidly transitioning to **"The Strong State." That transition is even recognized by crazy Trump.** One of his main surrogates, Rudolph Giuliani, former Mayor of New York City, and the author of the foreword to my 1999 book entitled **"Government Ethics and Law Enforcement"** admitted to this publicly.

Asked on November 13 about Trump's envisaged ban on Muslims, Giuliani, who might be considered for a high post in the Trump administration, his response was a testimony to the effects on America of **"the Strong State."** In effect, he **specifically cited Egypt as an example of the Arab State with which a Trump administration can vet** (scrutinize in advance) applicants for immigration to the U.S. Why?: **"Because El-Sisi government, a strong ally, has done a good job at combating the Muslim Brotherhood in Egypt."**

Where in his response do you find the value, any value, of **the Brotherhood megaphones** in Times Square, New York, or Washington, D.C.? **Gone with the wind.** In fact where in that early recognition of Trumpian recognition of Egypt as a Strong State is the effect of all the trash that **American non-governmental organizations** are heaping on Cairo for human rights abuses? **None!!** Why?

These NGOs are valuable to an interventionist America. **They are its cat paws.** The Obama administration has reduced their credibility. This is due to the Obama doctrine of **"leading from behind."** It also reflects

America's pivoting away from the Middle East and shifting those resources **to Asia and to trade.**

Those claiming that the Muslim Brotherhood is Washington's darling should learn an essential new fact about America and the world, especially the Middle East. That is that the American center is no longer the federal government. **The center now is defused among 50 states, calling themselves the United States of America.** By the Tenth Amendment of the U.S. Constitution, **powers not given by the Constitution to the federal government belong automatically to the States. (The Supremacy Clause).**

And as they say, **"the proof is in the pudding." Trump won the presidency by vilifying Washington, D.C.,** and gambling on his support from the State legislatures, fashioned, through gerrymandering, vote suppression, and the strongest voter ID requirements. **All of which are non-democratic methods.**

But it worked for him, and for the entire Republican party which now has Republican governors in 38 states, majorities in the two houses of Congress, and now the Oval Office. **The party of Lincoln is now owned by Trump,** the man who ferociously attacked Hillary, the Yale Law graduate, and **cuddled Sarah Palin who could hardly know how to read the U.S. Constitution.**

A point of convergence between Cairo of today and Washington of Trump is the emphasis on **"jobs and the economy."** For the opposition in Egypt claims that more than 25% of Egyptians are below the poverty line, so does the opposition to Obama claiming that 40 million America children go to bed hungry. Bill Clinton, a southern governor from Arkansas, won the presidency twice largely on the slogan: **"It is the Economy Stupid."**

No wonder that the chief operating officer of a major American bank (Pharos Investments) spoke optimistically about Egypt which has been approved to receive $12 Billion as a loan from the International Monetary Fund. Mr. Angus Blair, reflecting the attitude of fellow bankers about the New Egypt's floating its national currency, said: **"They are pleased that there is new thinking which is what Egypt needs."**

Please, Mr. Banker, say this to the doom and gloom sayers in Egypt. Tell them to leave Cairo and go visit the country side. This is where Egypt's pulse is. Even a weak pulse is a sign of life. A life of a new rebirth of the Strong State, now recovering from 60 years of military

dictatorship.

The New Egypt should rid itself of the stale thoughts of the past. **Replacing those thoughts and resultant mythology by facts that matter.** Together with a convalescing economy and a strong army, ensuring non-porous borders, **Egypt needs opinion-makers trained in connecting the dots.**

They say that camels walk faster at the sound of the flute. **Let Egyptian writers play their flutes to help that caravan move forward across even non-chartered deserts.**

Opinion-makers in America expect trouble in Trump America. Describing Trump's victory, one of them, **David Remnick of the New Yorker magazine,** characterized it as "an American tragedy." Then went on to call it "an event that will likely cast the country into a period of economic, political and social uncertainty that we cannot yet imagine."

Uncertainty about America does not augur well for the rest of the world. In fact, within 96 hours of his victory, **Trump, on TV, proved that his ultra-right bluster during the campaign threatens to become policy.**

In that TV interview he: **affirmed that the wall between America and Mexico shall be built,** from 2 million to 3 million illegal immigrants shall be the first installment of deportees, and looking menacingly through the cameras, he sternly ordered the anti-Trump demonstrators **"Stop It."**

He is already proving those who are writing to me that **"his bark is more threatening than his bite,"** or that **"the lady would have been much worse than him"** are dreamers.

With internal instability being ushered to the American streets, **countries like Egypt should, as of now, double their efforts to rebuild themselves from within.** It has always been my belief and advocacy that **national deliverance happens from within,** and that planning on the basis of reliance on help from beyond the border is a national gamble.

Even Emperor Donald J. Trump has admonished States relying on American defense: **"Go Defend Yourselves Or Pay Us."**

Observing our world of today, it doesn't take much thoughtfulness to conclude that **the world is pivoting to the right.** From America to

Europe, both west and east, to Russia to India to Japan, **the right is ascending. From globalism, our world is, in many ways, returning to tribalism.**

That is why the sovereign response at the national level is the Strong State. Alliances between strong states, whose national interests intersect, shall last as long as that intersection lasts.

For the Arab people, following the settlement of their national upheavals, **their future as a regional grouping shall only be served by the fulfillment of an old dream: the formation of the United Arab States (UAS). Not a union, but a federation** where the internally sovereign State shall go on, with the sinews of foreign affairs and defense are in the hand of a federal council.

This is the Swiss model of cantons, adjusted by the American constitutional model of supremacy for the individual State where powers are not allocated to the federal council. **Is this an Arab mythology? Maybe. But it is more logical than the present do nothing League of Arab States** where the future of some of its members is being shaped by non-Arab States.

For a United Arab States, the Arabs have the fabric. But so far, neither the will nor the tailor!!

To those who write to me saying that Hillary would have been worse for America than Trump, I say: You don't understand America. Comparing Hillary to Trump, is like **equating between experience and demagoguery.**

What has occurred in America on November 8, 2016, has been described as **"an epic mistake"** (Paul Krugman, Nobel Laureate in economics). Within 24 hours of that characterization, **Trump appointed Stephen Bannon as his Chief White House Strategist and senior counselor.** Bannon, the chief editor of Breitbart News, is the guru of white supremacists, the propagator of Islamophobia, and a man who made of hate an industry.

By such indicators, Trump is not embarking upon healing America's wounds. He is **launching a reign of racial, ethnic and religious hatreds, thus raising the specter of civil strife.**

For now, **rage has overcome sanity, and ignorance is about to**

overwhelm recognizable norms of governance. As the least politically experienced president-elect in modern American history, Trump is especially known for his **"I alone can fix it."** A most pretentious bombast.

A number of Arab leaders are scampering today to befriend Trump. Trying to get to his boat by climbing over the edges. To them, I offer the following:

• Remember that **that boat has a hole in its bottom.** Allowing the waters of Islamophobia, racism, war mongering, and the Trump family business, to rush through it;

• Remember that, under a Trump administration, **"America First," "deals are people,"** and sudden changes of mind, are Donald's political persona;

• **Remember that Trump's history reflects no lasting loyalties;**

• Remember that, by all means, **a changed America might still offer opportunities for an Arab renaissance subservient to no outsider.** For in this period of world tribalism and rage, **the way to national success is to put diplomacy in the service of clearly defined national goals. Trump is temporary. And Hillary is gone. But prudence calls for expecting a furious return of the Democrats** under a new leadership to oust the regime that came to power in spite of the popular vote.

• *Remember that under the U.S. Constitution, the federal government is one of enumerated (i.e. limited) powers. The States, and by extension, the cities, are where most of the powers reside. New York City, for example, has already defied Trump on immigration. Its police is not federal. Nor is its educational system. Nor is its voter ID system.*

Because of Trump, the United States may constitutionally be reverting to Athenian democracy: The City State. Back to the future!!

LAUNCHED BY TRUMP, A WAR OF CULTURES HAS BEGUN!!

Friday, December 2, 2016

One has to be blind not to see in the utterances of Trump and his coterie **the launching of a war of cultures!! A war against Islam, Blacks, Jews, and all non-whites.** Words have consequences, and appointments by Trump underline the gravity of those consequences.

Trump began his campaign for the presidency by calling for **"a Muslim ban on entering the U.S.,"** thus converting **Islamophobia into one of the fronts in his war of cultures.** From fear of Islam into a declared aggression in the form of singling out **Muslims as enemies of America.**

The Trump movement did not stop there. His appointee to the post of national security advisor, **General Michael Flynn publicly declared that "Islam is not a religion, but an ideology."** Elaborating on his Nazi-like pronouncements against the faith of 1.7 billion Muslims, Flynn called Islam **"a malignant cancer."**

Former Secretary of State **Colin Powell** described Flynn as a **"right-wing nutty."** Flynn circulated a video declaring: **"Fearing Islam, which wants 80 percent of humanity enslaved or exterminated, is totally rational and hence cannot possibly be called phobia."**

As a national security advisor, Flynn is charged with **guiding the president on all foreign policy matters.** Furthermore, that extreme anti-Islam propagandist is the coordinator of all foreign policy across all agencies.

Soon the **cavalry of hate, spearheaded by cultural warriors was given formal recognition** through another appointment. That of **Steven Bannon** to the White House post of **chief strategist for the President.** Bannon has worked for 11 years as the editor of **Breitbart News,** a medium for the **Alt-Right** -a fascist entity advocating that **"America is for the whites only."** In addition, Bannon is well known for **his unalterable anti-Islamic views and prejudices.**

So now you have two of the most senior staff positions in the Trump White House qualifying for top aides in the new war of cultures.

Logically, behind the forward leadership of the shock troops come the foot soldiers. People like **Richard Spencer, head of the National Policy Institute.** To his audience who raised their arms in **the Nazi salute** on November 20, Spencer declared as follows: **"White identity is at the core of both the alt-right movement and the Trump movement, even if most voters for Mr. Trump aren't willing to articulate it as such."**

Spencer's audience full throatedly screamed: **"Heil the people. Heil victory."** It was the perfect environment for **hysteria befitting the harangues of Goebbels.** In a cultural war, you need first to **attack the credibility of the media outlets of your opponent.** Thus Spencer pivoted to attacking the American mainstream media which Trump has systematically attacked as **"the media is crooked."**

The response of the Spencer rally was not disappointing. For he, with the swagger of a winning boxer, demanded an unequivocal endorsement of his racism. Said he: **"Perhaps we should refer to them (the media) in the original German." "Lugen presse."** To this stimulation, they roared back mimicking the Nazi-era term for **"lying press."**

Of course, in Trump's newly-launched cultural war, **fact-checking is a poisonous tool, as the big lie technique should stand unchallenged.** How enraging it must have been for Trump and his cohorts to be challenged by both **Fact Check and Buzz Feed.** These two organizations have determined that **more than 50% of Trump's pronouncements were blatant lies.** Including his assertion that he saw **"Thousands upon thousands of Muslims dancing in New Jersey at the collapse of the World Trade Center."** It never happened.

No exit from the scrutiny of a free investigative press of the stream of lies is overlooked. There are the Trump surrogates to explain that Trump was misquoted or misinterpreted. Or **"It was never said."** Or, frequently in the case of Trump: **"I don't recall,"** or **"I was told,"** or **"why are we focused on this issue"** (as in the case of 12 women complaining of Trump groping them). And if all else fails **"I shall sue,"** and **"I shall never settle."**

Well, **Trump was forced to settle the Trump University scandal for $25 million.** Refunds were arranged for the thousands who were fraudulently enticed to pay tuition in return for the **illusive quest for getting rich quickly through learning Trump's Art of the Deal.**

Note that for **Trump, the law is a construct of loopholes to be exploited** in order to evade paying taxes. For that tax evasion, Trump was described by one of his hired guns, **Rudolph Giuliani, "a genius."**

Well, if Trump who claims to be a billionaire, is applauded by a former Mayor of New York City, what do you think of the impact of that spin on the average citizen who is obliged by law to pay taxes in accordance with his/her level of income? Undoubtedly, **non-observance of the law would become a national practice!!**

Speaking of the law, as Trump thrusts this great country in a war of cultures, let us examine **his appointment for the post of Attorney General.** It is none other than **Senator Jeff Sessions of Alabama.** An avid **anti-black racist** who, as attorney general of Alabama had this to say about a defense attorney. **"He is a shame to his race!!"** That attorney was white, his clients were black. Later, Sessions who later sat on the **Senate Judiciary Committee,** called a black attorney **"boy"** -a term reserved in the south for black men.

In no way could Sessions, if confirmed by the Senate, in his capacity as head of the Department of Justice, divest himself from his anti-black past. Jeff Sessions, in 1986, had the dubious distinction of being rejected by that Committee as a nominee for a federal judgeship **"due to his racist comments and behavior."**

The would-be chief enforcer of the law in America **has associated with FAIR (the Federation for American Immigration Reform)** which is hostile to immigration and is committed to racial selectivity. Its founder, **John Tanton** has **repeatedly expressed the wish that America** remain a majority-white population.

The anti-Islamic, Mike Pompeo of Kansas, is now Trump's nominee for Director of the CIA. He believes that **"most Islamic leaders across**

America were complicit in terrorism."

The election of **Obama** to the presidency had the **effect of baring the racial and religious divides in America.** Racism, in particular, has now bubbled in the open, pointing to a sad fact: **The South, at least at the local levels, is still fighting the American Civil War by other means.**

And Trump, sensing that tilt at the local and State levels, found a wave which he could surf to the top. The Democrats failed, as they focused on the elite, the urban, and the college-degree holders. The blue collar workers, left behind by globalism, and **hungry for change, any change,** were lured by Trump's **"Make America Great Again."**

Through Trump's victory, this mantra has become **"Make America White Again."** A catch-all phrase for a battle cry in the rush toward a war of cultures. A war in which the **perceived enemies are local: From Jews, to Muslims. From Blacks to Latinos. From the Brown to the hyphenated names and foreign accents.** The early skirmishes incidental to the larger battle are on:

- 31% increase in hate crimes; 701 incidents have already been recorded;
- **Swastikas** have been scrawled **on synagogues;**
- **"You could kiss your visas good-bye"** is now frequently hurled at Muslim taxi drivers;
- **False claims** by General Flynn and others that **Sharia is spreading in America. It is not.** In fact, 38 states have either legislated, or on their way to legislating that the word **"Sharia"** cannot be mentioned in their courts. They, ignorantly regard it as antithetical to American values and the Constitution;
- Now there is **Trumpian conversations about registering Muslims in America, and even applying the U.S. Supreme Court decision in the Korematsu case to Muslims.** That is the Supreme Court's infamous 1944 Japanese internment decision. Approving the herding of hundreds of thousands of Japanese Americans into detention camps following the 1941 **Japanese attack on Pearl Harbor.**
- That decision has not been repealed, thus **potentially allowing it to apply to Muslim Americans.** Such threats are legally considered an assault, especially when accompanied by **"the apparent present ability to give effect to that attempt if not prevented."**

Those fears had, on Friday, November 18 **brought together Muslim,**

Jewish and Christian clergy members and lay leaders to gather in front of a mosque in Washington in a demonstration of mutual support. Sensing the dangers of the Trumpian threatened measures, they formed an inter-faith group called **"Shoulder to Shoulder."**

Their call on Trump is clear and simple: **"Keep your promise that you shall serve as the president of all Americans."**

The question here should be centered on the cultural war. Analyzing Trump from this perspective is challenging. Not because his racial and ethnic preferences are not already clear. But because Trump is showing the face of a normalized Trump in contacts with some of the foreign powers.

Trump who manifests friendship to **Egypt, the Emirates, and Japan,** is a different face. For the appeasement of the Republican party, the protection of his 110 businesses in 22 countries, **including the far-flung Muslim world, and the need to give priority to jobs in America,** all combine to give diplomacy a seat at the Trump's table.

As a deal-maker, Trump by core beliefs, practices, appointments to his administration, and to his populist base, is possessed of two personas: **the one inside America, divisiveness on the basis of ethnicity and religion** is to become the norm. And one for the outside, provided it does not project weakness.

The issue here is beyond diplomacy where negotiations or force may be employed. The issue is that a war of cultures inside America shall undoubtedly have grave repercussions, especially in the world of Islam. His top lieutenants have already withdrawn their recognition of Islam as a religion. Thus enabling ISIS which is now splintering into poisonous units all over the world. But through Trumpian hallucinations are provided fresh oxygen for recruiting, funding, and operating.

In this connection, Trump and his team are reading **"The Islamic State"** backward. To them, it is **"The State of Islam."** For the Trumpists, being hostage to social media, the very tool of ISIS franchises, have become **brainwashed by the narrative of terrorism.**

As such, the Trumpian narrative about Islam, nurtured by the ISIS narrative, **is blind to the present New Religious Revolution waged, primarily, by Al-Azhar in Cairo, and its Rector, Dr. Ahmed El-Taiyeb.** The tenets of this counter-jihadism are centered on:

- **Islamic law is supplemented by legislation;**
- Equality among all faiths is built on Islamic jurisprudence;
- **"Allahu Akbar"** means that all **humans are equal in the eyes of the Creator;**
- Justice and knowledge are essential to Islamic practices;
- Regardless of variety of practices in the geographic expanse of Islam, **gender equality is guaranteed;**
- No **"holy war"** in Islam; **only self-defense within your boundaries;**
- Removing a dictator is a religious duty, providing that such action **would not result in Fitna (self-help without the benefit of law);**
- Cooperation within a community and inter-communally must be **premised on the public good;** and
- Respect for local laws is incumbent upon a Muslim residing in non-Muslim countries.

Just read about that Religious Revolution set forth in four statements recently made by the Grand Imam of Al-Azhar in **Nigeria, Germany, France and Russia (Chechnya).**

How very alien are these tenets from the false advocacy of the likes of Bin Laden or Al-Baghdadi of ISIS!! And how ignorant is Trump's war of cultures of these principles!!

No wonder that a writer for the Op Ed page of the **New York Times, Charles Blow** commented in the issue of November 21 on the orange color of Trump's face: **"That orange glow emanating from the man is the sun setting on America's progress, however slow and halting, on race and gender inclusion and equity."**

Responding petulantly to such assessments, **Trump, the king of tweeting,** responded angrily: **"The New York Times is a failing newspaper."** *He* *even chided CNN for only showing bad angles of his face. How pitiful and silly for an American president-elect to be enamored with his facial looks more than with his threatening substance!!*

The **foregoing is not a hateful analysis. It is the analysis of hate.** Mr. Trump: Your enmity towards **"the other"** can be seen through the naked eye. Your first salvo in your war of cultures was the declaration of a Muslim ban.

While **Bush junior,** even in the heat of 9/11, declared that **"we are not at war with Islam."** But Donald declared, 15 years after 9/11, that the **problem with US Security was Islam.** His National Security Advisor, General Flynn, declared that **"Islam is not a religion, it is an ideology."**

So here is a mini-lesson for those who wish to read about the **history of the global Muslim reaction to terrorism from which the Muslim World had suffered the most:**

- **In 1997, the first head of State to call for a global effort against terrorism was Egypt's former President, Hosni Mubarak.** That call came from the rostrum of the US General Assembly.
- Before that 1997 global call from Egypt, which now, under President El-Sisi, is in the throes of combating terrorism on its own territory, was a **Mubarak presidential decree of 1996.** It was to the effect that all terror incidents should be brought, **not before civil law courts, but before military courts.** That was Egypt's response to the **Saber Farahat terrorist attacks on the Semiramis Hotel (Cairo) in 1993,** and later on the visitors of the Cairo Egyptian Museum in 1996.
- Farahat was apprehended, brought before a military tribunal and executed. I was the attorney for the US attorneys who were claiming, for the foreign victims at Semiramis, monetary compensation from Egypt. The Egyptian Court of Cassation offered the maximum under Egyptian law; I counselled acceptance; the US attorneys on the case demurred; an **a federal court in New York City gave them zero.** Saying: **"The case has already been decided by the Egyptian judiciary -a competent judiciary."**
- And in **1998, the League of Arab States adopted the first international regional convention on terrorism; followed in 1999, by a similar convention adopted by the Organization of Islamic Cooperation** (57 States), based in Jeddah, Saudi Arabia.

- All the while, the U.S., governmental and non-governmental entities were howling **"foul"** at these timely anti-jihadi efforts. **Reason: the wrong reason. They were placing due process for the individual ahead of due process for the community.**

- **When 9/11 happened, a major crime against humanity,** and in which hundreds of Muslims perished as a segment of the 3000 victims, Saudi Prince **Walid Bin Talal offered Mayor Rudolph Giuliani $10 million to** aid the first responders.

- Giuliani rejected that humanitarian effort for a flimsy reason. Prince Walid, in a TV interview had been asked: **"Do you think that 9/11 happened because of US policies favoring Israel?"** Bin Talal replied: **"I can't exclude it."**

- A few years later, **Giuliani, now chosen by Trump for a top security post in his administration, went to the Muslim region to make millions** of dollars through consultancies and speeches. **General Flynn was not too far behind in making lots of money through counselling Turkey -a Muslim majority country.**

- Thousands of Muslims are now serving in **various American police departments and in the US armed forces. Millions of US Muslim civilians are daily contributing to US advancement. Steve Jobs, the father of the digital age, was a Syrian.**

Mr. Trump: Before you open your mouth with assaults on Muslims and other American minorities, know that you yourself seem to have little regard for US laws: Not only on tax laws; on contract law; on due process law; on entitlements law; on anti-discrimination law; on religious liberty laws.

Even in regard to conflict of interest laws, you, at present, are refusing to separate between your personal wealth and America's commonwealth. Your family, which is your primary source of counselling, cannot run your business as of the moment you take the oath of office on January 20, 2017.

Mr. Trump: Your ignorance of the law is documented by your lack of knowledge of your own presidential powers. Were you to stop for a couple of hours in order to read the U.S. Constitution, you shall find that you have only **ONE POWER. The power of pardon.** (It is a well known fact that you do not read.) The **Supremacy Clause of the U.S. Constitution does not mean you, Mr. Trump.** It means **the States** where powers which are not allocated to the federal government become automatically State powers.

Now the cities and mayors are rising up to defy your plans for mass deportation of millions of undocumented immigrants. **The United States is fast becoming "The United States of the City States."** The States have the exclusive powers on their police forces.

And if you can spare more time for a modicum of studenthood in international trade law, you will find that your bluster against international trade agreements is nothing but ignorant Trumpese.

Rejecting the Trans-Pacific Partnership by you is a hollow threat. China has already cordoned off America through her proposal for a **"Free Trade Area of the Asia Pacific."** Both Peru and Chile are anxious to join it.

Your empty rhetorical nonsense about China, whose steel built your gambling casinos, has been ridiculed by experts who dismiss your bombast. The Peterson Institute for International Economics has concluded that **"a full-blown trade with China and Mexico would push unemployment in the United States to nearly 9 percent, in 2020, from 4.9 percent today."** What would the millions of working-class Americans who voted for you say to that, Donald? **"Defrauded Again!!"**

And Mexico has now undervalued its currency. Thus making its products more competitive, and its territory more inviting to American manufacture. The Ford Motor Company is planning to have its small cars assembled, not in America, but in Mexico. Labor in Mexico is paid only 15% per hour as compared to labor pay in the U.S. It is Mexico that has already built its wall, an economic wall, not the Trump wall, at the southern border.

DR. YASSIN EL-AYOUTY, ESQ.

In the **New Yorker** of November 25, Ali Fitzgerald posted this headline: **"Post-Election Nihilist Horoscope."** Then predicted: **"The new orange-tinted moon of November 8th will usher in an age of extreme darkness -lighting only the houses of racism, misogyny, and gross red hats."**

Donald: You often repeated "I love wars!!" Regardless of any Trumpist spin which you and your team might employ, wars shall not "Make American Great Again."

UNDER TRUMP, THE ARRIVAL OF A CHAOTIC "AMERICAN SPRING!!"

Monday, February 20, 2017

This is a **"Made In America"** American Spring. Quite different from the Arab Spring. **Its participants are not the masses. They are the billionaires.** Its ethos is not democracy; it is the gradual destruction of democratic institutions, with the freedom of the press, a constitutional right under the First Amendment, as a primary target.

As in the Arab Spring, there is no recognizable spokesman. Though Trump is the President, who gushes out daily with **"alternative facts"** (meaning falsehoods), the White House staff spins what the Donald says. This is while the Cabinet reshapes those utterances in various forms. In the meantime, **the civil service**(two millions of them in various departments) **ignores those directions,** or at best, kills them by a deliberate slow motion.

In the midst of this chaotic American Spring, the masses **(65% of the American public no longer trusts the man in the White House)** use the weekends to fill the American equivalents of Tahrir Square. A movement which resists Trump's espousal of Putin's style of leadership, his Muslim ban, his wall at the Mexican border, his attacks on the judiciary, his non-divulgence of his taxes, and his assault on the Affordable Care Act (Obama Care).

There are variables between the American Spring and the Arab Spring. But they share in one primary quality: One does not know their final outcome. The fragmentation (in the Arab world, it is called **"sectarianism"**) in America is the real **"creative chaos"** which

Washington had used as descriptive of the attempts to effect change in the Middle East. However, **in the American Spring, it is a constitutionally induced chaos.** Here is why.

In the American Constitution, there is a **"supremacy clause"** -the Tenth Amendment. For its importance to understanding the American Spring, it merits quoting: **"The powers not delegated to the United States by the Constitution, nor prohibited by it to the States, are reserved to the States respectively, or to the people."** So it was difficult for me, when lecturing at the Cairo University School of Law, the pearl of Arab legal education, to explain to my students that **"the American federal government is a government of limited powers."**

Here we have to bear in mind that the masses of the American Spring draw their power not only from **"the right of the people peaceably to assemble"** (The First Amendment to the Constitution). **The practical source is the state which controls the police** (not federalized in America), **the education** (controlled largely by local school boards), **state legislatures, state taxation, state licensing** of businesses and corporations, **state election of non Article III judges.** Huge powers. By contrast, the federal government, among other things, controls: foreign policy, foreign and interstate commerce, immigration, coinage of money, post offices, promotion of intellectual property, and war declarations.

This is a very broad and thus incomplete comparison between state powers and federal powers. But guess what? In the American Spring, stimulated by the election of Trump in consequence of this period of American rage, **the State flags are flying high:** The mayors of many cities and the governors of a dozen American states have ordered their police forces not to cooperate with the feds in certain activities; sanctuary cities are resisting Trump's draconian methods of deportation; Times Square (the new American Tahrir Square) is proclaiming **"We Are All Muslims Too."**

Allies of the masses in the American Spring are: **the federal judiciary, the free press, the constitutional provisions** on the separation between church and state, the civil service below the billionaires who now compose the cabinet, the on-going investigations in Russia's intervention in the American presidential elections.

Add to the above, the 17 American intelligence and security services about which Trump had frothed at the mouth in petulant anger. They, when confronted by a President about whom **impeachment is already publicly discussed after only four weeks of his administration** (called

Trump Inc.) are opting for selective briefs to Trump. These are tailored to protect America from leaks to its adversaries.

In his book **"The Art of Intelligence,"** Henry Crumpton who spent his life in the CIA's Clandestine Service, manifests the huge gulf between **"The Art of Intelligence"** and Trump's **"The Art of the Deal!"** Trump's **"America Uber Alles"** is relying on megaphones from Trump Towers. **The masses are relying on resistance from the ground up.**

Commenting upon the chaotic national scene in the Trump era, Daniel Gross sounded the alarm in the **New Yorker magazine.** Under the title of **"The German National Anthem and 'America First'"** he said: **"Political language, when misused, can turn healthy patriotism into toxic nationalism."** And the **New York Times Magazine** of February 12, festooned its cover with one word: **RESIST.**

DR. YASSIN EL-AYOUTY, ESQ.

UNCANNY SIMILARITY BETWEEN DONALD TRUMP AND DEPOSED EGYPTIAN PRESIDENT MOHAMED MORSI

Friday, March 17, 2017

They don't look alike. But are as unfit for presiding respectively over America or Egypt, they match.

Trump puts himself above the law, saying, in critical cases, it does not apply to the President. **So did Muslim Brotherhood Morsi in Egypt.** Trump sees no conflict of interest in mixing between the business of his 550 companies and being the President of the United States. So did Morsi when he declared, during his presidency, that he was above the law.

Perceiving Russia as in loco ally of the U.S., Trump has seen no problem in Russian slicing off of part of the Ukraine, **"Wouldn't it be nice to get along,"** he intoned. In Egypt, Morsi, during the **Brotherhood's reign of darkness (2012-2013),** saw in Turkey and Pakistan foreign policy extensions of Cairo.

Morsi did not have the material riches of Donald Trump. Far from it. But in **Khairat El-Shatter,** the Brotherhood's money bags, there was an equivalency.

The Brotherhood's coffers were supplemented by unaccounted for financial dollops from overseas. The State's Central Accounting Office in Cairo was barred from even raising questions. These were regarded as **"charitable contributions"** from abroad, and the hand of the State could not reach them for counting or accounting.

How similar is that to Trump's non-divulgence of his taxes either before the elections or after his elevation to the post of president. **"We are being audited by the Internal Revenue Service"** -he posited. No proof on that. And if a proof is produced about that feigned audit, no conflict in divulging the amount and sources of his claimed riches **for both transparency and payment of US taxes.**

Trump came to the Oval Office, **not through the majority of the popular vote on November 8, 2016.** His non-merited ascendancy to the most influential executive post in the whole world came through **a Constitutional gimmick called the Electoral College.** An appendix in the American Constitutional structure which had been intended by the founding framers to **keep mobocracy out of ruling America.** Well, that safety valve has malfunctioned, as it backfired through the enraged mobs being counted for the purpose of satisfying the Electoral College.

In Morsi's case, the route to the presidency in Egypt was circuitous, but led in the same direction. First **Morsi was not the first choice of the Muslim Brotherhood.** (Nor was Trump for the Republican establishment in America. **Sixteen others competed with him for the coveted prize**). But once Morsi was chosen, his gaining over his opponent, **General Shafik,** left the **legitimacy of the vote count in doubt.** Even with one and a half percent edge in the popular vote over Shafik, the ballot boxes were not secure. And **judicial monitoring was not geographically even.**

Both Trump and Morsi have a distinct propensity for war. Trump has declared **"I love war;"** and Morsi beat the drums for warring against Ethiopia over the construction by Addis Ababa of **the Renaissance Dam over the Blue Nile. "Egypt will go dry -a catastrophe,"** screamed Morsi. Yet all the while, Morsi looked the other way as Hamas denied the very existence of Israel with which Egypt has a peace treaty.

The **two men share the same perception of brotherly movements abroad as means of legitimating their rule** over their respective countries. Trump sees in the British Brexit and the rise of the right in Europe a vindication of the neo-isolation of America. The deposed Egyptian President saw in a mythical Caliphate over all Muslim lands **the road to the resurgence of Islam,** as interpreted by the Muslim Brotherhood.

It is interesting to note that neither Trump nor Morsi has an inclination to read. Trump has openly manifested that. But Morsi has proved it by circumstantial evidence. **Morsi claims a Ph.D. in engineering from California.** The question is this: Has he written that dissertation? Or was it written for him on commission. For if he had written it, then where is the proper English language which surely develops and expands in its vocabulary through the arduous self-authorship of a Ph.D. dissertation?

In a small pamphlet titled **"Accomplishments by President Dr. Mohamed Morsi,"** nearly 500 projects are listed. From dredging a canal in Upper Egypt to the repair of the railroad between Cairo and Alexandria. All by Morsi!! So are Trump's claims to great accomplishments within 50 days. Pre-election plans for industrial expansion by large US companies are immediately claimed by that narcissistic president to be a part of Trump's achievements.

Anxiety reigns over America since the assumption by Trump of the U.S. presidency. In certain instances that anxiety translates into outright fear, experienced by immigrants worried over deportation for the flimsiest infraction. Included in those widening circles of fear are Muslims, due to the Muslim ban, compounded by raising red flags over the misnomer **"Islamic terrorism." As if terrorism has a faith!!**

So was the case in Egypt, during the Islamist reign of obscurantism of the Muslim Brotherhood. **The targets were the Copts, the liberals, the other secularists, women.** Tourism dried up, compounding the economic woes of Egypt of 100 million. Attackers of **churches, Shiis, unveiled women, and the very message of Al-Azhar** went unpunished. It was the reign of impunity gone mad!!

Neither Trump nor Morsi saw in the judiciary a co-equal branch of the Government. In Egypt, the **Supreme Constitutional Court was besieged for weeks by Brotherhood hooligans.** The Brotherhood controlled both the executive, and its own Brotherhood majority parliament. As for Trump, judgments by the judiciary were attributed to the ethnic background of one federal judge, or to incompetence as in the case of freezing the Trumpian executive order affecting the freedom of movement in and out of the U.S. Trump called the orders issued by the U.S. judiciary, whether in Washington State or in Hawaii, **"judicial over-reach!!"**

One more thought remains: **The Egyptian Revolution of June 30, 2013 has resulted in the removal of Morsi, thus saving Egypt from the possibility of civil war.** In America, the nation is deeply divided; the three branches of government, including the judiciary through the possible confirming of a very conservative ninth justice for the Supreme Court; the growing anxiety over Russia's influence and possible blackmail over Trump, are all the kinds of drip drip drip which may end up in **shortening the tenure of Trump's presidency.**

Similar features of governance by Trump and Morsi are manifest in two critical areas: They both have failed in keeping religion and State separate. And they both seemed to treat the armed forces of their respective countries as if they were their personal institutions. Witness the oft-repeated Trump's reference to: **"My Generals."**

Am I forcing similarities between Trump and Morsi **into my own perception of dislike for both? Possibly.** Of course, Trump may yet declare the Muslim Brotherhood a terrorist organization **-a measure worthy of the just war on terrorism.** But whatever happens, with such actions, I cannot avert my gaze over two presidents who have acted similarly in a variety of issues.

In life, similarity of circumstances, especially in governance, generally leads to similar outcomes. **The parallel of the Trump and Morsi trajectories is difficult to ignore. Both of them have rested their thrones on the perilous grounds of "I won!!"**

Both Trump and Morsi live on the same oxygen. Their oxygen is called the mob. They both draw their fancied approval from the howling masses. **For Morsi it was Rabaa and El-Nahdha. For Trump it is Nashville, Tennessee and Michigan.**

The Trumpists, **especially Steve Bannon, Trump's highest adviser,** are calling for **"the destruction of the administrative State."** This anti-State call evokes the horrible memory of a Muslim Brotherhood earlier call. **"Toz Fi Misr" (to Hell with Egypt)** which was uttered by a Muslim Brotherhood Supreme Guide.

There could be nothing either "supreme" or "guidance" in belittling Egypt of 7000 years of existence.

FAKE NEWS ABOUT TRUTH AND VICTORY, ACROSS PAGES OF MODERN HISTORY

Friday, March 31, 2017

Fake news, like fake material, are contrived to look like the real thing. Those who create them, especially in the age of social media, are fakers engaged in deception. **Most of fake news are the stuff from which propaganda is made.** A cover for defeat, or unfulfilled promises, or an inducement to feel good especially when the outcome is terrible.

Fakers come from all cultures, and all geographic regions, especially when a dictator is actively seeking a cover-up. **This is different from purposeful deception in times of armed conflict, because war strategy invariably looks for fooling the enemy.**

In the age of Donald Trump, the issue of fake news has become a special industry. Trump and his supporters, whether in America or elsewhere where xenophobia is ascendant, **have made faking a substitute for either truth or experience.** Such fakers begin by attacking the credibility of proven truths as lies (fake news) to allow their own lies a space in the public square.

A most recent example about Trump as a faker is when, on March 20, his health care plan was withdrawn from the House of Representative rather than suffer certain defeat. Thus the Obama Care (Affordable Care Act), which Trump has vowed to **"repeal and replace, from Day One in the Oval Office"** continues to be the law of the land. Faking victory, in spite of that major defeat, Trump described the Democratic leadership **"the real losers."**

Deeper cover-ups by Trump are his denials of any contacts by him or members of his team with any Russian officials to help him win the Oval Office, his description of the Muslim Ban as "a security shield for America," his igniting hatred of Muslims by saying "they hate us, and want to kill us."

Laughing about these racist claims, the American comedians on the TV series **"Saturday Night Live"** had a response for Trump. On March 25/26, they said: **"If 1.7 billion Muslims want to hurt you, there must be something wrong with you!!"**

And how can the world ever forget a **historic Iraqi faker called Al-Sahhaf?!**Information Minister for Saddam Hussein who in April 2003, he declared in Baghdad: **"We are surrounding the Americans, crushing them!!"** This is while the American tanks were rumbling in Baghdad at a stone throw distance from Al-Sahhaf, now known as **"Baghdad's Bob."**

In a similar vein of faking the news was **Nasser's justification of the outcome of the Six Days War which lost Arab lands to the Israeli military juggernaut in June 1967.** He declared: **"We were expecting the enemy to attack from the east, but they came from the west!!"** How unbecoming for a military leader to justify that terrible defeat through an obtuse ignorance of what his Arab forebears have always declared: **"War is cunning!!" (Al-Harb Khudaa).**

Ironically it was Nasser's **under appreciated successor, Sadat, who through the adoption of a grand deception plan, was able in October 1973 to regain for Egypt's military both dignity and confidence.** But not before historic damage was done elsewhere. Lost, at least for now, is Arab sovereignty over **the Golan, the West Bank, and East Jerusalem.** A huge cost due to mismanagement by Nasser as of April 1967 when he precipitated the removal of the UN peace keepers from Sinai.

The same disease of faking news has **plagued Hamas** which is in control of Gaza in competition with Fatah in Ramallah which is no less faker of news than Hamas.

Hamas, the **"Islamic Resistance Movement,"** feigns victory in the midst of disastrous consequences. In its confrontation from 2008 to 2010 with Israel which besieges Gaza, Hamas leaders **claim success in the form of tunnelling for safety.** One does not expect Hamas to hold Israel, the 4th largest military machine in the world at bay. But how can the **total**

destruction of 14000 Arab dwellings in Gaza be measured by Hamas as a military success?

That pattern of deception by Arab leaders, **particularly in Syria, Yemen and the Sudan,** cannot be less comical. **Bashar,** even after the most brutal civil war in world history would have subsided, shall never be expected to rule over a non-divided Syria. And the **war against the Houthis shall not end in a Yemen Republic of a united North (tribal) and South (progressive).**

In the Sudan, Bashar's rule whose longevity is approaching that of the defunct Mubarak rule in Egypt, is presiding over a country which is preoccupied with this question: **"Which province is expected to split away next from Khartoum: Darfour or Kordofan?"**

Here the fake news in the Sudan are centered on **"the national dialogue"** about **"the earlier national dialogue,"** about **"the earliest national dialogue."** It is the same dreary song and dance about Palestinian national unity by Abbas in **"the State of Ramallah,"** and Mishaal in **"the State of Gaza."** Fakery can never be guidance toward national cohesion and progress.

So is in the grand case of the Muslim Brotherhood: Faking the news of being a social humanitarian movement while empowering its fake news machine to claim legitimacy in the face of the opposition by 35 million Egyptians in June 2013. That protest movement against turning cosmopolitan Egypt into an Islamic Emirate forced the Brotherhood to shed its humanitarian veil, revealing its true conspiratorial terroristic ethos in the land of the Nile. **Legitimacy can never spring from the muzzle of a gun or the explosion of a device by the road side.**

It was Kissinger who called for America's exit from Vietnam in the early 1970s. But that was also through **"fake news."** Stalemated by the Vietcong, and with more than 50,000 American military death count on the battlefield, Kissinger advised: **"Why not declare American victory then depart from Vietnam?"** It worked, but only in terms of **"the departure"** part of the Kissingerian equation. Ho Chi Minh knew that he had to deflate the claim of victory through the imposition of his **tough terms during the Paris negotiations in the mid 1970s.**

Faking news about non-achieved victories is like opium administered largely by failing leaders. It makes the populace feel good for a while. But the hangover lasts much longer **causing real damage to the fabric of** confidence between the Ruler and the Ruled.

But the prize for the most egregious and dangerous faker in modern history **shall go to Donald Trump,** the 45th president of the U.S. A book by an American author has hit the shelves in early March 2017. It is about Trump being the least fit president in US history. Its title is **"How The Hell Did We Get Here?"**

Getting **"here"** was due largely to decades of **"spin."** Such as **America encouraging Saddam to attack the Islamic Republic of Iran in 1980? Then to turn on him in 2003** on the fraudulent claim of possessing **"weapons of mass destruction."**

Should I stop here?! Perhaps not. **The New York Times Magazine** of Sunday March 19, 2017 carried a lengthy article on Egypt. With a title of **"Generation Jail,"** I recorded no less than **10 errors of fact (fake news).** These **included the fallacy that President Adly Mansour (2013-2014) was installed by the military, not through a broad national consensus.**

It also included the **hoax about the severity of the Egyptian law regulating demonstrations.** Really? Just compare that law with the American law. You shall quickly find that the **American equivalent is in fact much more restrictive than the Egyptian one.** Especially in regard to: **"Time," "Place,"** and **"Manner"** of holding an approved public demonstration. We all remember what happened to the **"Occupy Wall Street"** movement. Forget about the fraudulent testimony of some faculty members at the American University of Cairo (the AUC).

Lies have a very short shelf life. But their after effects could be very lasting. Just remember the horrible fake episodes about "the humane treatment" of detainees at Abu Ghraib and Guantanamo!! I can build a whole graduate course of study around these two black holes!! An appropriate title for it might be "The Hate and Fake Interdependency."

STRIKING SYRIA IS A LEGAL STRIKE FOR HUMANITY!!

Friday, April 7, 2017

This is not in praise of Trump. It is a salutation for the doctrine of **"international humanitarian intervention."** It is easy to understand. When a State commits genocidal acts against its own citizens, it is lowering the walls surrounding it **(we call it sovereignty)** for the outside world to jump over them and say **"enough."** **Bashar Al-Assad** has used against his own citizens chlorine bombs, nerve gas, and now, in **Idlib,** has used Sarine gas. On Tuesday, April 4, about 100 victims, including dozens of children, have suffocated.

By doing so, he has proved that, to him and his supporters, **sovereignty meant a fake license in the hands of the State** (and Syria is no longer a State except in name only) **to kill en masse.** How obtuse for him to miscalculate in a big way: that the Trump search for accommodation with Putin is a shield for his murderous regime; that the non-action by Obama on crossing **"red lines"** shall hold under Trump; that Trump's support for that inaction before the Trump's presidency shall hold; and that the **justification used by him as his war on ISIS shall save him from being considered a war criminal.**

Launching 59 missiles by the US navy on April 6 against the **Syrian Shayrat airfield** from which the Sarin attack on Idlib was launched demonstrates a general fault line in Arab thinking about America. That **comprehension deficiency boils down to the non-understanding of the U.S. as a compartmentalized State.**

Because of the decline in education in the Arab homeland, the process of thinking about issues is very linear: **things are either white or black;** relations are based on being a friend or a foe; if you take from me, it is a zero-sum situation whereby I lost totally and you gained totally. **No nuancing, no compartmentalization.**

How is America compartmentalized? A modern State can do many things simultaneously, regardless of the surface appearance of contradictions. Here are actual examples from the recent episode of striking Syria **-a strike which may lead to other strikes in the coming days:**

- The **US national security council** has just been reorganized: separating national security from politics;
- **The professionals of the 17 US security agencies,** together with the Pentagon and the military contracting industry have chased away the opponents of globalization, like **Steve Bannon,** from meddling in war and peace issues;
- The **"America First"** of Trump has been re-interpreted to mean: **yes** for rebuilding the infra-structure, but **no for disengagement from the world;**
- Investigating the connections between the Trump team and Russia shall go on, while Trump is allowed to garner the glory of a tough America to himself;
- The UN could be downgraded, while **Nikki Haley, the US Ambassador to the UN, is upgraded to have a seat on the US national security council;**
- The issue of human rights within States can be ignored as encumbering US diplomacy with those States. But the Syria attack on the **UN Convention Against the Use of Chemical Weapons** cannot be set aside;
- While Trump was dining with the Chinese President at his Florida privately-owned southern White House (Mar-A-Lago) -the U.S. navy was **nullifying** through that missile attack on the Assad regime, the **presence of fixed Russian bases on the Syrian coast.**

This is the essence of American **mixing of party politics, strategy, national interest and diplomacy** in a composite whole with so many facets that rotates all the time like **a strobe light in a darkened night club.**

As a result of this constant dynamic, the American strike on the **Syrian**

Shayrat airbase, is expected to be followed by others. For the message telegraphed by American compartmentalization is not aimed only at **Bashar who can no longer aspire to rule over a united Syria.**

The message is complex as it is directed, not from the White House, which under Trump is a house divided onto itself, but from the myriad of tissues which can only be deciphered by constant analysis. **Deciphering here means being turned into ordinary writing,** whose impact may last only for a short period, only to be replaced by fresh analysis.

This is a message that says, for now, the following:

- **To the Gulf:** there is no American abandonment; just pay for your own defense, and America, with two huge navies in the Mediterranean and the Gulf, shall keep its finger on the trigger;
- **To Russia:** there is a difference between asserting your power in your **"near abroad"** (the Ukraine...etc.) in the south, and your pressure on the **"near abroad"** (the Baltics ...etc.) in the north. The latter is shadowed by NATO, through **Poland and Scandinavia;**
- **To North Korea:** watch out, Pyongyang, we are watching. We have 37,000 American troops in South Korea. And your emboldened nuclear missile technology is a threat to East Asia and America's west coast. **The time has come for planting nuclear weapons in South Korea;**
- **To ISIS:** you may live on as free lancers of marauding hit and run; but **Mosul (Iraq) and Raqqa (Syria)** shall be over-run; and
- **To regional strong Arab States, such as the New Egypt:** we can cooperate in specific well-defined areas. The war on terror and American private investments are examples.
- The Russian thesis of **"no intervention in internal affairs"** has been well served by the Soviet and later Russian use of the veto in the UN Security Council. A non-changeable thesis since 1945. **But this doctrine draws its life from another doctrine, namely, sovereignty.**

But Moscow, on its attack at the UN Security Council on the American strike, **ignores the growth of the doctrine of international humanitarian intervention.** A doctrine which has grown out of the **Geneva Conventions of 1949 (protection of civilians in times of war),** augmented by the **UN Conventions against genocide, civil and political rights, the use of chemical weapons, and the non-resort to weapons of mass destruction.**

Russia's present resort to the UN Security Council shall be of no avail. And if push comes to shove militarily in the eastern Mediterranean, **America's military and economic power shall overwhelm Putin's Russia.** Putin may have overplayed his hand, thinking that a Trump-Putin detente might preempt America's military actions.

Even a possible Putin blackmail of Trump for the latter's presumed sexual indiscretions while in Moscow in 2013 might cause the Trump administration to look the other way. It shall not.

While Putin may be the sole actor in Russia, **Trump is beholden to the complexity of a compartmentalized America** -a country of 50 States stitched together in one. The economy of California alone is bigger than the economy of France. And the **half trillion dollars budget of the Pentagon makes America militarily ahead of the next 20 sovereign States of today.**

Should America be the world's gendarme? No!! But at these times of our world being in disarray, a swift military action by the US is intended for several purposes. High among these purposes is **the projection of US military power. This power is exercised now without a Congressional declaration of war.**

For the enemy is diffuse, terrorism has neither boundaries nor uniforms nor real faith, unpredictability by a receding ISIS is outmatched by the unpredictability of a constantly innovating military **"lean and**

mean" American machine.

Syria is expected to be hit again and again. The Syrian UN representative might babble on at the Security Council about **"criminal aggression."** But who is listening and what could an enfeebled international organization do, except to record a hollow speech?

"Take Assad's air force out" is the new norm. The real action on Syria is now in Washington, D.C., and Moscow, and Brussels (on billions of dollars for reconstruction).

In the era of "universal jurisdiction," any State can act. Yet, in the Arab world, complexities are tiresome. Analysis is deficient. Resort to vocalization is a national pastime. Arab media are nearly comatose!!

DO NOT BLAME INSTABILITY ON FOREIGN CONSPIRACIES - BLAME IT ON MARGINALIZING MINORITIES

Friday, April 28, 2017

Attributing instability to foreign conspiracies is like blaming your household problems on your absent neighbors. **Conspiracy advocates are essentially escapists.** They are also brainwashed by the old colonial narrative. But if a nation looks at itself from within, it shall soon discover that salvation comes from within. No conspiracy has a chance for success unless a nation is so fragmented that a conspirator could come in through national cracks.

Take a broad look at the history of the Middle East. The Ottoman Empire collapsed (1516-1916) because **it abused its minorities. Al-Astanah (Constantinople)** regarded the Greeks, the Serbs, and the Arabs as empire-servers, not empire co-builders. The so-called Ulamas (Islamic scholars), through their deep ignorance of Islam, **advocated disengagement from the west. Those Ulamas were the forefathers of Boko Haram (Western learning is sinful).**

But Turkey revived in 1923 with **Ata Turk ending the Caliphate and made Turkey secular.** The imperial period was no more. However denying the Kurds the right to use their language and have an autonomous status in this 21st century will keep Ankra as the capital of **a country which is in constant battle within itself.** And if **Ordogan** fancies himself as the new Islamic Sultan, he must be smoking some strong weed (hashish).

In Syria, now flattened and fragmented, the minority (the Alawites-Shiis) are brutalizing the majority (Sunnis). Under Bashar, a war criminal, Syria has descended from **"a failed State"** to a **"non-State."** Bashar (ironically it means in Arabic **"good tidings"**) might keep on fighting. But what he shall end up with is a **partitioned Syria,** with an Alawite enclave protected by a Russian base and is smaller than Lebanon. Again the disappearance of Syria did not result from foreign machinations. It is the inevitable outcome of a **lopsided power sharing between an oppressive minority and an internally-colonized majority.**

So it is laughable to still read banners at the entrance of Damascus declaring a blatant fiction: **"One Nation With An Eternal Message!!"** (Ummatun Wahidah That Risalaton Khalidah).

An Eternal Message has been bequeathed to the Muslims in **the Quran - DIVERSITY.** For Islam is not **"a faith and a State."** It is **"a faith and a Nation."** Islam does not create a State. The Quran gives clear evidence on diversity being both a natural human phenomenon the respect for which is a predicate for good governance. **"If your Lord had so willed, He could have made mankind one nation."** (Chapter II, Verse 118)

The terms **"minority"** and **"majority"** might also apply to women in Saudi Arabia. In spite of the huge oil wealth, the **Kingdom of Saudi Arabia has a bifurcated governance:** The Governorate in **Riyadh,** and the Wahhabis in **Diriyah.** Riyadh rules, and the Wahhabis run the country's social life with a belief in denying gender equality. Whereas women sat on the councils of the **Prophet Muhammad,** today's Saudi women are subjected to walls, to totally covered faces except for eye peep holes, and to total rule by their male folks. **Can this last forever? Impossible.** Is 50% of the Saudi population a minority? Yes, a minority in being deprived of rights equal to those enjoyed by the male half of that population.

This may explain why, in Egypt, recent attacks on the Coptic minority (10% - 15%) of the nearly 100 million population have triggered the declaration of emergency laws by the government. Reporters of the **New York Times** based in Cairo, such as **Declan Walsh** do no justice to that paper's motto **"All The News That Is Fit to Print."** It is misleading to read a headline in that paper's issue of April 11, 2017: **"Attacks Show Isis' Strategy for Egypt: Gaining Ground by Killing Christians."**

Rubbish!! Does ISIS, a faction on the run, has a strategy? Are they gaining ground in Egypt? **Could hits and runs or suicide bombings be a strategy -a term reserved for structural command and control?** It is ominous for world peace to find the America of Trump so divided upon itself to the point that **its unstable President could not accomplish through his first 100 days one single piece of legislation.** And daily descriptions in US media of El-Sisi as having engineered a military coup in July 2013 against the Muslim Brotherhood shall have no effect on the New Egypt. Egypt is now becoming **the only strong State in that volatile region.** It is demographically cohesive.

For within the space of a few years, we might have **a new Sudan (without Darfur and Kurdufan); a new Libya** (back to 3 provinces); **a new Yemen** (South Yemen and North Yemen); **a new Iraq** (Kurdistan is gone, and might be followed by a fictitious sectarian divide between the Sunnis of the north, the Shiis of the south). And the non-reconciled Palestinian **statelets of Ramallah and Gaza.** All the historic outcomes, not of foreign conspiracies, but of uneven minorities - majorities relationship.

But Egypt is, and shall remain, a different story. Though with impoverished educational and public information systems, its DNA of national unity is **always pumping reflexive energy.**

This energy could be augmented by an Egyptian one person lobby in Washington, D.C. -A Copt, preferably a female, speaking good "American" as Ambassador.

That would be an enlightened response, representing a true "thinking outside the box." A monumental return to the Egypt bequeathed by Muhammad Ali. From 1832 to 1839, that Egypt has nearly conquered the ailing Ottoman Empire. Cairo's weapon was diversity!!

SERIES OF FAILED MISCHIEF BY THE MUSLIM BROTHERHOOD IN EGYPT AND ABROAD!!

Friday, May 19, 2017

Here is a great Arab proverb in my translation: "Like the ram attacking a mountain, breaking its horns, but not the mountain."

The Muslim Brotherhood, once mixing faith with politics, has signed on its warrant for gradual extinction. Not only in the New Egypt, but anywhere it claims representation. Born 88 years ago near where I grew up in Egypt, it started with advocacy for Islamic reform under the guidance of Hassan El-Banna. Then degenerated into a call for Islamic rule.

The murder in 1947 of Egypt's Prime Minister, Al-Naqrashi Pasha by the Brotherhood signaled its descent on a slippery slope to an accelerated end. Under Prime Minister Ibrahim Abdel-Hadi, Al-Naqrashi's successor, secular Egypt liquidated Hassan El-Banna in 1948. That revenge took place only hours before El-Banna was about to flee to Syria.

Al-Hodheibi, as a successor of El-Banna, was less militant. But the seeds of suspecting every move by the Brotherhood had already been sown. The fact that the Brotherhood had infiltrated Egyptian impoverished masses throughbread, sugar, tents and aspirin was of no use for its longevity.

Its penetration of the armed forces led to a short period of good feelings about the movement. The shot fired at Al-Manshiah, Alexandria, in 1954, at Nasser, who had dislodged Naguib out of the leadership of the coup against the monarchy, was a shot heard around the Muslim world. Whether it was a real or a fake attempt on the life of that rising dictator, cannot be proven by probative evidence.

What is ascertainable is the placement of the Brotherhood under a ban since 1954 till the January Revolution of January 25, 2011. Nearly 6 decades out in the cold. In spite of Nasser's liquidation of the great judge Abdel-Qader Auda in the 1950s and Sayed Qutb in the 1960's, the Brotherhood continued to cater to the religious masses.

The assassination of Nasser's successor, President Sadat, in October 1981 at the hands of Al-Islambully, an Islamist, jolted the Brotherhood into silence verging on being underground. But again, that historic crime signaled two convictions: the sword was a Muslim Brotherhood tool of last resort; and that the Brotherhood's Guidance Bureau was divided upon itself like a Mafia family.

From 1981 to 2011, a period of 30 years of being "the Disbanded Group" (Al-Jamaa Al-Monhallah), the Brotherhood under Mehdi Akef kept its head down, unable to match the power, the resources, or the discipline of the Egyptian Armed Forces.

Then the Brotherhood took two roads, both of which led to dead ends.

The first path to nowhere was reliance on internal as well as external funding. But funding does not create lasting loyalty. It only provides temporary energy for mercenaries (the Mamelouk phenomenon). The second path to nowhere was reliance on public propaganda, especially in Asia, Europe and North America. Their megaphones inflated their numbers in Egypt to 30% of the population.

That percentage is a big fat lie. There are no 30 million loyal Brotherhood adherents in Egypt. How do I know? As an attorney, when you do not have the census to provide evidence, you rely on circumstances. There has never been social science research in Egypt to prove by figures who is who, politically and socially.

Thus the smoke screen of the Brotherhood was the rally (like the Trumpist rallies of disaffected Americans).

But rallies do not legislate. They only indicate the popular depth of attitudes. As in the case of 35 million Egyptians rising on June 30, 2013 against the Brotherhood's rule. That was a corrective revolution constituting lawful popular recall of Morsi as president, in the absence of a Constitutional provision.

After the Battle of the Camel in Cairo on January 27/28, 2011, the Brotherhood which had described the rebellion against Mubarak unislamic, joined the Revolution. It was the winning side. And the Brotherhood, being imbued by opportunism, and getting recognition and the protection of the Armed Forces, sought to become the post-Mubarak regime.

Egypt obliged. The elections, pitting Muhammad Morsi of the Brotherhood against General Shafik, were held in June 2012. That was before the Constitution was drafted and legislated. A typical case of putting the cart before the horse. I voted for Morsi -a big mistake!! But within 5 months of Morsi becoming President, he pre-empted the Constitution by declaring himself in November 2012 to be exempt from the application of the law. A new combination of Sultan and Califah was now in power.

The Islamic Constitution of 2012 was not "Made in Egypt." It was "Made By the Brotherhood." And it ran counter to Egypt's DNA -a 7000 year secular State. Islam did not create a State, it created a community; Egyptian sovereignty does not permit of ceding Sinai to Hamas immigration; and the Armed Forces are the guarantor of that sovereignty, their being the only permanent institution in terms of cohesion and loyalty to the motherland. Above all, diversity of faith has always been an Egyptian hallmark.

The companion revolution of June 30, 2013 against the Islamic rule was a revolt against the Brotherhoodization of Egypt: No to the creation of Brotherhood militias; no to suppression of the Copts, women, and Shiis; no to any affinity with ISIS marauders; no to having Qatar or Turkey or any outside entity dictating how should 100 million Egyptians govern themselves.

And no to a white robe, a long beard, a pair of sandals, a raisin-like spot on the forehead, and a skull cap being the manifestations of authority. Faith and governance cannot mix; religion has been defined as "how others are treated" (Al-Din Al-Moaamalah); and Sharia is supplemented by legislation.

The expulsion of Morsi and Islamic rule on July 3, 2013, was a classic process of recall by the popular will manifested on June 30, 2013. The Islamic Constitution of 2012, now replaced by the secular Constitution of June 2014, contained no provision allowing for a legislated recall of Morsi.

Abdel-Fattah El-Sisi, together with an amalgam of civic, secular and religious leaders, including the Coptic Church, failed through 4 days of negotiations with Morsi to start again through a new plebiscite. The Brotherhood refused to participate in those attempts as they regarded the presidency of Morsi as the only legitimacy (Shariyah) they can recognize.

To them the majority of the Egyptian people, including the Armed Forces, were usurpers. Even clearing the Brotherhood occupation of the Rabaa and Al-Nahda public squares in August 14, 2013, was propagandized by them as a brutal attack on human rights.

How can that be? Two main public squares in the capital of Egypt being occupied by a Brotherhood rebellion for six weeks!! Declared them Islamic Emirates was a case of internal rebellion presaging civil war. Throughout those six weeks, the Government continuous appeals to the marauding occupants went unheeded. So went the Brotherhood's calls for external intervention by force in Egypt under the false label of "humanitarian intervention." The mere passage of American naval vessels in the Suez Canal was hailed by the Brotherhood as the start of a forceful abrogation of the new secular established order!!

In Rabaa, hundreds died. Not by Government designs, as the Brotherhood propagandizes. But by the criminal designs of Brotherhood gangs who, like ISIS and its affiliates, sought victimhood (Shahadah) as a means of legitimation.

Yet more Brotherhood propaganda spewed out, especially abroad, that El-Sisi's presidency lacks legitimacy!! More advocacy by some Egyptians in New Jersey, such as a TV broadcaster named Ayat Orabi, declaring on social media obscenities such as "the Egyptian Armed Forces are a collection of whores!!" More visits to Washington by Brotherhood sympathizers to demonstrate against El-Sisi!! All in vain!!

Secular Egypt marched steadily on. The administration of interim President Adly Mansour handed power to its successor administration, that of El-Sisi. These steps came about after approval by plebiscite of the 2014 secular Constitution. These were open and fair elections (El-Sisi vs. Hamdain Sabbahi). El-Sisi, the former Defense Minister and the mediator with the Brotherhood for participation, was the choice of the majority.

El-Sisi did not come to the presidency on top of a tank. He was given the baton in an orderly democratic process of post-Islamization in an Egypt which was spared the agony of civil war.

A series of failed mischief by the Muslim Brotherhood which, among other things, tried to marginalize Al-Azhar Al-Sharif, the citadel of an inclusive and universalistic Islam. Jihadism is now being confronted by "The New Islamic Religious Revolution" on which I am authoring a book.

The word "Idea" comes from the Greek "to see." It is a pattern that enables you to understand the true nature of a phenomenon.

The phenomenon of the Muslim Brotherhood, now declared in its birthplace, Egypt a terrorist organization is not hard to understand. Its idea is "Islam as a path to a fascist theocracy." The firewall against its conversion of Egypt into an emirate is the Armed Forces. Its enablers, especially those in America, such as Ayat Orabi of New Jersey, and Sheikh Salem Abdel-Galeel in Cairo are, judging by their false propaganda, sheer haters of interfaith harmony.

With the Egyptian arena preempted by secularism, the Muslim Brotherhood is in hot pursuit for life support overseas. Their megaphones, whether in Qatar, Turkey, or America, produce echo chambers. Collapsing the New Egypt is nothing but a pipe dream.

Their abuse in America of the freedom of speech is an overreach. It has turned into calls for violence against Christians, into a jihadi call for criminalized hatred.

Their mischievous veil of "political opposition" behind which they hide their calls for sectarian violence might be pierced through legal means. They have no idea (means of understanding) of the consequences of their unending mischief.

"Virtue" in Latin means "strength." Just show me one single virtue which the Muslim Brotherhood can claim!! Even the "Rabaa Salute," depicting their claimed victimhood at Rabaa Square on August 14, 2013 when hundreds died, is a crooked finger!!

DR. YASSIN EL-AYOUTY, ESQ.

THE NEW AMERICAN REBELLION: CITIES AND STATES AGAINST TRUMP

Friday, June 2, 2017

The man is out of control. **"Make America Great Again"** is his call. Its practical effect is **"Make America the World's Pariah."** Trump may be impeached before too long. His swagger in public maybe a mask of his fear of eventual humiliation. The appointment of a special prosecutor, Robert Mueller, to investigate the possibility of a Trump-Putin axis signals the ultimate check on a president gone rogue.

The recent straw straining the American camel's back is Trump's abandonment of the Paris global climate accord of 2015. Resorting to a junk misinterpretation of that 195 States voluntary accord on the reduction of fossil emission, Trump declared on June 1 at the White House that that agreement was an economic straight jacket. **"I was elected to represent the citizens of Pittsburgh, not Paris."**

The rebuke of that isolationist move against combating global warming came fast and furious. Not only from heads of State, especially those who lead the **"least developed countries;"** but also from American business, corporate executives, climate activists, and American state governors and city mayors. **A new American rebellion of cities and States against an erratic president is now afoot.**

Led by former New York City mayor, Michael Bloomberg in the east, and Governor Brown of California in the west, the rebellion is a practical application of the Tenth Amendment of the US Constitution. It reads: **"The powers not delegated to the United States by the**

Constitution, nor prohibited by it to the States, are reserved to the States respectively, or to the people."

From his campaign for the presidency (June 2015 to November 2016), it became clear that **Trump is not conversant with the Constitution.** A Muslim father of a US army officer killed in Afghanistan, Mr. Khan, angered by Trump's foolish call for a Muslim ban on entering the US, posed a challenge to Trump at the Democratic National Convention. Flourishing a copy of the American Constitution, Mr. Khan posed this historic challenge to Trump: **"Have you ever even read the U.S. Constitution?"**

The fact that the federal government in America is one of **"enumerated"** (limited) powers, has created for the states and cities which are in favor of the Paris climate accord the requisite space for this new check on Trump's **"act of gratuitous destruction"** (to quote Paul Krugman, a Nobel Laureate in economics).

This challenge by city mayors and state governors to Trump's headlong isolationism has been in the making since their opposition to Trump's executive orders for the deportation of **"illegal immigrants."** In one of the so-called **"sanctuary cities,"** Mayor De Blasio of New York City led the charge. He instructs the New York Police Department **not to cooperate with federal agents attempting to arrest persons who lacks documentary evidence for being in America.**

In America, police departments (47000 in all) are not controlled by the federal government. They, as in the case of education, are subject to control only by cities (in the case of the police) or by community school boards (in the case of public education).

The spark that has further ignited the states and cities rebellion against Trump's **"reckless climate decision,"** has been described by John Niles, the Director of the Carbon Institute of California, in these words: **"Mr. Trump's decision is not only an arrogant abrogation of science and cooperation, but also defies logic. Ignoring the opportunities in clean innovation and relying on 18th century technologies is a mistaken bet to 'make American great again.'"**

This new assertion of local power over federal power in America, is taking place against **a series of Trumpist isolationist moves which have created voids now filled by China.** Trump's avoidance of reaffirming US commitment to NATO, his abandonment of the Trans-Pacific Partnership, his reduction of the budgets of the State Department in favor of a 10%

increase in the military budget, have alarmed an **America whose leadership has, since 1945, been the mainstay of the postwar world order.**

As of now, former New York City Mayor Bloomberg, together with 30 mayors, several governors, 80 university presidents, and more than 100 businesses, are now negotiating with the UN to formalize their contribution to the Paris climate deal. Declared Bloomberg: **"We are going to do everything America would have done if it has stayed committed."** It is incorrect to claim that such an initiative has no formal mechanism for entities that were not countries to be full parties to the Paris accord.

Although the UN is an inter-state system, its Charter, a World War II document dating back to 1945, declares in its preamble **"We the peoples of the United Nations determined ... to promote social progress and better standards of life in larger freedoms."** The cluster of US cities and states now rising against Trump in support of the climate accord endorsed by 195 States, falls in that category of legitimated UN participants. This is particularly so because such an American cluster includes states whose status under the US Constitution is regarded as **"supreme."**

Adding to that relevance to UN purposes is the continuous creation by the UN of new mechanisms to overcome the strictures imposed by the literal interpretation of the UN Charter. The most important examples are the creation of peace-keeping operations (there is no mention in the Charter of the term **"peace-keeping"**); the expansion of the authority of the UN Security Council to impose travel bans on individual citizens of sovereign States; and the avoidance of voting in the Security Council for fear of paralysis through the veto, by creating **"presidential statements"** to replace formal decisions.

Add to the above is that **Mayor Bloomberg is a UN envoy on climate change.** In that capacity of improvised American leadership outside of a White House going backward on international commitments, Bloomberg declared his approach to the UN was **"a parallel pledge."** Declared California's Governor, Jerry Brown: **"If the President is going backward, we are going forward."** California's economy is the 6th largest economy in the world.

In America, that fight has now **shifted from the federal government to lower levels of government including academia and industry.** This is a rebellion whose vanguards include Governor Jay Inslee of Washington State, Governor Andrew Cuomo of New York, and Governor Jerry Brown of California. All of them, democrats, have **declared an alliance committed to upholding the Paris accord.**

Now we have new European allies for the new American rebellion of cities and states against Trump. France's president, Emmanuel Macron welcomed that uprising in these words: **"I want to say that they will find in France a second home... I can assure you that France will not give up the fight."** And during her meeting in Berlin with India's prime minister, **Narenda Modi,** Germany's chancellor **Angela Merkel** pledged her support, and distanced the European Union from Trump. **This is while she welcomed China's leadership in the global push for action on climate.**

Under Trump, America is being transformed. Not in the way the Trumpists have hoped. **But in the rise of new checks and balances not before used to chain a president who thinks that running a country is akin to running a company.** As a country of laws, the system may yet force Trump out of the White House which he has recently dubbed **"The People's House."**

The U.S. Constitution begins with these words: "We the people of the United States, in order to form a more perfect Union ..." It now looks that the "more perfect Union" is in the making via this new cities and states rebellion.

THE IMPERIAL PRESIDENCY OF DONALD THE MINDLESS

Friday, June 23, 2017

In the early 1960's I sat at the UN to interview **Mohamed Ali,** the world boxing champion. Warming him to that interview in a UN Radio Studio, I humorously asked him: **"Do you really think that you are the greatest?"** With humility and a smile, his response was: **"It is the world that says so!!"**

The greats hardly ever describe themselves as such. Trump is an embarrassing exception. His call to **"Make America Great Again"** does not mean what it says. Its practical meaning is: **"America shall be for whites only."** All others are potentially un-American.

Never in the history of the cabinet meetings at the White House has there been one like that held by Trump in June. It was for the sole purpose of having himself being praised by members of his own cabinet. It was a disgusting show of servility. Cravenly submissive to the narcissist, egocentrism of Trump, they bathed him, one at a time, in adulating **"thank you for the honor of serving under your leadership."**

One of the most sickening behavioral traits of **that mindless American President** is his lashing at any critic. On May 13, he spoke at the commencement exercises of **Liberty University,** a bastion of religious evangelism. In that address, he said of criticism:

"Nothing is easier or more pathetic than being a critic, because they're people that can't get the job done."

Yet it is well established that the **primary lesson of a liberal democracy is how to live with critics.** It was the composer **Jean Sibelius** who quipped: **"No one ever put up a statue of a critic."** Egomaniacal Trump has his name on every building or a golf course he owns, leases, or has licensed his name to be stamped on it. This is typical of **Trump's delusional mental disorder that is marked by infantile feelings of personal omnipotence and grandeur.**

Trump's famous **"I alone can fix it"** could now be added to **"I know more than the generals know."** This is to appreciate the total nonsense of these irresponsible utterances revealing the gap between his empty words and their empty results.

His first baptism by fire was in Yemen where one of the seals was killed. But Trump blamed that mishap on the Pentagon.

Now finding it expedient to leave the generals face the blame for future mishaps, he has n ow ceded his central function as Commander In Chief to General Jim Mattis, his Defense Secretary.

It is now the Pentagon which would decide on a useless military surge in Afghanistan of 5000 more troops to be thrust in that unwinnable 16-years-old war. A war that rages on without any American arching strategy, and from which Obama had wisely begun to disengage as a gradual exit strategy.

Nonetheless, Trump focus on being not responsible for any bad outcome **(his sole focus is on garnering ritualized flattery),** shall not shield him from what **The New York Times** of June 16 has aptly characterized. The paper mocked Trump's self-absorbed tweet celebrating the 242nd birthday of the US army. Trump, the **Tweeter-In-Chief** has said: **"Proud to be your commander-in-chief."** This is the man who sought multiple deferments from military service. Thus the paper mocked his escapist decision to give General Mattis **"the authority to determine troop levels in Afghanistan."**

In the 1950's I witnessed as a UN staff member the Permanent Representative of **Israel disparaging Saudi Arabia** by a novel attack. He, in effect, said **that the only UN member which is a family business is Saudi Arabia.** Well, by that measurement of statehood, it would not be far fetched to apply it today to the Trump administration. But not as a State, but as a government. Trump's daughter Ivanka and her husband, Jared Kushner, partake of official meetings with visiting Heads of State.

The fact of that **American family business masquerading as the apex of executive power in the US** is more compounded by other factors outside of blood relations. The intertwining of family and State business, representing violations of both ethical and legal nature, has been **tolerated by a supinely-submissive Republican controlled Congress.** A collective exhibition of mutual and moral slackness.

With the accumulation of portfolios of vital national interest in the hands of Kushner, from government organization to Middle East peace, comes the issues of conflict of interest. Trump and his enablers have vouched for a legal impossibility: **The President is immune from conflict of interest. By what legal standard? None,** except by dictatorial fiat. As a mindless president, Trump has declared that he could run his world-flung business and the U.S. simultaneously.

From all indications, especially through the avalanche of executive orders, paraded before cameras as Trump jabs his pen on folders bearing his tower-like signature, **Trump fancies the US a corporation. His cabinet is his corporate board, his angry look as a threatening menace.**

In his hallucinatory state of mind, Trump believes that his signature moves programs forward. **No major legislation has so far moved forward,** especially in the areas of health care, tax reform, trade promotion and national security. Only in the matter of appointing a very conservative justice to the Supreme Court, deregulation to benefit Wall Street, and environmental degradation through exiting the Paris accord on climate change.

All are nearly negatives, which Trump counts as **"fulfilling my promises to the American people."** The outcome has been the federal judiciary issuing stays of the application of his bans, including the Muslim ban which he declares to be not a ban. This is while his acolytes claimed it to be a non-ban. **But the courts took Trump's own words as evidence of unconstitutionality.**

This is while we see the rise of states and cities declaring their own defiance of federal power regarding rounding up illegal immigrants. Their police departments shall not cooperate with federal authorities in the pursuit of unconstitutional measures.

The American Declaration of Independence unanimously approved by the 13 United States of America on July 4, 1776 includes several passages which in their totality constitute obstruction of justice when violated by the Executive. One of these refers to endeavoring **"to prevent the population of these states,"** through **"refusing to pass (laws) to encourage their migrations hither."** Trump bans against Muslims and plans to build walls on the Mexican-American border should be taken by the judiciary into account with these passages in mind.

As to the Constitution, Article III, Section 3 states: **"Treason against the United States, shall consist only in levying war against them, or in adhering to their enemies giving them aid and comfort."**

President, Donald Trump, assisted by others like General Flynn, his former national security advisor, have by Trump's silence on Russia's interference in the 2016 elections, given eloquent evidence of culpability. Not one word of protest against Russia's cyber attack during the campaign and transition has issued from the mouth of that mindless president.

- His firing of FBI Director, **James Comey,** for investigating what Trump called **"the Russia thing."** By his own admission in a TV interview with **Lester Holt,** he provided the Russian investigation as the reason for that firing;

- During his testimony on June 8, 2017 before the Senate Select Committee on Intelligence, the question of Trump's attempt to have Comey abandon the Flynn investigation was confirmed. An honest finger pointing to **Trump's attempt at obstruction of justice;**

- During that historic testimony, the former FBI Director called Trump's trail of statements by which that mindless president tried to put the onus of firing Comey on Rod Rosenstein, the Deputy Attorney General: **"Those were lies, plain and simple."** For the first time ever has an American president been called **"a liar,"** repeatedly before Congress by an officer of the U.S. ;

- Trump, by his professed anger at **Comey's refusal to publicly disclose that the President was not personally under investigation,** has made himself actually the target of investigation.

- The revelation that Trump has cajoled Comey to pledge **"loyalty"** to him could not but point to the bubble in which Trump exists as a **pretended potentate.**

- Instead, Comey, being the then director of an independent law enforcement agency, promised only his **"honesty."** Not enough for Trump **"the Predator in Chief."** An apt characterization by the **New York Times** of June 9, 2017.

- The day following Comey's testimony, Trump accused the dismissed FBI Director of lying. At a rambling press conference in the White House Rose Garden, Trump, in the presence of Romania's President said: **"Yesterday showed no collusion (with Russia), no obstruction."**
- Then he hinted that he had tapes of his conversations with Comey. Comey, in his testimony, said: **"I hope there are tapes."** Various challenges to Trump to produce these tapes have gone unheeded. Pure bluster!!
- The misdeeds committed by Trump's aides and close associates shall, under agency law, be regarded as amounting to impeachable offenses. Said Elizabeth Drew in her article in the **New York Review of Books** of June 22, 2017. **"Mike Flynn, Trump's former campaign adviser and dismissed national security advisor is obviously a problem for the president."** Her article is titled **"Trump: The Presidency in Peril."**
- **No less than seven Trump associates have been linked to Russia including his own son-in-law, Jared Kushner.** Kushner is now a subject of a criminal investigation. He is suspected of having discussed with Russia's Ambassador to the US a secret back channel using the Russian Embassy as a conduit. **The purpose is to deny US Intelligence Services the possibility of tracking those channels.** If such an infantile attempt at hiding secrets from the powerful American intelligence community (16 such organizations) is proven, **it could amount to a charge of espionage.**
- With Trump and his entire phalanx and Trump himself lawyering up, important Republican Senators, and even senior Cabinet officers (e.g. Defense Secretary Mattis), are beginning to distance themselves from that toxic president.
- In a rare such example, Republican Senator **Richard Burr of North Carolina** presiding over the Intelligence Committee, asked Comey: **"Do you have any doubts that Russia attempted to interfere in the 2016 elections?"** Comey's response was a single lethal word: **"None."**

The list of examples of Trump digging deeper a hole for himself can go on and on. The appointment by Deputy Attorney General Rosenstein of **Robert Mueller** Special Counsel to investigate the components of the dark cloud surrounding this fake presidency is a turning point.

Trump's test balloon launched on June 13 by **his friend, Christopher Ruddy, suggesting that Trump may fire Special Counsel,** Robert Mueller, is either a phony attempt at intimidation, or a terrible misreading of the pulse of the American people. They will have to conclude that **their president is a crook.** That admission by Ruddy may also indicate that Trump uses and abuses his executive privilege which prevents the divulgence of private conversation with the president.

Loosening that rule is also a manifestation of Trump's **mistaken belief that he is above the law.** He, as the saying goes, could run, but can't hide. His attempt to protect Flynn, his chipping away at the elaborate American civil rights edifice, his feverish attempts to dismantle the Obama legacy including the opening to Cuba, and his calling the investigations in the Russian connection a **"witch hunt"** is a reminder of a **concerned rat moving in all directions in the hope of escaping capture.**

Donald: What is happening in the way of multiple investigations is not **"a witch hunt."** It is a hunt for the truth. And the only recognizable truth about your five months presidency is what your main strategist, Steve Bannon, has admitted to: **"The destruction of the administrative State."**

That administrative State seems to be marching towards an inevitable goal: Putting an end to the charade of the presidency of a mindless president.

Statistical fact checking shows that **Trump has lied 500 times since June 2015.** The most recent lie being his bluffing that his conversations with Jim Comey had been taped. **Now under the pressure of a Congressional subpoena to force Trump to disgorge these tapes,** he came out on June 22 admitting that there were no such tapes.

The implication of that forced divulgence from the American Liar-in-Chief is clear: He intentionally meant that lie for possibly these purposes: **(a) to intimidate Comey into silence; (b) to distract public attention away from the Russian investigation; and/or** (c) to heap scorn on law enforcement.

There is a new theory called **"Mindfulness."** It advocates knowing yourself as a means of constructive engagement. By that standard, Trump, through his utterances and actions, is entitled to the counter-theory: **"Mindlessness."** It advocates self-absorption combined with always being on the offensive.

Donald the Mindless has been, if not on the defensive, in a constant attacking mode: From **"crooked Hillary,"** to **"I have inherited a mess."** From **"That judge is Mexican,"** to **"The intelligence services have failed."** From **"The Muslims hate us,"** to **"China is ripping us off."** From: **"The Media is the enemy,"** to **"I heard it from someone."**

The superlatives are his lexicon. His imperial presidency is not to **"Make America Great Again."** It is to **"Make America Hate Again." Where are all the allies gone? Even Mexico and Canada are no more America's longest unarmed borders.**

DR. YASSIN EL-AYOUTY, ESQ.

THE FIFTIETH ANNIVERSARY OF THE ARAB CALAMITY CAUSED BY NASSER

Friday, July 7, 2017

That was the Six-Day War, begun by Israel on June 5, 1967. It ended by its occupation of Sinai (Egypt), the Golan (Syria), the West Bank (Jordan), Gaza (Egyptian administration), and East Jerusalem (Jordan and the Muslim world). Israel was the aggressor; Nasser was the unwitting creator of those circumstances. **Thus in mere 6 days, Israeli administered-territories quadrupled.**

Yet there has never been an Egyptian commission of inquiry into **Nasser's huge miscalculations** whose disastrous consequences are still plaguing the Arab world. Nasser's leadership, though still perceived as gaining honor for the Arab homeland, gained that homeland neither muscle nor relevance to the world community or to regional or universal institutions.

In a historical summary, **Nasser was largely about Nasser being seen as the Arab** world leader. It was a fake leadership: The Egyptian-Sudanese unity collapsed as Nasser pushed President Naguib (of Sudanese parentage) out; the cozying up with Russia translated into anti-west; the union with Syria into a United Arab Republic lasted only for 3 years (1958-1961). **Then came the intrusion into the civil war in Yemen (1962-1967)** causing a rupture with Saudi Arabia and the rest of the Gulf; the enthusiasm for the 1969 Qaddafi rise to power in Libya was mere empty optics; and the coddling of Arafat of the PLO was at the expense of both Jordan and Lebanon.

There is no doubt that internally in Egypt, Nasser caused the **re-start of Egyptian industrialization;** the construction of the **Aswan dam;** the launching of **agrarian reform;** the moving forward with the **Egyptian nuclear program** for energy; and the inclusion of the **peasants and workers into parliament.**

There is also no doubt that Nasser **did not steal** from the public treasury; stimulated **free university education** for all; and garnered respect for Egypt as a **player in African unity,** and in the non-aligned movement.

These are achievements whose roots were mostly planted prior to his military coup of July 23, 1952 (65 years ago). And **the price** for whatever was achieved under his leadership internally **was inordinate:** the abrogation of the historic Egyptian Constitution of 1923; the muzzling of all voices of dissent; **the disbanding of the vestiges of Egyptian democracy (1922-1952).**

There was also the encouragement of the Islamists in order to counter the influence of the communists; the break-up of viable agricultural land holdings in favor of micro-agricultural land holdings of 5 acres or less; the improper ascertainment of the adverse effects of stopping the silt from the Nile water behind the Aswan dam.

Under Nasser, Egypt with its vast and underused human intellectual resources, **became a one-man show.** The show was called **"the struggle,"** and was given a cliche by the Nasser mouth-piece, Mohamed Hassanain Haikal, in the propagandistic words: **"No voice is above the voice of the struggle."**

And officially, the propagator was **Abdel-Qadir Hatem** who refashioned the Egyptian Information Department in the model of a Goebbels Nazi operation. Lies by **Ahmed Saeed** of the **"Voice of the Arabs"** were given credence. Calling **Saudi King Faisal, Jordan's King Hussein, and Tunisian President Bourguiba "traitors"** was common currency as a Nasser means of intimidation of whoever in the Arab world dared to say, **"Gorilla!! Your Eyes are Red"** -an Egyptian saying.

As the only **dinner** guest to dinner hosted by Haikal in Cairo on a Friday 1969, my host asked for my opinion of his weekly column **in Al-Ahram newspaper.** It was entitled **"Frankly Speaking"** (Bissarahah). Its heading in that particular issue was **"The Four Traitors."**

I have cited above three of those four, but the name of the fourth escapes me. My response was: **"How do you measure treachery? There is no agreed pan-Arab definition, as each Arab sovereign State pursues its policies guided only by its national interest."**

Measuring Nasser's achievements against Nasser's blunders, I find **the scales tipping heavily on the side of blunders.** For those affected a whole region, and decided the history of hundreds of millions for years to come. **Nasser was not a very educated** man. He was ill-fated by a conspiratorial mind. That mind dictated his preference for persons whom he trusted over persons who possessed experience.

Haikal is a prime example: a high school graduate; with no university education; but with self-education **focused only on copying (Naql),**translation, and plagiarism (no attribution to original sources). A story teller in the mode of **"Ali Baba and the Forty Thieves."** The author of Nasser's **"The Philosophy of the Revolution."**

In it, there is a vacuous blueprint consisting of **aspirational generalities. A Bla Bla Bla that glitters but does not educate.** Its real companion, though more in the superlatives, is Qaddafi's **"Green Book."** Two books considered by their die hard fans historic, yet you find them today in the dustpan of history.

More strategically located **beside Nasser was General Abdel-Hakim Amer,** commanding ill-equipped large armed forces. Amer's education in military strategy and military intelligence could not be compared to that of his Israeli counterparts. The latter were methodically sent for specialized education at the Massachusetts Institute of Technology (MIT), USA.

That is while Amer was dispatched by Nasser to **the Northern Region (Syria)**during the short-lived United Arab Republic. (Egypt was the Southern Region). As Amer in Syria (1958-1961), assisted by the then **Syrian Interior Minister, Abdel-Halim Al-Sarrag,** was turning Syria into a security State, Israel was innovating militarily.

The flow of US armaments into Israel was the price which **Ben Gurion as Prime Minister had extracted from President Eisenhower** for withdrawal from Sinai in 1957. Israel had, at that crucial junction, shifted away from France and refocused on the innovative American military technology. By comparison, **Egypt was reliant on Soviet weaponry: simpler to use, but technologically inferior to the American arsenal.**

The stage was set for the Israeli historic strike of June 5, 1967 against all its

Arab neighbors. **Nasser was preoccupied with his war in Yemen where napalm was used by Egypt against opposing Arab forces;** Amer of Egypt was no match for General Moshe Dayan; the Baath Party of Syria which collapsed the union with Egypt was **taunting Nasser as a paper tiger because of the stationing of the UN Blue Helmets** on the Egyptian side of the line of demarcation with Israel.

With Nasser's ego being nearly the size of the Giza pyramids, and **against the quiet advice of the experienced Egyptian Foreign Ministry,** he forced the withdrawal of the UN forces from the scene. And with the Nasser megaphone, false Egyptian claims of having closed the Gulf of Aqaba, were magnified. That played well in the hands of Israel. At the UN, Aba Eban, Israel's then Foreign Minister declaimed. **"Israel is besieged."**

American **President Lyndon Johnson, together with UN Representative, Ambassador Goldberg,** must have known that a big push by Israel against the Arabs was in the making. The USSR could only give lip service to their Arab allies. Russian global strength was receding; American hegemony was on the rise; and Israel was a willing strategic American ally. New American war weapons were tested in Israel held territories.

And on June 5, 1967, the Israeli air force struck all Egyptian airfields destroying Egypt's aircraft as they slept on their tarmacs. By noon, Nasser's Egypt had no air cover, and that great country laid defenseless. But Nasser had an obtuse explanation: **"We expected the enemy to come from the east; it came from the west!!"** DA!! Our Arab forebears have counselled: **"War is trickery."**

But Nasser had little education in culture. His education was in how to pretend that the Arab calamity could be repackaged to the Egyptians as only **"a set-back"** (Naksah).

Has the October War of 1973 which was astutely planned by Sadat, Nasser's successor, mitigated that Arab disaster of 1967? Not really!! It led to Egyptian recovery of its territory through the Peace Treaty of 1979 with Israel. But other Arab territories are still under Israeli suzerainty.

That 1973 war also led to a later treaty of peace between Jordan and Israel. These peace moves, combined with the absence of a meaningful Palestinian leadership, have drastically redrawn the Middle East map for a long time to come.

Nasser, in effect, was a phantom leader. "Eternally-Remembered?" How misleading!! Nasser was nearly all throat and imagery. Substance was not his substance.

DR. YASSIN EL-AYOUTY, ESQ.

Perspectives on Egypt, Islam and the Dark Era of Trump

PEERING THROUGH MIDDLE EASTERN FOG: WAHHABISM RECEDING, OTTOMANISM RISING

Friday, July 21, 2017

On the one-hand, Wahhabism was originally forged by a reformer. Muhammad Ibn Abdel-Wahhab sought an Islam based on its sources: **The Book (the Quran), The Sunna (Muhammad's tradition) and The Hekmah (common-sense interpretation).** Earned high praise by **Sheikh Muhammad Abdoh**-the all-time Egyptian reformer and liberator.

On the other hand, Turkey, once relieved by **Ata Turk in 1923** of the yoke of the Caliphate, began to move on as a secular State. Secularity, supported by its armed forces, was its way forward, straddling both Asia and Europe.

But then, as of the 1920's, the unification of most of the Arabian peninsula by **King Abdul-Aziz Al-Saud** came at a heavy cost. The cost of ceding to the Wahhabis (Al Alsheikh) all matters relating to Islam. About the same time frame, Turkey's stabilization came also at a heavy cost to secularity: **No tangible civil rights to either opposition or to the Kurdish minority.**

In both Riyadh (Saudi Arabia) and Ankara (Turkey), the sword became the arbiter. That is the sword of a repressive Islam in Riyadh, and the sword of a repressive secularity in Ankara. **In both countries, the contents of Islam was converted into non-Islamic authoritarianism.**

Yet after nearly 100 years, something happened in both capitals. On the way to the 21st century, a new ideology came to the Saudi government as of the reign of King Abdullah **-openness.** But to the Turkish scene, came **Ordogan, bent on closing the door to secularity, and espousing Islamism.** From King Abdullah to King Salman, the road was leading to cutting Wahhabism down to size.

But in Ankara, under Ordogan, the road was leading through dictatorship and Islamism. Expunging secularism for the sake of an Ottoman-like revival.

The two opposite currents had a direct effect on the Muslim Brotherhood and its sanctuaries in both Qatar and Turkey, among other places. In tandem with the New Egypt, **Riyadh closed its door to the Brotherhood.** That was a historical extension of King Abdul-Aziz's famous retort to the Brotherhood: "**Why a Brotherhood center in Riyadh, when we all are Brothers and are all Muslims!!**"

The reverse took place in Ankara where, Ordogan raised his hand of four fingers **in a symbolic salute to the Brotherhood.**

From reading the tea leaves of the future, the gradual shrinkage of the Wahhabi role in governance is most likely to succeed. Riyadh now seeks **true integration in the modern world community.** By contrast, the gradual islamization of the new sultanate of pro-Ottoman Ordogan, is most **likely to falter due to the historic inculcation of the Ata Turk secularism.**

It is a tradition built in the Turkish Constitution as being the **sacred trust of the huge NATO-supported armed forces.** It was nearly a year ago that a coup against Ordogan nearly succeeded. Its reversal by Ordogan came at the cost of more than 250 people killed and more than 2000 injured.

Reflection on the happenings in both Riyadh and Ankara is a comparative way of guessing at the future in the entire Middle East, **following the liberation of Mosul (Iraq) and Raqqa (Syria).** While the destruction of the so-called caliphate of ISIS in its two centers of power is a most welcome development, one has to wonder as to what next?

What can the future role of an islamized Turkey and of a less-Wahhabi Saudi Arabia be? In Riyadh, we have a crown prince, Muhammad Bin Salman, seemingly **bent on a Saudi Arabia for the 21st century.** Can Syria or Iraq remain territorially united? And if not, what might be the effects of an independent Kurdistan in northern Iraq, or of Kurdish nationalism in Turkey? Could the **diplomatic isolation of Iran in the New Middle East** last while the influence of Tehran in Damascus, Baghdad, Beirut and Sanaa (Yemen)** is a fact of political life?

For now, such questions have to remain unanswered. What is assured for now, is that Islam, whose main thesis is unity, shall continue to be divisively interpreted. Especially in the holy land of Mecca and Medina, and in the land of the neo-Ottomans!! **No relation or linkage to the Fourth Caliph after Muhammad: Othman Ibn Affan.** He was an enlightened leader. **The Ottomans, whether old or re-invented, are not.**

THE OTTOMAN EVIL SPIRIT IN TRUMP'S WHITE HOUSE

Friday, August 4, 2017

President Trump may not need a chief of staff. He is his own chief of staff. But he may need an exorcist to free him from the Ottoman evil spirit. The manifestations of that spirit have multiplied. Creating a White House in turmoil.

What should that exorcist, if found, be armed with: His holy water is the U.S. Constitution; his luring Trump into exorcising sessions should be in the pre-dawn hours when Trump is about to tweet his crazy statements; his voice should be soothing with words of adulation for that perplexing Commander-in-Chief.

Above all, the exorcist should use some Russian words, because no Ottoman (Turkish) spirit could bear the sound of the Russian language. First Lady Melania from ex-Yugoslavia might assist in keeping the Donald from frothing at the mouth during that ritual.

That Ottoman evil spirit has so far replicated in the White House what the Sultans in Istanbul (Constantinople) had done for 500 years:
- All senior White House staff distrust one another;
- Your opponent is someone with easy access to Trump;
- Making the Sultan (Trump) fearful of the intrigue by others outside of the Oval Office is a national duty;
- Lying to the President, or by the President, or for the President to the nation and the world is loyalty, honor, and courage; and

- Back-knifing is a patriotic sport.

Above all, the exorcist should ignore Trump's tantrums and vulgar language. The more that filth pours out of his mouth, the closer the exorcism is to a happy end: Trump, now hopefully cured, is out of the White House.

His embodiment of the Ottomans, brought about in part by General Mike Flynn, a foreign agent for Turkey while becoming a national security advisor, has brought unspeakable harm to America and the world:

- The turmoil of successive firings of a dozen senior staff has stalled work on the national agenda: jobs, health, the economy, taxation, infrastructure, and security;
- The obsession with repealing the legacy of President Obama, including its signature legislation in the areas of health care and the environment, has led to a rupture of Congressional bipartisanship, attacks on Obamacare while being the law of the land, and threats by the Executive against Congress -a co-equal branch of government;
- The repeated attacks on the integrity of the judiciary and the institution of free press have given life to the agenda of the ultra conservatives led by Steve Bannon, chief strategist for the President. Its main tenet is **"the destruction of the administrative state;"**
- The abuse by the President of laws against nepotism and conflict of interest through appointing his daughter, Ivanka, and son-in-law, Jared Kushner, as senior presidential advisors. These violations constitute a danger to the trust in government and in the Rule of Law; and
- The calls by the President for condoning of violence against protesters, suspects in police custody, persons perceived as immigrants, are attacks on a national environment of law and order.

Such palace authoritarianism mentality, coupled with silence on the vulgarity of Anthony Scaramucci, former Director of Communications, has led to:

- Congressional defiance of Trump especially through sanctioning Russia for, among other things, meddling in the 2016 national elections. The near unanimous resolution on these sanctions was made veto-proof by Trump;
- Trump's forced signature on that resolution, now made law, was bemoaned by Trump as an unconstitutional interference in his foreign policy making;

- Resort by the Senate to staying in pro-forma session to prevent Trump from attempts at removal of the Attorney General as a means to derailing investigations into Russia's role in the 2016 elections;

- Expansion of the investigations by the Special Counsel beyond potential electoral conspiracies to also cover Trump's business and family finance has become public knowledge. This in spite of Trump's description of that investigative expansion as **"red lines"** -another aspect of Congressional defiance to this rogue presidency.

- The convening by special counsel of a grand jury, or his resort to empowering an existing grand jury sitting in Washington, D.C. are clear indications that those investigations are robust. Subpoenas have already been issued. They are the primary method by which prosecutors gather evidence in criminal investigations.

The international repercussions of the Ottomanism of this presidency are legion:

- Russia's reaction to American punitive sanctions, especially in the areas of energy and banking, has been swift. Russian actions against American diplomatic presence on Russia is only the beginning. Giving up on the prospects of warmer relations between Moscow and Trump's Washington, Putin derided anti-Russian sanctions as **"Russophobic tools;"**

- Trump's calls for China's help with restraining North Korea from posing a nuclear threat to America's mainland were quixotic. His attacks on China as a currency manipulator, the naval confrontations by the two powers in the South China Sea, and the flow of American arms to Taiwan, have all made such calls contradictory. President Xi's rebuff to Trump was made public in late July by Chinese media describing the Donald as **"green horned"** -a novice;

- Even in America's neighborhood to the North (Canada) or to the South (Mexico), the thrust of dealings in regard to trade has now sidestepped the federal government and refocused on directly contracting with individual American states.

The gravest aspect of this presidency remains its daily affront against the Rule of Law. Washington, D.C. is not the Astana of the Ottomans, although there is a strong whiff of it over this White House.

In and op. ed. page article in the New York Times of July 29, Sally Yates, a former Deputy Attorney General, leveled these attacks against

Trump: **"He's ripping the blindfold off Lady Justice and attempting to turn the department into a sword to seek vengeance against his perceived enemies and a shield to protect himself and his allies."**

And on July 31 came the revelation that Trump has personally written the cover-up statement of his son, Donald Jr.'s liaison with Russia.

Finding himself in early August besieged by multiple investigations, Trump fell back on an old Ottoman device: Ascending the pulpit to harangue his devotees that attacking him is an affront to legitimacy **-a political apostasy bordering on insurrection.**

That Ottoman evil spirit was in plain sight inhabiting Trump at his rally in West Virginia on August 4.

Time to fire that exorcist as weak and ineffectual. The evil that Trump knows is better than the evil that he doesn't know!!

JUDGING BY HIS UN SPEECH, TRUMP SHOULD BE CERTIFIED "INSANE"!!

Friday, September 29, 2017

If in doubt, read his declaration of wiping off North Korea off the map. And if still in doubt, read his attacks on Iran, and Venezuela. Still in doubt regarding the U.S. President gone rogue? Read his declaration at the U.N., an organization of equal state sovereignty, about **"America First."**

Could it be the stress of multiple investigations in his possible collusion with Russia to put him on top in the 2016 elections? Or could it be that his flaunted wall on the American/Mexico border cannot be funded? Or that his son, Donald Jr. and his son-in-law, Jared Kushner are now in the cross-hairs of multiple investigators? With no hope of eventual pardons by Trump, unavailable at the New York State level?

To fathom how **"Trump is the shame of America,"** compare his UN speech with that of a leader, El-Sisi, of Egypt -a developing nation!! For content analysis is a useful tool for comparing two speeches given at the UN on September 19 from the rostrum of the General Assembly. I served there for more than 30 years and wrote many speeches for the UN Secretary-General and for other presentations in his name. As a long-time insider, I know how leaders often talk, behave, interact and project. By these standards, I judge **Trump as the American Idi Amin of Uganda, or Qaddafi of Libya, or Chavez of Venezuela. The Fraternity of the Deplorables!!**

The UN Charter, in its Article I on **"Purposes and Principles"** provides for taking **"effective collective measures for the prevention and**

removal of threats to the peace, and for the suppression of acts of aggression or other breaches of the peace." That charter is a World War II document which was in the making since 1942, though signed in San Francisco in June 1945.

In spite of those provisions, Donald Trump stood under the dome of the UN General Assembly to shoot holes into that international treaty. Declaring war of annihilation of North Korea, he said: **"The United States has great strength and patience. But if it is forced to defend itself or its allies, we will have no choice but totally destroy North Korea."** An unequivocal threat to the peace in East Asia.

By comparison, the Egyptian President declared from the same spot on which the Trump's sabre-rattling took place: **"We are certain that the purposes and principles of the United Nations are still valid for the founding of a world which provides for all its inhabitants the opportunity for benefiting from ...the great potentiality of realizing the dream of a just and peaceful world order. An order of open interaction with all of humanity."** How more statesmanship can one hope for?

But that **direct threat of genocide, uttered by an unhinged Donald Trump, against North Korea** was not enough for the American President. Other verbal idiocies followed, as he castigated Venezuela, Cuba, Iran, Syria, and more. Armed with a teleprompter, but baffled by the lack of applause from a chamber silenced only by diplomatic protocol, he pontificated: **"If the righteous many do not confront the wicked few, then evil will triumph."**

It is said that Bush Jr.'s downfall began with his infamous description of **"Iraq, Iran and North Korea"** as the axis of evil. That slogan underpinned a non-winnable war of 16 years in Afghanistan, the sectarian mayhem in Iraq, the voids filled by the crazy jihadists, and the launching by both Iran and North Korea of the quest for an ultimate deterrent called nuclear armament.

Contrast this aggressive hyperbole from the US, reflecting disdain for a UN world of equal sovereignties, with what El-Sisi said only four hours after the Trump's shameful spectacle. The Egyptian leader said: **"In an interconnected and complex world, replete with challenges which are difficult to overcome by any single State, regardless of its capacities and determination, it has become logical for Egypt to aspire to implementing a development plan. Such a plan has to be intertwined** with an energetic foreign policy which draws its inspiration from a moral code entrenched in our heritage and culture. Such a policy closely adheres to the legal principles of the world order to which Egypt has contributed to its emergence."

Well!! Haven't Trump invoked the concept of **"sovereignty"** from the UN General Assembly rostrum **20 times?** Sovereignty is not a weapon which is uncheased at will by the strong with a view to overwhelming the sovereignty of the weak. **The UN General Assembly is the world's house of commons where Malta and China have co-equal voting powers,** regardless of demographic size and influence.

That concept is also operational as reflected in Article I (par.2) of the UN Charter. That provision calls on all UN members **"to develop friendly relations among nations based on respect for the principle of equal rights and self-determination of peoples, and to take other appropriate measures to strengthen universal peace."**

An important mechanism for fostering that coveted **"universal peace"** is to respect the sanctity of treaties and international agreements. At law schools, we drill in the minds of our students the Latin phrase: **"Pacta Sunt Servanda."** (Pacts must be observed). But Trump has consistently demonstrated that pacts are a process whereby their terms must remain open for possible unilateral change.

An ominous demonstration of that Trumpian trait is his attacks on the Iran nuclear deal. Assailing that agreement, which had been ratified in 2015 by the Security Council, nitwit Trump declared at the UN: **"The Iran deal was one of the worst and most one-sided transactions the United States has ever entered into."** Then looking straight in the direction of Iran's seats in the GA hall, he belligerently fulminated: **"Frankly, that deal is an embarrassment to the United States, and I don't think you've heard the last of it, believe me."**

Unbelievable!! The parties to that historic deal are all the five permanent members of the Security Council, plus Germany and Iran. **America alone cannot undo that agreement.** Moreover, the International Atomic Energy Agency has verified Iran's adherence to that agreement which postponed for 15 years Iran's non-enrichment of uranium.

The reaction by both Iran's President Hassan Rouhani and its foreign minister Mohammad Javad Zarif was swift. Rouhani warned that America's exiting that agreement would lead to **"no one will trust America** again."** Less diplomatically, Zarif who negotiated that agreement for two long years said: **"Trump's ignorant hate speech belongs in medieval times -not the 21st Century UN."**

But El-Sisi speech at the UN in regard to **"Pacta Sunt Servanda"** belonged to the 21st Century UN. Referring to the Egypt-Israel treaty of 1979, he directly addressed both the Palestinians and the Israelis. To the Palestinians he said: **"Your unity is most important for achieving your goal. Do not waste any more time in readying yourselves to co-exist with the Israelis in security and peace."**

And for the Israelis, El-Sisi said: **"I address this call to you directly. We, in Egypt, have with you a great experience -living in peace with you for forty years. It is an experience which, once more, can be replicated -security and peace for the Israeli citizen living side by side with the Palestinian citizen."**

Where is scatter brained Trump from the President of a country in transition **"From Chaos To the Strong State,"** as I described Egypt in my 2016 book by Amazon? The Greeks invented the term **Enosis** as a movement for unity -unity between Greece and Cyprus. El-Sisi and many other leaders like him made of enosis a global cause in their UN speeches. **Who is Trump kidding** when he told the General Assembly: **"The United States will forever be a great friend to the world, and especially to its allies!!"** Really, Mr. President?! Your own Chief of Staff, General John Kelly was observed bringing his head between his two hands while you fulminated nonsense as if in an American campaign rally.

At the UN, by his measured statement on September 20, **Hassan Rouhani of Iran** proved that Trump was irrelevant to the very concept of the UN. His words rang true as he said: **"The ignorant, absurd, and hateful rhetoric with ridiculously baseless allegations that was uttered before this body yesterday was not only unfit to be heard at the UN which was established to promote peace and respect between nations. But indeed also contradicted the demands of our nations from this world body to bring governments together to combat war and terror."** And **"the prize goes to"** --the leader wearing a turban!!

In the New York Times of September 25, 2017, Peter Baker, the author of **"Obama: A Call to History,"** said about Trump: **"He has made himself America's apostle of anger, its deacon of divisiveness ... Mr. Trump has attacked virtually every major institution in American life**

... even the United States of America."

DR. YASSIN EL-AYOUTY, ESQ.

A FOOLISH AMERICAN INTERPRETATION OF EGYPTIAN-RUSSIAN RELATIONS

Saturday, December 9, 2017

It is foolish because it is as old as the 1950s. Out of sync with the march, always accelerating, of the global political life. Judging should be based not on yesterday's facts. It should be based on the facts of the moment, even when you glance at the prior cases.

The New York Times of December 1 headlined on its first page: **"Egypt Agrees to Open Bases to Russian Jets."** A neutral headline, followed by the imperial interpretation of yester years. Here follow the points where the reasoning is as old as a museum piece telling how the past was:

- "The agreement would give Russia its deepest presence in Egypt since 1973;"
- The U.S. has provided Egypt with more than $1.3 billion a year for four decades because that aid "secures the use of Egypt's airspace and bases for the American military;"
- Analysts "characterized the preliminary deal as the latest sign of the waning influence of the U.S.;"
- Then quoting from a former American deputy assistant secretary of defense, the paper bolsters its foolish interpretation by his imperial language. **"Power abhors a vacuum, and when the United States pulls back, we can't be under the impression that the world is going to stand by and wait for us."**

These are pitiful points of reasoning because **they reflect mental sclerosis regarding Egypt.** That country, throughout its long history has never been a client State of any power. **No foreign military bases have ever been allowed by any Egyptian government,** monarchical or republican. Not even during the 400 years of Ottoman nominal rule (1517-1917). No bravado in this. Only historical facts.

In fact, it was the Egyptian army of modern Egypt, built by Muhammad Ali as of 1805, that punched through the Ottoman Empire in 1832 to punish an impudent Sultan. Marched as far as only 60 miles from the seat of that Empire. British troops were stationed in Egypt as of 1882 as an occupation presence, and were gone by 1956. And the U.N. Peace-Keepers, in Egypt as of 1957, do not constitute occupation since the host country can always invite them out.

This phenomenon of Egyptian freedom from clientism or, for this matter, occupier-inclination in the modern era, cannot be due only to one single factor. Among the multiple factors, account should also be taken of: **the longevity of the deep historical State (7000 years); demographic cohesion; the nilotic tendency to stay close to home; the intercontinental bridge between 3 continents,** thus heightening the innate apprehension of suffering, say, the history of **Poland or the Korean peninsula.**

And when Rommel, the German brilliant general, pushed eastward from Libya into Egypt, reaching less than 100 miles from Alexandria in 1942, **we, as high school students donned military uniforms to fight him.**

Hence the fallacy of the rationale of the New York Times experts as they make the facile claim of: **"The danger and the reality (of landing rights in Egypt for Russian military aircraft in Egypt) is that other countries will take advantage of the opportunity presented when America chooses to pull back."**

Even the linkage between this new facet of Egyptian-Russian relationships to the Cairo/Moscow agreement to have **Russian building nuclear power facilities at Al-Dhabaa** is patently counterfeit. For what does Cairo's search for energy has to do with the implied claim of subjugation of Egypt to the will of Putin's Russia? **A contradiction of today's revelations about the Trump's administration feverish search for Russia's helping hand to put Trump into the Oval office.**

Getting away at this juncture from these deceptive claims to the content analysis of this imperialistic posture, we find the unmistakable resurrection of **the colonial notions of:**

- **The Russia/Egypt agreement is a symptom of a power void.** There are power voids only in failed States due to their inability to conduct foreign affairs. **Not applicable to Egypt;**
- Egypt entered into that agreement with Russia to **boost its tourist industries.** The plain fact is that tourism is rebounding in Egypt mainly from Arab and other Asian arrivals.
- The **relationship between Cairo/Washington/Moscow is a zero-sum relationship. A gain by Moscow in Egypt is perceived as a loss by D.C. Not so.** In Cairo, there has been a strategic shift away from non-alignment under Nasser, to multi-alignment under El-Sisi. Purchasing **military hardware from Moscow and Paris,** while keeping the contracts with Washington intact in the areas of maintenance and fresh supplies.

Even Saudi Arabia under King Salman, has pivoted in the same direction. The King was the first Saudi monarch to pay a State visit to the Kremlin last month. That is after he teamed up with Trump in Riyadh in a sword-dance, and multi-billion dollars contract for modernizing the Saudi arsenal. **In Analysis, which also goes by another name, interpretation, one has to seek not only what was said, but also what was not said.** Of the latter category, there is plentiful of **examples:**

- The worrisome ups and downs in Congressional attitudes towards aid to Egypt. Though contractual and linked legally to the peace treaty of 1979 between Egypt and Israel, it has become akin to a ball in the field of **competition between American special interests, lobbies, and stable foreign policy;**

- The constant drumbeat emanating from Washington questioning the **legitimacy of the elevation of El-Sisi to the presidency of Egypt.** That process was **not,** as those nay-sayers claim, **a military take-over.** It was the **result of the implementation of the Egyptian secular Constitution of** January 2014: a fair and open election contest between El-Sisi and Sabbahi;

- The **continuous intrusion in the internal affairs of Egypt through American governmental actions** (the annual assessment of human rights in Egypt by the State Department) **and non-governmental organizations like Human Rights watch;**

- In a country like Egypt, where **terrorism has felled hundreds of casualties,** the country has perforce to put societal right to security, ahead of individual rights, in the context of emergency laws. The American Civil War of the 1860s witnessed the partial suspension of the US Constitution. **And where is American due process and the jurisdiction of Habeas Corpus in keeping Guantanamo open since 2002,** even when the American judiciary asserts the viability of application of these basic rights to Muslim detainees?! These helpless victims **have not even been** charged by military commissions;

- Add to the above the manifestations of anti-Islamism exhibited nearly daily by President Trump, members of his administration, and his supporters?! This is no longer freedom of expression under the First Amendment of the US Constitution. Calls to hate have increased the volume of incidents, both anti-Semitic and anti-Islamists. These go largely unprosecuted. They are lumped together within the Nazi-like call for **"Save Us From Islamization;"**

- **Muslim bans are, in effect, igniters of ISIS-like terrorism** as they become fodder for jihadi propaganda helping recruitment and funding;

- **And how could Trump's ill-considered decision to declare Jerusalem, whose eastern part is occupied territory since 1967, the capital of Israel advance the cause of peace generally, or of American/Egyptian amity, specifically?**

In all of this, one sees America's lurch to the Right, staggering towards white nativism which seeks in the old imperial lingo a mode of self-assertion. This is the essence of hegemony. America today has military presence in more than 100 countries.

There is no American physical retreat. Only a retreat from rationale regarding other sovereignties claim to the right to action independent of the wishes of other sovereignties. Facts are facts. They are not alternatives.

Alternative facts are falsehoods. Including foolish interpretations deriving from the bygone days of the Cold War of a bipolar world.

And one has to be blind not to admit that America under Trump is now experiencing a period of irrational governance. This great country is divided between right and left to the point of outright tribalism. Trump, lacking the power of inquiry, is following what appears to be a formula for destroying "the administrative State."

With an approaching constitutional crisis, how can America's allies rely upon Washington's promises? **On December 1, General Michael Flynn, Trump's former national security advisor, pleaded guilty in federal court to lying to the FBI about conversations with Russian officials regarding elimination of sanctions** imposed by Obama, prior to Trump becoming president.

The claim by Trump on December 3 that Flynn's life is unjustly being destroyed by the judicial system is manifestly bogus. It puts the American President in further legal jeopardy.

Commenting on this State of chaos in the White House which can only become worse, **Garry Wills in an article on Trump in the New York Review of Books dated** December 21, 2017, says: Trump's **"neglect of necessary requirements for governing offers in itself grounds for impeachment."**

DR. YASSIN EL-AYOUTY, ESQ.

A RARE ARAB OCCURENCE: JUDGING LEADERS BY THEIR PEFORMANCE

Friday, January 5, 2018

How refreshing. Part of the mobocracy in the Arab world is to judge leaders by hearsay, not by performance. There is a weakened sense of nationalism in a 400 million population of whom 40% are illiterate. A combination which makes the rumor and personal interest the parameters for judging leadership performance. Yet, I was lucky enough to look up the sky when a shooting star was streaking across that darkness.

That was an article in the e-journal of Al-Qabas of Kuwait by a leader whom I have known for years to enjoy the gift of critical thinking. It is Ambassador Abdullah Bishara, former Kuwait representative to the UN, and later, the first Secretary-General of the Gulf Cooperation Council (6 Gulf States). I always read his stuff and learn from it: the graceful Arabic rendering; the political analytical approach; the absence of pandering to leadership.

Bishara, as the founder and president of the Kuwaiti think tank of diplomatic and strategic studies, has been, and rightly so, critical of Egypt under Nasser (1950-1970), and aficionado of the democracy of Egypt before the Nasser Coup. On that plane, he and I, friends since 1968 (50 years ago) are on the same page. The ideological and contentious trajectory of Nasser's Egypt, and the lack of attention to the sovereignties of other Arab States caused the Egyptian public plenty of headaches.

Under Nasser, the great educational edifice crumbled. It was replaced by the rantings of hucksters, such as Mohamad Hassanain Heykal of Al-Ahram newspaper who sermonized that Arab leaders who did not accept Nasser's approach to Arab events were **"traitors."** I had once confronted Heykal at a dinner in Cairo in 1969 about the destructive hegemonic of attributing **"treason"** to others.

There has never been a consensual definition of **"treason"** which the Arab community of nations has reached. Nor can that be reached as each of these countries values its independence as an insulator from outside intervention under the guise of the controversial term **"pan-Arabism."**

Under Nasser, Egypt became saddled with the inordinate price of his seeking to be a pan-Arab leader. The results were a series of catastrophes: The Sudan split from Egypt; Yemen descended into its first civil war (1962); Israel quadrupled its size following the 1967 war (the Six-Day War). The Arab leaders in Khartoum in 1967 declared: No negotiation, no recognition, no peace. That was at a time when Israel was ready to deal; but Nasser, and behind him, a corrupt Palestinian leadership, were after their image, not after an honorable accommodation.

Three years later, Arafat tried but failed to take over Jordan; the PLO immigrated to Lebanon; and Sharon of Israel, though through genocide at Palestinian refugee camps in Lebanon, forced Arafat and his corrupt coterie to flee to Tunisia. At every step, that failed Arab leadership assigned the word **"victory"** to every defeat. Even the massive defeat of 1967 was called **"the setback"** (Al-Naksah). The Nasser scene was one of phony image, but no substance. **"The voice of the Arabs"** was nothing as radio broadcasts more than unworthy propaganda in the service of Nasser.

Then in 1970, an Egyptian regeneration occurred with Vice President Sadat succeeding Nasser who passed away that year. An under-valued leader, the son of a Sudanese mother, whom the Nasser goons had disparaged and defamed as unfit to fill the shoes of his towering predecessor.

Being the heirs to the legacy of bombast, they were proven wrong. There was talk of attempted coup with Aly Sabri ready to assume the helm. Sadat, unexpectedly struck back; the armed forces stood solidly behind the legality of succession; and the suspected perpetrators ended up in jail, including the real author of **"The Philosophy of the Revolution,"** Heykal.

With the era of pretended leadership of the fractious Arab world gone, Sadat, a true Egyptian patriot, saw in his presidency two vital goals: Regain Sinai from Israeli occupation, and rebuilding his country through economic and financial opening. As to the Arab world, Sadat ended any form of intervention, whether by the military, by the intelligence services, or by pretentious inflated propaganda.

Egypt, under Sadat, was not above other Arab countries; it acted as an example of a sovereignty which respected the sovereignties of its Arab sister States. Soon the era of good feelings generated by the Sadat regime (1970-1981) paid its national dividends, especially through Saudi Arabia under the enlightened leadership of King Farsal Ibn Abdel Aziz. His generosity was crucial to rebuilding, not only Egypt's economy, but also its demoralized huge armed forces.

With the Soviets dismissed by Sadat in 1972, the Supreme Armed Forces Command planned and successfully executed the crossing of the Suez Canal on October 6, 1973; destroyed the Israeli Bar Lev lines and partially penetrated Sinai. Egyptian honor was restored because that was not a fight, a la Nasser in Syria or Yemen. It was a fight by Egyptians, assisted by other Arab countries, for Egyptian liberation. The final outcome was peace with honor in the form of the Egypt-Israel Peace Treaty of 1979 which is still standing.

From Sadat, to Mubarak (1981-2011), to the Supreme Council of Armed Forces (2011-2013), to the transitional government of Counsellor Adly Mansour (2013-2014), to El-Sisi (2014 to the present). The Sadat approach to Egyptian leadership held.

This brings me to the thoughtful assessment by Ambassador Abdullah Bishara of Kuwait in Al-Qabas newspaper in December 2017. Entitled (in Arabic) as **"El-Sisi's leadership and Reforming Egypt,"** the author, eloquently, hit all the right keys. Bishara states that

- Modern Egyptian history records the names of two leaders who relieved Egypt from unprecedented burdens: Sadat, the liberator of Sinai; El-Sisi as Egypt's reformer;

- As the preparations for Sinai liberation distanced Sadat from the woes of its declining economy, El-Sisi came to give that economy his full attention;

- In the process, El-Sisi boldly relieved Egypt's economy from public subsidies for food stuffs, gas, electricity and water;

- Simultaneously, El-Sisi relentlessly pursued all those corrupt officials who have tarnished the dignity of Egypt and its public. There was no truce with those suspected of corruption whhom he exposed to public view;

- Referring to the other national preoccupation of El-Sisi, namely combatting terrorism, Bishara rightly points to El-Sisi perspective on terrorism as a retardant of Egypt's development.

Bishara's conclusion, which happily conforms to the reality of President El-Sisi, is that he is a true Egyptian leader, deeply immersed in his country's economic and social progress. Within that frame of mind, El-Sisi has patterned his diplomatic road map to align it with the improvement of the lot of his people.

Thus, Bishara, finds in El-Sisi approach a negation of the adventurism which characterized earlier regimes. The author sees in that sane and pragmatic approach the best way to stretching the hands of friendship and cooperation to all capitals. The goal, Bishara says, is to gain for Egypt access to technology and investments. For under El-Sisi, Cairo has become a capital with no enemy capitals abroad.

At the same time, Bishara sees the urgent need for Egypt to deepen the culture of investment. Laws, by themselves, are not enough. The educational process in regard to investment needs the elucidation of a philosophy which suffered greatly under Nasser. Nasserism has wrongly painted investment as a disease which robs Egypt, weakens its national resolve, and conspires against its security.

The remedy, as seen by Ambassador Bishara, is to inform the nation that investment creates job opportunities, opens up foreign markets, and introduces the new arts of management and technological innovation.

Only through such approaches, asserts the author, could Egypt create global partnerships which uplift the status of Egypt. This is feasible. Such a regime, which is confident in its capabilities and is a believer in the worthiness of its national program, can find in the societies of the private sector a true collaborator.

To Bishara, the yardstick for measuring the performance of El-Sisi government is: the educational and institutional innovations of Muhammad Ali Pasha, the founder, since 1805, of Egypt's last royal family. Then as now, seeking knowledge and education everywhere abroad, was the norm.

His parting shot in that seminal article in **Al-Qabas** of Kuwait, is a **"We stand with Egypt, as we understand the nature of the leadership weight placed on the shoulders of President El-Sisi."** This is particularly so after the terrorist massacre at the mosque in North Sinai -a massacre perpetrated by the devils of assassinations.

"May God Save Egypt and the Egyptians" was Bishara's prayer at the end of his article.

It is refreshing and inspiring to have such an Arab thinker, like Abdulla Bishara of Kuwait, pick up his pen to assess the Egyptian leader in terms of performance, not in terms of the dying personality cult and fake propaganda.

WITH TRUMP AS CAPTAIN, THE SHIP OF STATE IS SINKING

Saturday, February 10, 2018

At least Captain Ahab had a single obsession: To destroy a killing whale that interfered with safe navigation. But Trump has shown that he is plagued with various obsessions. Shifting whimsically from one to another. The obvious result is that the American ship of State is in dire peril. Whether he stays or goes, the damage to the Rule of Law in the U.S. shall outlast Trump's tenure.

Institutions like checks and balances, federal and state interaction, constitutional observance of limits of presidential power, respect for the Department of Justice, and non-interference with the freedom of the press, taking together, have been the hallmarks of American governance. They, not Trump single-handedly, have made America great.

But the very notion of **"Make America Great Again,"** in the Trump era, is a revisionist vow to undo the America of 240 years of tradition. Only to replace it with an America gone rogue. Internally and externally. Never in my 66 years of life in the U.S. have I felt that the warning uttered in 1954 by one of my professors at Rutgers University, New Jersey's State University, might actually become real.

Professor Sidney Ratner, for whom I was a teaching assistant in American economic history, said at one of his seminars: **"Under our Constitution, the President, if he is so inclined, could become a dictator."** We thought that Ratner was being hyperbolic. Now I could see in Trump the very materialization of a dictator. For the Donald, the primary concern is loyalty to him, not to America's decades-old institutions.

No more can the word of Trump as president, be credible. Buzz-feed and other fact-checkers have attributed to him no less than 2000 lies, deliberately uttered in 2016 and 2017. A conman by both upbringing and temperament, like the Donald, shall eventually go down in history as a charlatan whose age's of one darkness.

Citing selectivity some manifestations of Trump's America gone rogue, one might start with the phenomenon of the House Speaker, Paul Ryan, choosing to stand aside as Trump treats Congress as if it were a subsidiary of the Trump organization. The episode of the release of a document impugning the credibility of the Department of Justice and the FBI, in spite of the opposition of those law enforcement agencies, is truly shameful.

That shame is allowed to envelope today's America, without a whimper by the House Speaker, shall forever attach. For the only beneficiary of that flagrant violation of America's need to protect its national secrets from the mischief of a hostile foreign power, Russia, shall not soon be forgotten. Saving Trump from the possible results of the ongoing investigation by the special counsel, Mueller, has become to the Republican establishment of today more important than protecting America's democracy.

In Trump's first State of the Union message, delivered on January 30, there was not even one word by that fake president against Russia. That is although no less than 517 votes were cast in the House of Representatives for the imposition of sanctions on Russia for its imperial designs on Europe. It is truly laughable.

Full throatedly in his State of the Union message, Trump characterized his efforts to place himself above the law as **"our new American moment."** Then, after applauding for himself in the style of a cheerleader, he declared: **"Together, we can achieve absolutely anything."**

So let us look at Trump's view of **"Our new American moment"** in the context of today's American realities.

Disposing of the veracity of the phony rallying cry of **"Togetherness,"** no American president before Trump has ever divided this great nation. His **"America First"** is no more than a code phrase for **"America is for the Whites only."** He has supported the extreme American right, equated between American Nazis and American supporters of diversity, and lambasted African States as **"shit hole States."** Trump has stood with the deprivation of minorities of the right to vote through gerrymander and vote-suppression. And has hatefully claimed that **"the Muslims hate us."**

As to **"Our New American Moment,"** it is **"his"** not **"our"** American moment. His guru, Steven Bannon, has called for **"the destruction of the Administrative State,"** and his spokesmen have railed against **"the deep State,"** a code name for **"conspiracy"** built in the State Department, the Department of Justice, and the 17 security agencies of the US, including the FBI. The Trumpist efforts are aimed at diversion, disbelief in the free-press (he called it **"enemy of the people"**), and preparation for either dismissing the Special Counsel, or casting doubts on the outcome of his investigations.

Today's Trump fascism has become clear in various ways: Indicators of his involvement in the obstruction of justice multiply. Whatever the outcome of the Mueller investigation, Donald Trump shall forever be stigmatized, at least as a non-convicted felon. For that rogue White House occupant has:

• Demanded from James Comey, former FBI Director, at the White House on January 27, 2017, a pledge of loyalty. At that time, Comey was overseeing the investigation of the Trump campaign;

• On February 14, 2017, Trump, acting in a mafia-mode, directed several officials to leave the Oval Office so he could be alone with Comey. At that unlawful tete-a-tete, he asked Comey to **"let"** the investigation of Michael Flynn **"go."** Flynn (the instigator of **"lock her up about Hillary"**) had resigned the previous day as Trump's national security advisor.

• But that resignation had come about eighteen days after Trump was warned by the Department of Justice about Flynn's criminal involvement with Russia, in detriment to American national interest.

• With Comey standing his constitutional grounds, as his oath of office as FBI Director was to uphold the US Constitution and laws, Trump, on May 9, fired Comey.

• On the following day, the President of the United States told the Russian Foreign Minister, Lavrov, and the Russian Ambassador to Washington that the firing had **"taken off the great pressure"** of the Russian investigation. No US press was allowed to witness that treasonous admission. Only Russian media was permitted to record that unbelievable obsequious self-prostration in the mode of a Putin agent.

• No loyalty to country, to flag, to an oath of office, or to the Constitution. Article II, Section 1 of the US Constitution, provides for the following Oath or Affirmation by the President-elect at inauguration: **"I do solemnly swear (or affirm) that I will faithfully execute the Office of President of the United States, and will to the best of my abilities, preserve, protect and defend the Constitution of the United States."**

- On May 11, 2017, Trump told NBC News for the whole world to see, that the firing of Comey was because of **"this Russia thing."** Being unfaithful to your country, Mr. President, is not a **"thing."**
- If proven, your collusion with Russian interference in the 2016 elections, if proven by the ongoing Mueller investigation, (forget about the sham of congressional investigations) is an impeachable offense. It falls within **"Treason, Bribery, or other High Crimes and Misdemeanors."** (Article II, Section 4 of the US Constitution).

Trump is still exploring various options to regain control of the Mueller investigations, including his attacks on the Attorney General, Jeff Sessions, on the Deputy Attorney General, on the FBI, and the indirect firing of Andrew McCabe, the FBI deputy director. Bulldozer Trump shall not stop at anything or anyone who is not on the **"Trump team."**

Trump's totality of illegal actions shall have to be judged by the same standard used in Nixon's article of impeachment. It reads as follows: **"made false or misleading public statements for the purpose of deceiving the people of the United States."** At the Constitutional Convention, when the framers were debating impeachment, George Mason asked: **"Shall any man be above justice?"**

To that basic principle on which America was established, I should add these words of Daniel Webster: *"There are men, in all ages ... who mean to govern well; but they mean to govern. They promise to be kind masters; but they mean to be masters... They think there need be but little restraint upon themselves... The Love of power may sink too deep in their own hearts..."*

In North Korea, Kim is reported to kill those who do not applaud him with gusto. And in America, Trump has called the Democrats who did not join in applauding his **"State of the Union"** message last month **"un-American"** and even **"treasonous."** Conclusion: Kim and Trump, as dictators, are on the same page. Though not fully on the same authoritarian page. Kim is slightly better than his American clone. He does not attack his own law enforcement agencies.

In only one year of his chaotic presidency, Donald J. Trump has sunk even below the limits of **"love of power."** *His narcissism, his divisiveness, his steering the ship of states over the shoals of destructive boulders, his kindness towards hostile foreign powers, and his mischief abroad, including his declaration of contested Jerusalem as the capital of Israel, are all sure signs of an unhinged potentate.*

One of the recently published books sums up this dilemma. It is by David Frum, titled: **Trumpocracy: The Corruption of the American Republic.**

GETTING TO KNOW THE STATE OF KUWAIT

Friday, March 2, 2018

While I was Secretary of the Board of UNITAR (The UN Institute for Training and Research), I was tasked with supervising a special study. It was (in short) **"issues of Small States."** Its drafter was an Eritrean scholar, friend of mine, by the name of Dr. Berhan Andemicael. Later, Berhan headed the NY Liaison Office of International Atomic Energy Agency (IAEA), as I moved from UNITAR to establish the first Peace Research Center within the then UN Department for Secretary Council Affairs.

This is the context of this monthly blog, entitled **"Getting to Know the State of Kuwait."** Reason: Kuwait is described by the Kuwaitis as a **"Small State."** I beg to differ. States, in my own definition, are neither big, mid-size, nor small. Each State from Monaco to Russia draws their description from two sources: The character of their people, and the contribution they make towards internal welfare, and external management of their foreign affairs.

With these parameters in mind, I have observed Kuwait through its presidency of the UN Security Council in February, as well as through its celebration of its Liberation Day on February 26, 2018. Not only did I observe both the Foreign Minister, Sheikh Sabah Al-Ahmad Al-Sabah, as well as the Kuwait Permanent Representative to the UN, Ambassador Mansour Alotaibi; my gaze roamed beyond, as a search light, shining a spot on the totality of that environment of a State, whose origins date back to the mid 17th Century.

As I peered through the fog of the endless practice of UN compromises, a requisite for Security Council complex drafting and passing of resolutions, I detected Kuwaiti calm and well modulated voice from the presidential chair. No screams, no shouts, no pointing of blaming fingers on issues, such as Syria, Yemen, Libya, Central African Republic, Palestine and ISIS.

The outward motion hummed on noiselessly. Its combustion engine was not that of a tractor, but of a Mercedes Benz. The goal was to move things forward, even through the boulders of big power rivalries seeking to score points, not necessarily moving towards the two principal objectives of the UN: peace and prosperity.

Not since the 1990s when UN Secretary-General Boutros Ghali issued his twin agendas, one for peace, the other for development, have I, as professor of international law and organizations, seen the likes of the Kuwait concept memorandum on energizing the peace and prosperity pillars on which the UN Charter of 1945 had been established. Seeing in it the spirit of a **"small"** but resilient State, I have assigned it a course of study for my spring intern from St. Francis College, New York City, Julia Cruet. Her successors (I only take one notable undergraduate each semester from St. Francis College -a class of one student!!), shall benefit by that historic concept paper introduced by Kuwait into the UN annals.

Beyond the UN realm, I came to discern in the public events organized by the Permanent Mission of the State of Kuwait to the UN, what I can only describe as **"the of sinews resilience"** of Kuwaiti Society. From that I learnt why the Iraqi invasion of Kuwait of 1990 had failed. That power grab by Saddam Hussein had collapsed, not only because of the collective military intervention by the UN. The roots of that failure, as I came to recently discover, grew deeper in the sands of Kuwait through a population that said: Saddam **"you can burn our oil fields. But you shall not extinguish our 350 years of Kuwait ID!!"**

How did I reach that conclusion? Not through fantasy of a person like myself who was born in the desert of an Egyptian province called Sharqiah, west of the two Suez Canals. But through:
- Their orchestra playing in the UN General Assembly Hall;
- Their songs evoking the transition from the **"hard times,"** to **"the blessed times of plenty;"**
- Their diverse skin color which reminds me of the American and the Egyptian models;
- The engagement by Ambassador Alotaibi and his Deputy, Mr. Bader AlMunayekh of little Kuwaiti girls dancing to their native music;

- The teamwork of their diplomats who seem never to forget why they are in New York serving Kuwait and the world;
- The outward openness and affability of their ladies whether diplomats, spouses, advisers or local recruits;
- Their generosity writ large not only at the Mission; but also worldwide through the **"Kuwait Development Fund."** They have even contributed significantly in 2018 towards the rebuilding of Iraq;
- Their national dress, especially the head gear, black AQAL (thick cord) holding in place a snow white Kaffieyeh covering a man's head, and needing constant adjustment with a flourish;
- Their security guards who never fail to greet every permitted visitor with the equivalent of the song in Oklahoma: **"Oh What a Beautiful Day!!"**

I am finally getting to know the State of Kuwait through only two weeks of residence at the Permanent Mission.

So please note: Kuwait is not only a State; it is "a state of mind!!"

ABSOLUTE JUSTICE FOR ALL: THE ISLAMIC JUDICIAL MAGNA CARTA OF OMAR, IN THE 7TH CENTURY AD

Friday, March 30, 2018

It was promulgated 500 years before Magna Carta was issued in 1215. Magna Carta was extracted by British nobles from King John on behalf of human rights for his subjects. Omar Ibn Al-Khattab, the second to succeed the Prophet Muhammad, as the second of four Enlightened Caliphs, had a sense of absolute justice.

With law being basically an equalizer, the motto **"Justice Is the Pillar of Governance"** was Omar's creed. Unsurprisingly, it appears on the wall of every Arab court behind the judge's bench. In Arabic it says: **"Al-Adl Asas Al-Mulk."**

With our present world in disarray, especially in these waning days of jihadism, I opted for translating Omar's judicial creed from Arabic into English.

And for a suitable location for that first-ever translation, I annexed it to my book, recently published by Amazon. The book's full title is **"War on Jihadism By Ideology: The New Islamic Religious Revolution."** That publication has been dedicated to Al-Azhar in Cairo, and to its Grand Imam, Dr. El-Taiyeb.

Of course, Omar's judicial creed is the very anti-thesis of the catastrophe for justice and human rights summed up in one word: **"Guantanamo."** For it reads as follows as instructions for a nominee for a judgeship in Kofa, Iraq:

Here follows its full text:
- "From Omar To Abu-Musa Al-Ashaari: Peace Be Upon You!!
- Know that judging is a firm religious duty, and a tradition observed. Be sure to understand the pleadings delivered before you. And when you reach a decision based on evidence, implement it. For there is no use in speaking about what is right if it lacks execution.
- Maintain a neutral face while on the bench, performing the role of a judge. This ensures that the powerful shall not aspire to your siding unjustly with them. Nor shall the powerless despair of your rendering justice unto them.
- The burden of proof is upon the plaintiff. And those impeaching that evidence should take a solemn oath that their denial has merit.
- Conciliation is permissible between litigants (referred to in general as Muslims). That is unless it is on a basis disapproved by Islamic jurisprudence, or denying what is permitted under that jurisprudence.
- Do not hesitate to review and amend a judgment which you might have reached the day before, only to discover, through your sense of fairness, that it was in error. That is because what is right does not age by the passage of time, as nothing could invalidate an obvious right.
- Returning to the zone of what is rightfully just supersedes any continuation down the path of what is unjust. And if someone claims a right that has not been uncovered before a proof was available, give them a time limit to provide such evidence. If they succeed, rule in favor of restituting to them those rights. But if they fail, they lose their cause. Thus no pretexts can stand, and no blindness to what is evident can prevail.
- Comprehension, comprehension of the pleadings in your court. Especially whatever is in those pleadings which is not based on text either in the Quran or in the Prophet's tradition. In these situations, resort to prior cases decided by unanimity (ijmaa) or by analogy (quias). Educate yourself about those precedents, then make the judgments which seem to you to be supported by the Quran, as close as possible to the word of God, and nearest to the concept of fairness.
- People (the faithful) have a sense of what is right within their society. With the exception of those whose testimony had been previously impeached as false, or those previously convicted, or those whose sense of loyalty or family lineage is subject to doubt.

- Only God knows what people harbor in their bosoms, and He is the One who shields them from punitive measures. That is with the exception of situations where there is probative evidence and proven faith.
- You are hereby instructed to avoid becoming angry or anxious or bored, or upset by adversaries, or by turning your back upon issues of conflict. That is because good judging on issues of right and wrong is what God dictates to you, and is what you shall be remembered by.
- This is applicable to judges who are endowed with good will and who might rule even against themselves. It is the way prescribed by God for any relationship between a judge and his community.
- But those who resort to mere appearances which they know to be non-reflective of their true feelings, shall not be favored by God. Only honesty can be favored by God, and that is where God shall favor those who adhere to it, rewarding them in their livelihoods and through his limitless mercy.

Peace Be With You."

> بسم الله الرحمن الرحيم
>
> رسالة عمر بن الخطاب
>
> إلى أبي موسى الأشعري عندما ولّاه قضاء الكوفة
>
> "من عبد الله عمر أمير المؤمنين
>
> إلى عبد الله بن قيس"
>
> سلام عليك ...
>
> أما بعد – فإن القضاء فريضة محكمة وسنّة متبعة فافهم إذا أُدلي إليك والفذ إذا تبين لك فإنه لا ينفع تكلّم بحق لا نفاذ له.
>
> آس بين الناس في مجلسك وفي وجهك وقضائك حتى لا يطمع شريف في حيفك ولا ييأس ضعيف من عدلك.
>
> البيّنة على من ادّعى واليمين على من أنكر، والصلح جائز بين المسلمين إلا صلحًا أحلّ حرامًا أو حرّم حلالاً ولا يمنعك قضاء قضيته بالأمس فراجعت فيه نفسك وهديت فيه لرشدك أن تراجع فيه الحق فإن الحق قديم لا يبطله شيء.
>
> والرجوع إلى الحق خير من التمادي في الباطل ومن ادعى حقًا غائبًا أو بيّنة فاضرب له أمدًا ينتهي إليه، فإن بيّنه أعطيته حقه وإن أعجزه ذلك استحللت عليه القضية، فإن ذلك أبلغ للعذر "وأجلى للعمى".
>
> الفهم ... الفهم فيما أُدلي إليك مما ورد عليك مما ليس في قرآن ولا سنّة ثم قايس الأمور عندئذ واعرف الأمثال ثم اعمد فيما ترى إلى أحبّها إلى الله وأشبهها بالحق. للمسلمون عدول بعضهم على بعض إلا مجربًا عليه شهادة زور أو مجلودًا في حد أو ظنينًا في ولاء أو قرابة، فإن الله تولى من عباده السرائر وستر عليهم الحدود إلا بالبيّنات والإيمان.
>
> وإياك والغضب والقلق والضجر والتأذي بالخصوم والتنكّر عند الخصومات فإن القضاء في مواطن الحق مما يوجب الله به الأجر ويحسن به الذكر فمن خلصت نيته في الحق ولو على نفسه كفاه الله ما بينه وبين الناس ومن تزيّن بما ليس في نفسه شانه الله فإن الله تعالى لا يقبل من العباد إلا ما كان خالصًا فما ظنك بجواب عند الله في عاجل رزقه وخزائن رحمته.
>
> "والسلام عليكم ورحمة الله"

From the above, a global legal conclusion emerges. Equal protection of the law, otherwise referred to colloquially as **"no one is above the law"** is the substance of Omar's judicial decree. At that time, mid of the 7th Century AD, judging was integral to rulership.

Prior to the promulgation of Omar's judicial decree, which adorns the entrance to the Institute of High Judicial Studies in Abbasiyah (a Cairo district), the Prophet Muhammad had planted the seed of that concept.

In appointing Moaz Ibn Jabal judge for Yemen, to succeed the Prophet's cousin and protege, Ali Ibn Abi-Taleb, he urged the pursuit of a novel concept for finding the law. In summary, he urged that if the judge cannot discover the rule of law applicable to any case, in either the Quran or the Sunna, he should extrapolate it through common sense -in Arabic **"Al-Hekmah."** Thus the Prophet made Al-Hekmah the **modus operandi** of Al-Ijtihad, which in effect is the brain of **Sharia** (Islamic Law).

From the 7th Century (Omar's decree in Arabia) to the 13th Century (Magna Carta in England), to the 19th Century, when the U.S. Constitution embraces the same concept, the thread holding that legal necklace is one and the same. For the 14th Amendment, ratified on July 9, 1868 provides for **"any person within its jurisdiction the equal protection of the laws."**

So, never accept the ancient Roman saying: **"In times of war, the law falls silent."** It never does!!

Ibn Al-Khattab put his declared faith in **"equality before the law"** in practice. Not only was he one of only 17 men in his tribe (Quraish) who could write when Islam began, thus able to enhance the enforcement of his sense of justice. Omar was also a dedicated protector of minority rights.

He chided and punished his appointed governor to Egypt in 641 AD for injustice to an Egyptian Christian subject (a Copt). Omar's words, on that occasion, shall always stand as testimony to **"justice is the pillar of governance."** For he told the errant Governor: **"Why do you enslave people who were born free by the very fact of their birth!!"**

GUANTANAMO BAY? HUMAN RIGHTS LAWS HAVE NEVER LIVED THERE!!

Friday, April 20, 2018

It is the darkest stain on America's human rights record!! Opened in 2002 in a fit of rage over 9/11, a criminal act to which neither Islam nor the Muslim world is related, it is still open. Challenging every Rule of Law. Obama tried to close it; Trump declares that he shall repopulate it. This is no way to MAGA (Make America Great Again). It is a way for ISIS to justify its lunatic existence.

Why is Guantanamo a human rights hell hole? The reasons are diverse, but their centrality resides in the following:

- Scooping whole populations in Afghanistan and Pakistan in a massive American dragnet? A nasty violation of the American Constitution injunction against **"attainder."** What is attainder?: **Grabbing a person anywhere and hauling them to prison without notice, arraignment or charges.**

- **No habeaus corpus application.** What is that? **Enabling the detainee to appear in a court of law to challenge the cause of their loss of freedom.** No Guantanamo detainee (their number has once exceeded 700 Muslims) was allowed that legal relief.

- Who caused the deprivation of that elementary human right, which, in English, means **"you have the body of the detainee?"** By legislation of the US Congress, the legislative arm of the US Government. What was the reason for such unconstitutional legislation?: **The laughable claim that these Muslims are neither American citizens, nor are they on US soil!!**

- **Really?** But then what are they, and where are they on the part of the planet Earth called Guantanamo Bay, Cuba? They, from the ludicrous view violating human rights, are not American citizens, but **"economy combatants."** Thus, that foolish view goes on to say: these Muslims are not entitled to Habeaus Corpus application.

- But isn't the designation of **"enemy combatant"** the prerogative of a congressional action? **Yes, but this is total war (where there is no distinction between military and civilian).** So Congressional action has been dispensed with. Furthermore, so the lawless argument goes, **those Muslims are not on American soil!!**

- Oh My God!! Are you claiming that habeaus corpus can only apply on American soil? **But Guantanamo Bay is American soil!!** How do we know that?: The American flag is fluttering over it; the US Defense Department controls it; the Cuban Government has no scintilla of control over it; **and the US Supreme Court had in 2004 dealt directly with it.**

- **How did SCOTUS (the Supreme Court of the US) deal with it?** In the famous case of **Hamdi v. Rumsfeld** (2004). (Hamdi was a Guantanammo detainee; Rumsfeld, the Secretary of Defense), the Supreme Court required the Defense Department to provide Hamdi with the opportunity to challenge his classification as enemy combatant.

- The importance of that case lies in: (a) the Court's recognition of Guantanamo as **"territory of the US.;"** (b) confirmed the lawful **extension of Habeaus Corpus to anyone detained in such territory;** (c) **four of the Justices relied on the Geneva Conventions (1949)** as a source of due process; and (d) declared that the term **"enemy combatant"** does not exist in those Geneva Conventions.

- Here we should note that since 2003, the year of the American war of choice on Iraq, those conventions were downgraded to things of the past (depasse). And therefore not applicable to what the Justice Department and White House counsel called **a new type of war:** non-conventional, since the adversary (the terrorists) wore no uniforms; held no recognizable boundaries; and had no clear command and control hierarchy. As could be seen below, **these are all bogus claims rebutted by international rules of laws of armed conflict.**

The Supreme Court cases of **Rasul v. Bush** (2004) and **Hamdan v. Rumsfeld** (2006), proved that Guantanamo Bay, seen from the angle of human rights, **was no more than a legal swamp whose drainage was called for by the US Constitution, US laws, international conventions on human rights** to which America has affixed its accession.

- **Rasul v. Bush** (2004) held that America had sufficient sovereign control over Guantanamo. Thus justifying the extension of Habeaus Corpus to **"the foreign nationals seized in Pakistan and Afghanistan, during America's invasion of Afghanistan in 2002 and transferred to Guanatanmo."**

- And **Hamdan v. Rumsfeld** (2006) **denied the legality of the US establishment of "military commissions."** Said the Supreme Court that those commissions, established as substitutes for the regular US criminal courts to try the Guantanamo detainees, **were not authorized by the US Congress.**

- The link made by the Supreme Court between the US legal system and international conventions were at its broadest in yet another case. In **Boumedienne v. Bush** (2008), the Court recognized the challenge raised by foreign nationals to the concocted term **"enemy combatant,"** and to their endless detention at Guantanamo. Once more the absence of Habeaus Corpus application was noted, but on broader grounds. **The Court's holding in that case declared that that deprivation violated the US Constitution federal laws, the US treaty obligations under the Geneva Conventions (1949), and Customary International Laws.**

Guantanamo, the human rights catastrophe, has led to a Congressional act called the Military Commissions Act (MCA). MCA was declared unconstitutional by the US Supreme Court. Such act constitutes aggression against the Rule of Law. This is because it **precluded the federal judiciary from having Guantanamo detainees from bringing before it Habeaus Corpus challenges.**

Thus a totally non-Rule of Law structure has been built. Infecting both Congress and the Executive, as far as law and order are concerned, with the Guantanamo disease.

Not only have the Geneva Conventions (1949) been blatantly flouted. So, among others, have been the UN Universal Declaration of Human Rights (1948); the UN Convention of Civil and Political Rights (1966); the UN Convention on Economic, Social, and Cultural Rights (1966); and **the Torture Convention.**

Specifically on the Torture Convention: It is most ironic for a **former US**

Vice President (Cheney) to regard "water boarding" (subjecting a detainee to the simulation of drowning to force out confessions) **as not torture.** Torture, which has been the modus operandi in Guantanamo against detainees (all Muslims), is legally regarded **"a universal crime." A universal crime is defined as a crime punishable by any State anywhere.** Universal is universal.

A brief legal analysis of the Torture convention reveals: (1) The Torture Convention is an international treaty; (2) The US is a signatory of that Convention; (3) **Under the theory of integration, developed by US chief justice John Marshall, in the case Marbury v. Madison (1832), that Convention has become the law of the land;** (4) Under that Convention, torture is considered **"a universal crime;"** (5) Therefore, all American states are estopped from extraditing any individual, regardless of their status on American soil, to any other country where there are **"substantial grounds for believing that there is a danger of torture."**

It should also be stated that Guantanamo has not served to enhance US security; has resulted in the **conviction of only ONE detainee (out of more than 700), namely Khaled Sheikh Muhammad; has offered the jihadists, including ISIS and Al-Qaeda, justification for their existence;** has demeaned the claim by the US that it is a governance based on the Rule of Law, including supporting human rights laws.

Keeping Guantanamo open is akin to keeping alive the aura of suspicion on the part of 1.7 billion Muslims that **Islamophobia has, in America, become a war on Islam.** No system of international peace and security can be sustained world-wide **"without the gates of that hell hole been firmly shutdown."**

Even the Alien Tort Claims Act provides American federal courts with jurisdiction over any claim of a violation of the law of nations. (the Kadic Case). The time may not be far into the future to get ready for massive reparations. Accountability Matters!!

THE US SYSTEM OF JUSTICE IS NOT ON THE SIDE OF GUANTANAMO. WHY? BECAUSE HUMAN RIGHTS HAVE

NEVER RESIDED THERE. THE ONLY RESIDENT THERE GOES BY THE LONG NAME OF **"ANTI-MUSLIMS POLITICAL MANIPULATION."**

THE HISTORIC ABANDONMENT: THE PRESENT US DEPARTMENT OF JUSTICE NEITHER DEFENDS NOR ENFORCES CIVIL RIGHTS

Friday, May 4, 2018

The American Declaration of Independence (1776) was the promise. The U.S. Constitution (1787) was the fulfillment. The soul of both documents has always been ordered liberty. Expressed differently, Chief Justice Warren Burger (1969-1986) said it best: **"Ever since people began living in tribes and villages, they have had to balance order with liberty. Individual freedom had to be weighed against the need for security of all."**

Today's Department of Justice must be measured by these concepts. **For these measurements have made America, until the age of Trump, a unique environment.** That uniqueness stemmed from the creation of energies and talents of a **diverse population** of an ever-changing America.

Regretfully no more. The present Department of Justice, under the stewardship of **Attorney General Jeff Sessions** has, for all intents and purposes, abandoned its central mission. **It no longer defends nor enforces civil rights.** Though Trump has peddled his regime as one of **"law and order,"** the facts on the ground prove that the reality exists outside **"law and order."**

No legal argument can prove this point like the recently-published book entitled **"Fascism"** by Madeleine Albright, former US Secretary of State. **That book shall be reviewed** in a future posting of this blog. Other good books have been recently published along the same theme of Trump's failure to govern this great union of 50 States effectively.

The global effect of that failure? **America can no longer be a global guide to other sovereign States in the pivotal area of concern of the world of today -namely human rights.** What compounds this dilemma are the constant attacks by President Trump against the Department of Justice (DOJ) and its head, Jeff Sessions. Trump labels DOJ and Sessions as **"Disgraceful."**

In these thoughtless attacks by a President on his own cabinet member, Sessions, lies an irony. The U.S. President sees in DOJ a role which has never been intended for the executive branch of the US Government. Since its establishment, DOJ has been regarded as an independent cabinet department which is immunized from interference by the White House.

But not under Trump. He, with no prior experience in government, has regarded **DOJ as existing for his own personal legal protection.** This thinking has been evidenced by the first and only conversation between president-elect Trump and the then outgoing President Obama. This conversation has been reported as follows: Trump, referring to Obama's former Attorney General, Eric Holder, is reported to have extolled to Obama: how effectively has Holder protected Obama. The surprised Obama responded: **Holder was not there to protect me. He was there to protect the American people.**

So as the legal challenges to his presidency multiply, including the ongoing investigations into Russia's role in electing Trump president of the U.S., Trump has continually manifested his disgust with the Mueller investigations. These are focused on the alleged **Trumpian obstruction of justice and possible collusion with Russia in Trump elevation to the occupancy of the White House.**

The issues demonstrating the abandonment by the present DOJ of its historic responsibilities cover a very long list of items. This imposes on us the task of selecting only two primary ones:

Voting Rights:
The right to vote is the gateway to self-rule. Tampering with that franchise is the pathway to suffocating democracy. **Under Sessions, those rights have been under constant attack.** For twenty solid years, the Republican party has surpassed the Democratic party in building up its representation from the ground up: **from school boards to state government, to occupancy of congressional seats.**

The Republicans spoke the language of the changed American street. This is while the Democrats focused on urban cities and the language of the elite: urbane, nuanced, and nearly incomprehensible to the half-educated or even the non-educated populace. The most current phrase of the Tea Party, **which ushered in the Trump dark ages,** was: **"We need people who look and speak like us."**

The Republican Party of today, a winner among the non-elite, evokes the memory of the defunct **"Know Nothing Party"** of the American post civil-war. The Trump governance ethos, **now supported by 49 million Americans,** is "don't trust either institutions or politicians."

With the Trump rallies, **a modern Roman circus,** becoming the Trump's mass way of governance, **"America First"** now means **"America is for the whites only."**

- The **Voting Rights Act of 1965 was adopted in order to ensure and facilitate access to voting.** The ballot box is the ultimate container of the popular will. Texas, a traditionally **"red State"** (Republican) has now adopted voter identification requirements. The introduction by the Texas legislature of those requirements had the **hallmarks of racism as affirmed by a ruling by a federal judge against it.**

- DOJ has now abandoned its opposition to that measure of voter suppression, a shift in line with the preferences of Trump and Sessions. The **non-white population is known to vote democratic. This is an electoral fact** which has pushed Trump to claim that Hillary's surpassing him in 2016 in the popular vote by 3 million **has been due to millions of people voting fraudulently, a charge which is wholly without merit.**

- In Ohio, **about 50% of the population, like other Americans, don't vote.** It has been reported that 80 percent of the notices sent by the state to eligible voters were never returned. Though there was no indication that such result was due to voters' moving out of that jurisdiction, **Ohio took the drastic measure of removing them from the voting rolls.**

Thus the citizens of Ohio, upon presenting themselves at their assigned voting station, only to discover that their names were not on the record, were turned away from exercising their constitutional right.

The upshot was a Supreme Court case **(Hsted v. A. Philip Randolph Institute).** That case challenged in January 2018 Ohio's practice of purging voters from the rolls if they failed to vote and/or failed to return the voting notice mailed to them. **Remember that 80% of such notices were never returned.**

The DOJ during the Obama administration had supported that lawsuit. Its support was **solidly based on the National Voter Registration Act which clearly prohibits a State from removing voters from the rolls for failing to vote.** But with Sessions, the DOJ abandoned a position which it had maintained for two decades under both Republican and Democratic administrations.

Voter suppression, gerrymandering by States of electoral lines **in order to reduce the effect of voting by a browning America,** and non-substantiated charges of fraud, all point to one sorry conclusion. The Trump's Department of Justice's role in defending and enforcing civil rights, access to the ballot, and equal treatment, has nearly evaporated.

Trump's only ascertainable concern is for saving his own skin from the looming disaster of successful investigations by special counsel, Bob Mueller, into the alleged Russian intervention in the choice of an American president.

Justice System Reform:

The American Bill of Rights **(the first ten amendments of the US Constitution)** delineates the shape of America's respect for the rights of the accused. One is presumed innocent until proven guilty, through a fair and open court of law. Upon an arraignment of a suspect before a judge, the pleading of the suspect is invariably: **"Not guilty, Your Honor."**

Both Trump and Sessions have made the phrase **"tough on crime,"** the vehicle for **downgrading the right of the accused.** Not only has the DOJ been active in selecting very conservative federal judges. **The President himself has encouraged police officers not to be too concerned about injuring suspects during arrests.** And his Attorney General, Sessions, has never abandoned exaggerating the volume of violent crime.

• The **DOJ stands in opposition to bipartisan reform of sentencing guidelines.** This is evidenced by Sessions ordering all federal prosecutors across the 50 states to **seek the most extreme charges possible** against criminal defendants. That is regardless of any extenuating circumstances.

• By contrast, **Eric Holder,** the Attorney General under President Obama, **had a completely different approach.** Holder had directed prosecutors to stay away from filing charges which carry unnecessarily harsh mandatory minimum penalties. **That is with the exception of cases where the defendant had a significant criminal history, including gang leadership and drug trafficking.**

• The result of this shift in charging has been an increase in mass incarceration. Harsher charging decisions made by prosecutors in the age of Trump/Sessions have been the primary cause.

• Just look up the book by Fordham Law professor John Pfaff, titled **"Locked In: The True Causes of Mass Incarceration -and How to Achieve Real Reform."** It clearly demonstrates that charging decisions have been the cause.

As compared to Germany, for example, we find that **per capita, the American incarceration rate is nearly four times as large as in Germany.** Germany's emphasis is on rehabilitation and eventual integration in society, rather than on punishment and revenge. The law, if it is worthy of its name, is not meant to **"get even,"** but to **effect behavioral change.**

One of the most egregious attacks in America on reforming the criminal justice system is the **project of privatizing the prison system.** An owner of a private jail does not care about the legality of how his residents got to his jail. Like a hotel owner, he is focused on **"full occupancy."** The profit motive is the primary motivation. **The main loser is justice.**

It is a great irony that the reduction in crime in America, which began in the Bush/Obama era, is now bold-facedly, claimed by Trump as resulting from his being **"a law and order president,"** a leader who is **"draining the Washington swamps."** In reality, the age of Trump demonstrates that **the persistent swamp is located in Trump's White House. Including the racist and ethnic ban of citizens from seven Muslim-majority countries from entering America.**

Walling off of Muslims from entering America, is a part of the Trumpian march towards selectively disengaging the US from world affairs. Witness Trump's **persistent call for a wall on the American/Mexico border.** This reflects Trump's growing reliance on the popular myth that America is under attack.

The use of American laws as divisive tools within and outside America, especially when it comes to the Muslim world, ignores some basic American facts. In the US of today there are an estimated 3.5 million Muslims from 75 different countries (1% of the US population). Reporting on these facts, the American magazine, **National Geographic** of May 2018 said about them: **"They (the American Muslims) are forming communities, building mosques, and thriving."**

To this, I should add that many of these **Muslims are enrolled in police departments all over the US, as well as in the armed forces.** They included the son of Kizr Khan, formerly of Pakistan, an officer, who died in Afghanistan trying to save his troops from the carnage caused by a suicide bomber.

The **father** of that officer who died for the U.S. **remains a strong advocate in America for the Rule of Law.** His famous admonition to Trump shall live on for a long time. He shamed Trump at the Democratic National Convention of 2016 as he said: **"Sir!! Have you even read the**

U.S. Constitution?!"

Michael Hayden, a former director of the Central Intelligence Agency *has wondered in his forthcoming book as follows: "How do you brief a president (Trump) who isn't interested in facts?" The title of this awaited book is "The Assault on Intelligence: American National Security in an Age of Lies."*

BY INVITATION: IN JANUARY, THE RABBI WAS UNABLE TO GO TO AL-AZHAR, BUT IN MAY, AL-AZHAR WAS ABLE TO GO TO THE RABBI

Friday, May 18, 2018

When there is a will, there is a way!! Perfectly applicable to the mutual invitations between Al-Azhar and Rabbi Dr. Robert Widom of Temple Emanuel of Great Neck, New York and Al-Azhar through me.

During my visit in December 2017 with the Grand Imam of Al-Azhar, I was briefed on the plan for a global conference on Jerusalem that was to be held in Cairo in January of this year. The purpose was to invite me to it, and to have me recommend leaders of other faiths to be guests of Al-Azhar and to speak at that conference. My prompt response was: **"I would be honored to come, and to invite my distinguished friend, Rabbi Widom to join." A**s I sat facing Dr. El-Taiyeb, the enthusiasm for that response was palpable.

But the leader of that great Reform Temple, with which I have been associated as an **"honary member"** since 1974, had a conflict of appointments. He could not attend, but his support for a non-change of the status of Jerusalem as a shared capital for Israel and a future State of Palestine was well known.

It was Widom's fair-mindedness over the past 44 years of my proximity to him, to his thoughts, and to the congregation of Temple Emanuel, which led me to invite over the years senior Egyptian diplomats to address that congregation.

So from 1980 to nearly 1990, **"the pulpit"** of Temple Emanuel of Great Neck reverberated by the voices that authoritatively expounded Egypt's outlook on peace in the Middle East. Those voices belonged to the late Dr. Esmat Abdel-Mcguid, and to the then Ambassador Amre Moussa, Ambassador Abdel-Raouf El-Reedy and Ambassador Hussein Hassounna, who spoke at that time in the name of the League of Arab States.

It was that activity on behalf of an Egypt which has been for 7000 years a universal cultural bridge which the Muslim Brotherhood in Cairo has never recognized. For in 2007, as I was visiting the country of my birth, I was asked at a public meeting if I would visit Mehdi Akef, the then Supreme Guide of the Muslim Brotherhood.

In reality that invitation was a challenge couched in the form of an invitation. I instantly could perceive several pitfalls in such an encounter. Primarily, such a visit could not be of any assistance to the central purpose of my visit at that time to Cairo. I was in the process of gathering ideas and material in preparation for my new seminar at Fordham University School of Law in New York.

The graduate seminar which lasted from 2008 to 2015, was entitled: **"Islamic Law and Global Security."** My Cairo coordinator was my late beloved friend Dr. Mahmoud Mahfouz, former Health Minister.

Upon entering the offices of Mehdi Akef, who was surrounded by a dozen of his top lieutenants, Akef immediately shot an arrow across the bow of the conference. He asked me: **"Do you speak to the Jews?"**

As I learnt at the UN and through litigation as an attorney, an odd question belies an odd perception. And an odd perception, however offensive it might be, calls for a determined counter offensive. **"Supreme Guide,"** I responded, **"I am an honorary member at Temple Emanuel at a New York suburb. And why don't I interact with the Jews, any Jews, for the sake of mutual understanding in the Middle East. This is especially critical following 2 peace treaties between Israel and two Arab States: Egypt and Jordan."** Then a call to the Noon prayer offered me the chance of a quick exit.

It is such an obscurantist mind which has plagued the Muslim Brotherhood throughout its history since it began in 1928. That is even after its assumption of supreme power in Egypt from 2012 to 2013 under a misfit by the name of President Muhammad Morsi (now an Ex).

Now back to my comfort zone: my speaking on May 11 at Temple Emanuel, during religious services. It was on **"The New Religious Islamic Revolution."** That is the title of my recent book, authored as Trump was undeservedly elected President of the US and inaugurated in January 2017.

Trump and his base have disastrously converted Islamophobia in America in a war on Islam. Trump's first National Security Advisor, General Flynn, has declared that Islam was **"a cancer,"** and not a religion but **"a political ideology."**

Such malicious characterization, which was followed up by Trump's successive executive orders banning citizens of seven Islamic countries from US entry, was a clear signal on what was to come. The new American administration was victim of seeing Islam through the criminal eyes and acts of jihadis.

That circumstance was enough reason for me not only to write that book in response. It was also enough reason to dedicate the book to the Grand Imam of Al-Azhar, and to Al-Azhar itself, from which my late father had graduated.

Appearing at Temple Emanuel on the evening of May 11 was in essence Al-Azhar going to the Temple. The road of interfaith communication does not only run through the advocacy by Al-Azhar Al-Sharif of **"The New Islamic Religious Revolution."** That road also collides with the retrograde thesis of Sam Huntington in his book on **"clash of civilizations."**

At my presentation before the enthusiastic congregation at the Temple, I set forth before them the primary sources of my book, published by Amazon, in December 2017. These were the very words voiced by Dr. El-Taiyeb, in 2016 and 2017, before the European Parliament in Berlin, and in France, Russia, Nigeria, the United Arab Emirates. And in Cairo before leaders of the youths of Rohynga of Myanmar.

That torch held aloft by the Grand Imam of Al-Azhar, a graduate of the Sorbonne (Paris), as a trail blazer. His utterances were the essence of ideological attacks on ISIS, Al-Qaeda, and other criminal franchises. For those terrorists sought in vain to present Islam as a high dam separating Islam from the world of enlightenment.

Expressing that universalism at the Temple seems to have hit the mark: The

Temple had arranged for me a reception after my speech featuring tens of copies of my book for sale. It was the first time for me as an author of more than a dozen of books to be in the role of signing copies of that book to a long line of Jewish purchasers of a book stating in English the very theme of the Islamic Revolution -namely: In faith, all of humanity is one.

And this is how I began that presentation at Temple Emanuel:

"I kept on drafting, then redrafting my remarks for us tonight: The topic of "the oneness of faith" has multi-layered meanings. It encompasses the existential question of "what is faith." Is it allegiance to duty or a person? Is it fidelity to one's promises? Is it sincerity of intentions? Is it belief and trust in and loyalty to God? Is it a firm belief in something for which there is no material proof?

We were born to think. And if you think, you have to believe that others think also -thoughts that crystallize in complex beliefs which we call faith. And all the questions which introduced my remarks are, in their totality, facets of faith."

A credible advocacy of a global cause needs an articulation in a language with which the global audience is familiar. Good English is a vehicle, so is good Arabic. Except that what is said in the Arab and Muslim worlds in classical Arabic has to be imported to America in classical English.

Otherwise the great culture of universalism shall always remain hidden from view. Not only by geography. But also by recognition that effective interpretation of words and concepts are truly the sinews of global understanding.

In this historic search for universal understanding, Al-Azhar and Temple Emanuel are but one as vehicles of interfaith.

Perspectives on Egypt, Islam and the Dark Era of Trump

WHY IS AMERICA'S WAR IN AFGHANISTAN ANOTHER ENDLESS VIETNAM!! UNWINNABLE!!

Friday, May 25, 2018

I possess no military secrets, no capacity to read the future through analysis of tea leaves!! **But history is my sole guide when I say that America's war in Afghanistan is destined to be another loser.** The same was the case in Vietnam.

From the study of global conflicts, a valuable conclusion emerges: **the indigenous population rising to confront a foreign invader always wins.** It may take years for the Taliban in Afghanistan to overcome the American formidable military hardware, technology, and reliance on foreign and local intelligence. However such **American assets can never compensate for the Taliban knowledge of their mountains, valleys, tribal affiliation, and a long history of ceaseless combat.**

I am not evaluating the Taliban cause. I am assessing their assets, which are best expressed in Kipling's 19th century words about why Great Britain had suffered humiliating defeats in Afghanistan. This is not a question of valor. It is a question of the superior impact of a tribalized society forcing the Soviets to flee in the late 1980's.

Osama Bin Laden claimed that Soviet defeat was due to Al-Qaeda's combative resourcefulness. Bin Laden lied. **He and his fighters were only a part of that tribal resistance effort.** A supplementation, egged on by training by the Americans, the Pakistanis, the Saudis, and other actors. **The spinal cord of combat and sacrifice was the Taliban.**

As a term, Al-Taliban means **"two students."** A protest movement which capitalized on devotion to Islam, to hate for structure and institutions, to instant readiness to pick up arms. **There was also involvement by female units as back-up reserves.**

Their's is an economy based on opium production. Afghanistan is a multi-ethnic scene, versed in using the resources of India, Pakistan and Iran to great advantage. **Tribal affiliation is the glue which keeps alliances forming and, when weakened, dissolving.** To all of these human formations, Kabul, the capital, is where corruption resides. **Afghan is a complex fabric which is dedicated to the sword which is forever ready to slice through invaders.**

Afghanism is a blend of nativism, faith (mostly Sunnis; the west is Shii), and an outlook on life as a mere passage through an existence of intrigue. The only durable loyalty is to the core tribe.

It is the embodiment of what an Arab poet had once said about tribalism. **"They never ask their brother, who calls for help in adversity; How was he wronged, by his enemy?"**

There are historic icons, like **Jamalu-Din Al-Afghani (1838-1897).** His sole life, together with his companion, **Sheikh Muhammad Abduh** (a distinguished Egyptian Azhar scholar, 1849-1905), was **devoted to combating foreign intrusion in the lands of Islam.**

From this struggle, nurtured by these two reformers, grew **the notion of total unity of Muslim countries.** Unity in purpose, not in structure. **For Islam did not create a State.** It created a Nation.

From Muhamad Abduh and Al-Afghani, the central idea of Islam, namely the **"One-ness of God"** (Tawheed) became deeply ingrained. **All faiths are one, because God is one. But don't step over boundaries through aggression.** That would be a fight that shall end in the invader's exit, sooner or later. **This is the only unshakable pillar in the Taliban movement.**

Against this formidable background of tribal loyalties, combat resilience, and indigenous presence, **American military planning, surges, and war technology make America in Afghanistan the non-announced underdog.** Taliban casualties are quickly replaced; Trump's exhortation of Pakistan to do more in the Afghan struggle is **a useless call.** For it keeps the influence of New Delhi in Kabul at a minimum. Pakistan is a beneficiary of the Taliban movement.

9/11 was an understandable **casus belli** for American entry upon the invasion of Afghanistan in 2002. But after 16 years of American losses in blood and treasure, without a clear strategy except **"the defeat of the Taliban,"** there is no end in sight for America.

Yes, Bin Laden is dead (and good-riddance). But he was an Arab, a foreign element in an Afghani demographic landscape. They protected him as a Muslim who helped them defeat the Soviets and usher in the collapse of Soviet communism. **They were living up to a tribal code, not to an Al-Qaida affiliation.** Eventually Bin Laden was killed in Pakistan, not in Afghanistan.

From all indications, the effectiveness of the government in Kabul in fighting the Taliban is not greater than the effectiveness of government in Somalia in fighting Al-Shabab. The only difference between the dilemmas in Kabul and Mogadishu is that in **Somalia, a terrorist gang, Al-Shabab, causes mayhem in the surrounding area.** But in Afghanistan, the overwhelming sentiment is to rid the country of America's presence.

The war on the Taliban shall eventually lead to an American exit. Such an exit, ala Vietnam, shall also signify a clear recognition of the failure of **"nation-building."** The concept of **"nation-building" when introduced from beyond national boundaries, as in the case of Afghanistan, is ultimately a losing proposition.** The importance of the indigenous factor in all war-like situations, cannot be over-exaggerated. **That factor is the elixir which keeps the Taliban to never contemplate falling within the sphere of America's influence.** That is regardless of how many roads or schools America builds in Afghani ancestral lands.

The recent clear examples in the Arab world of the unvanquished resilience of the local populace confronting outside invasions are numerous. **They may be found in the Algerian struggle for independence (1954-1962); the October war of 1973 (Egypt v. Israel); and the second Gulf War of 1990 (Kuwait v. Saddam of Iraq).**

Rudyard Kipling (1865-1936), through poetry, has sung the praises of British colonialism. **But even he, in regard to Afghanistan, lamented the prowess of Afghani women preying on the hapless British soldiers as they lay motionless on the open fields of Afghanistan.** So did Arab women in Algeria during the war for independence. **There I was an eye** witness as UN spokesman in the early years of my UN career.

Scrutinizing the above statements, you might also have to conclude that America cannot win in Afghanistan. That is even when America uses non-military means which are known as **"sanctions."** For the ultimate goal of such methods is **"regime change."** A false coin.

When you flip the false coin of **"nation-building"** by an outsider, you shall find the term of **"regime change."** Again only sovereign people do their own **"regime change."** And again, if they need help from outside, especially when faced by a brutal dictatorship a la Saddam or Qadafi or Assad, that **help goes by a fancy but good legal term. It is called "international humanitarian intervention."** Cases in point: Kosovo; Iraq.

If you want to do nation-building, do it within your own borders. For nation-building has never been a matter for export. Otherwise it becomes imperialism.

Americans love fantasies. In films, theatre, novels, and even in foreign policy such as in the Middle East and the Pacific. Winning the war in Afghanistan is an American fantasy. Benjamin De Mott has noted that America was experiencing "a universal descent into unreality."

For his **op ed** column in the **New York Times** of May 25, 2018, David Brooks chose an apt title: **"Trump's Magical Fantasy World."**

Facts are difficult things to challenge. Their challenger is a fake peddler of falsities. Following history and tribal dynamics, it is impossible to see how America can win in Afghanistan.

FROM THE ABBASIDS (656-1258 AD) TO THE MUSLIM BROTHERHOOD (1928-2013 AD): THE ABUSE OF ISLAM AS A POLITICAL POWER TOOL

Friday, June 15, 2018

Happy end of Ramadan, the Muslim month of fasting and hoped for reflection. The New Islamic Religious Revolution (see my book on it at Amazon, December 2017), launched by Al-Azhar in 2014 has to contend with the abuse of Islam as a political power tool. A span of time of nearly 1400 years.

It should be noted that Islam did not establish a State. It established a Nation, now numbering 1.7 billion population, spread over every continent and region. Including Iceland where Muslims fast for 20 hours during the month of Ramadan (the sun there sets for only 2 hours). After the 4 successors of the Prophet Muhammad assumed the title of Caliph to stress continuity, though within an Arab context, **all so-called Caliphate which followed lacked legitimacy.**

That early continuity was demonstrated by burying Muhammad at where he lived with his wife Aisha in Medina. Next to his burial grounds were buried the first two Caliphs, Abu-Bakr, then Omar. The Arab line of succession within Quraish (the tribe in Mecca which dominated Islam from its inception in 593 AD until 661 AD), held fast. That is until the transfer of the capital of Islam (the capital of the Nation) from Al-Medinah in Arabia to Damascus where the Ummayiads held sway.

Yet the Ummayiads of Syria kept the leadership of the Muslim nation for nearly 160 years with the Arabs. The Arabs were then on top of the ethnic fabric of that nation. Even after conquering the four civilizations surrounding tribal Arabia. These were the Yemenis to the south; the Persians to the east; the Byzantines to the north; and the Egyptians westward.

Yes, the Bedouins of Arabia gained not only territory, but also diverse civilizations, especially in the art of governance and medicine and philosophy. Nonetheless, all non-Arabs to the East, to the North, and to the West were , though Islamized, Mawalis (meaning subservient). The ruling class were Arabs, and those who possessed better knowledge and organizational skills were the Mawalis.

That latter class, by the 7th century, were the majority of Muslims. The armed forces brought the Arabs and the Mawalis together under the banner of Islam. But the Mawalis, whether in Persia, Syria and Palestine, Egypt or Morocco, were deprived of: army pay equal to that of the Arabs; riding horses, even in combat; restriction of their service to infantry (foot soldiers); and no permission to intermarry with Arab women.

One may call this apartheid of the first order which went against the soul of Islam. For Islam stands for equality. But the Ummayiad structure was primarily monarchical, patterned after the East Roman empire. The leader was Arab, but the system was either Roman or Persian. And that is what collapsed the Ummayiads in 750 AD. So the pendulum swung again in the direction of Medina in Arabia, and towards the family of the Prophet Muhammad.

So far the battle for the soul of Islam remained within Islam itself. Other faiths were left undisturbed, with full respect for Judaism. Christianity and other beliefs. That inter-Islamic struggle was about who was to be on top after the collapse of the last Arab caliphate, namely, the Ummayiads. Those who established the Abbasids in 656 AD resumed the linkage to the line of the Prophet Muhammad, since Abu-El-Abbas, the founder, was Muhammad's uncle. But the backbone of that 600 year regime was Persian.

In fact the last of the Ummayiads Caliphs, Marwan II who fled for his life to Egypt, was pursued by the Mawalis of the Abbasids to the Egyptian province of Al-Fayyoum where he was killed at the village of Bu-Seer.

The manipulation of Islam through its politicization now began in earnest, basing itself from its initial capital of Khorasan (Persia), before moving to Baghdad. Baghdad became the historic Abbasid capital as of the 7th century AD -the persianized capital of the

Umma.

The Islam of Arabia which advocates inclusiveness was now the Islam of the Mawalis. The conquered became the conqueror. With that major shift in the fortunes of Islam, came also the repression of all those who spoke Arabic -though Arabic is the language of the Quran.

Power became the object of governance; the politicization of Islam by the non-Arabs proved to be a legitimating cover; the division between Sunni Islam and Shii Islam was advocated; those within the Shii branch were branded in part "Alawis" - the sect of Bashar Al-Asad; the sword, a word not mentioned at all in the Quran, became the instrument of enforcement, especially by the Ottomans, the Turkic races which swooped from central Asia on horseback to the Mediterranean and the Black Sea (the 16th century to the 20th).

Finally Islam, as of 1928, was co-opted by Egypt's Muslim Brotherhood whose logo is still two swords framing the Quran, with the fighting words **"Be Prepared" (Aaidoo)** at the bottom of that **trade mark of a wayward movement.**

The historic and ideological lineage of the Muslim Brotherhood should be traced to Abu-Muslim Al-Khorasani (653 AD) in Eastern Persia.

Under the Abbasids, freedom of thought was suppressed. Even Abu-Hanifah and Malik, the founders of two great schools of Sunni thought, were whipped. The framework of the Abbasid system was the glorification of those fake Caliphs who followed the first four succeeding the Prophet Muhammad.

Examples on the disconnect between Islam and the period from the 7th to the 20th centuries abound. Here is an early example. The response of Al-Mansour, an early Abbasid ruler to those who criticized his brutality was very candid: **"We are among people who saw us yesterday as ordinary street people and now we are their Caliphs. Such people shall never respect anything but punishment. So forget about forgiveness."**

The second dominant feature of the Abbasids is to clothe their politics with a Muslim garb. The Caliph propagated himself as the protector of Islam. They made the Sultan or Caliph the projection of God on earth.

Thus Abu-Hanifah and Malik were punished because they declined

Al-Mansour's invitation to be judges. Such declination, Al-Mansour feared, would signal to the rank and file of Muslims that the Abbasid Caliphate lacked legitimacy.

The basis for the dogma of the Muslim Brotherhood, though appearing 13 centuries later, is one and the same as that of the Abbasids. **To them, Islam is only a cover for raw power; the ballot box to them is the entry ticket to rulership.**

To them, Egypt, the State of 7000 years was no more than a launching pad for a mythical Islamic realm. And one of their supreme guides expressed this candidly but grossly: **"Hell with Egypt"** (Toz Fi Masr).

Such words have historic consequences. The Brotherhood's affinity to the brutal past, starting from the Abbasids and stretching to Ordoghan, the present Ottoman ruler, needs to be understood in the light of that horrid continuum.

Islam's abuse as a political football has indeed deep roots.

LIKE A PIECE OF SWISS CHEESE: AMERICAN DEMOCRACY HAS MANY HOLES IN IT!!

Friday, July 13, 2018

Trumpism did not arise from a vacuum. The 242-year old Constitution, plus judge-made law, lie at its roots. A great Justice of the Supreme Court, Oliver Wendell Holmes, once wrote of the Constitution: **"It is an experiment, as all life is an experiment."** Well, that **"experiment"** was expressed darkly by President Trump as he alluded to that great document as **"archaic."**

Trump is a president who was catapulted to the White House by less than the majority of those who voted. His adversary, Hillary Clinton for whom I voted, garnered 3 million more votes than that **"reality show"** host.

The Constitution intended to establish a government **"of the people, by the people, and for the people"** (the words of President Abraham Lincoln at his first State of the Union message.) But the electoral votes are counted twice: **once for citizens voting; the other for a non-democratic allocation by a pre-determined formula to each state.** The magic number of **270** is calculated through a non-elected body called the **Electoral College.**

It could therefore be said that the Trump presidency, though in accord with the Constitution, is a presidency that is **"undemocratic;"** when measured by the formula **"one man, one vote."**

So was the Bush presidency in 2000 during the Bush-Gore contest. But in that earlier instance, it was the US Supreme Court, a non-elected body of 9 justices, which ordered the **stoppage of recounting the Florida ballots.** The deciding vote was that of Justice Sandra O'Connor who tipped the scale of the conservatives on that divided 5 to 4 court.

This is where the **recent nomination by Trump of Brett Kavanaugh as Associate Justice of the Supreme Court,** replacing retiring Justice Anthony Kennedy, represents a further **politicization of that Court.** It pushed that body further to the right to serve a decidedly non-democratic purpose, namely-interpreting law, thus making law by a non-elected body.

A close reading of the Constitution as written **does not give the Supreme Court a clear right to give a final say over the meaning of the Constitution and federal laws.** Nor do they have the power to order state and federal officials to comply with its rulings. They can only make decisions on cases that are brought to them by in application a person who is actually affected by the laws. **So why is the practice different in application?**

It was in 1803 that Chief Justice John Marshall, in a case called **"Marbury v. Madison,"** interpreted Article III (of the Constitution) on the judicial powers to give the federal courts that final say. That opinion by John Marshall **made the Supreme Court a sort of a co-legislative branch of the U.S. system of governance.**

Herein lies the anticipated problem of possibly confirming Kavanaugh by the Senate. The extreme right in a highly tribalized America would then hold sway over the White House, Congress, and the Supreme Court. **This would be a sure recipe for a fascist-like America. No checks and balances.**

The Kavanaugh nomination caused Peter Baker of the **New York Times** of July 10 to describe it as follows: **"That has raised the stakes for groups on the left and the right, guaranteeing an incendiary, ideological, partisan and well-financed confirmation battle in a capital already driven by incendiary, ideological, partisan and well-financed politics."**

Speaking of **"well-financed politics,"** the U.S. Supreme Court, in the case of **Citizens United** had, in effect, **made money a decider of the outcome of American elections** at federal and state levels. The First Amendments which guarantees **"the freedom of speech"** has been re-interpreted to make the unlimited wealthy nonprofit corporations, with millions of dollars in assets, free to support without limits political action committees (PACs). **The dollar, now, has the unfettered freedom to speak on behalf of the causes of its donors.**

As to the sovereign right of all eligible voters to express their political choices through the ballot box, **we, in America, have the inequality of the application of that right.**

This has come about through **political gerrymandering** at the state level. Even the ultraconservative late Supreme Court Justice, Antonin Scalia had said in 2004: **"Severe partisan gerrymanders are incompatible with democratic principles."**

So what is a gerrymander? It is defined as **"the creation of a civil division of an unusual shape within a particular locale for improper purposes."**

This process, in which the right in America has, for the past 50 years, worked assiduously, **created legislative districts of unequal population.** Hence the constitutional rule of **"one man, one vote"** required by the equal protection of the law has been violated.

In his seminal book (2014) **calling for amending the US Constitution, retired US Supreme Court Justice John Paul Stevens** (a liberal) called for requiring federal judges to apply the same rules in cases challenging **political gerrymanders as those applicable to racial gerrymanders.**

The remedy proposed, but seems to be quite far from attainment, is that voting districts should be compact and composed of contiguous territories.

At present, **democracy in a disunited United States, suffers from destruction by the Republican Party,** now the party of Trump, of the pillars on which this great enterprise was launched:
- **The wall between the State and religion has been shaken to its foundation.** The primary example is the recent endorsement by the Supreme Court of Trump's **ban on Muslims from six States, from entering the U.S.;**
- The call by Trump for an **"America First"** is in essence a call for **"an America for whites only;"**
- The **tearing up of children from their parents** (3000 of these) seeking asylum at the southern border, dispersing them throughout the US

without much hope for family reunification, is **as close as possible to being a genocidal act;**

• The daily attacks by Trump and his **submissive** machine on the Department of Justice and the investigations presently conducted by special counsel Robert Mueller, are nothing but a direct vilification of the Rule of Law in America;

• The various legal infractions by **the Trump family and the Trump Foundation** are being overlooked as petty incidents by a so-called **"non-political"** president;

• The senate hearings, in today's America, have become devoid even of a modicum of due process to be accorded to witnesses.

• Powerful special interests, like the **National Rifle Association (NRA),** have amply demonstrated that they are able **to dictate to Congress legislation** in favor, not of the nation, but of their membership.

The party of Trump is no longer the party of Lincoln. Lincoln, the historic leader who ended slavery of the blacks in America. In his first State of the Union message to Congress in 1861, he set forth a legal standard for government. As the civil war raged, he inspiringly declared:

"It is as much the duty of Government to render prompt justice against itself, in favor of its citizens, as it is to administer the same between private individuals."

In the Trump era, that legal standard, on which American democracy was based, is no more. The sad fact is that America still regards itself as the world's mentor of liberal democracy.

"The carpenter has a house whose door creeks for lack of repairs!!" (An Arab proverb).

65 YEARS AGO, MY PROFESSOR AT RUTGERS UNIVERSITY PREDICTED THE EMERGENCE OF AN AMERICAN DICTATOR!

Saturday, July 21, 2018

That was Professor Sydney Ratner, for whom I was Teaching Assistant. The subject he taught was **"American Economics."** But, on that occasion, he was commenting on the American Constitution.

Ratner's prophesy was based on the **possible disappearance of checks and balances,** resulting from the concentration of power in one major political party, or the **manipulation of the Constitution** by an authoritarian Chief Executive. Or both factors.

America of today is what that professor, **who valued his patriotism and his Jewishness** had predicted. The America of Trump proved Professor Ratner to have been **a true Cassandra,** though not generally believed in 1953. As his **Arab and Muslim** disciple, I trusted somewhat in what he foresaw.

We now find at the White House, a President who **rules largely by executive orders,** without fear of a Congress which is controlled by a **party which he had bent to his ways.** It does not matter whether the Republican majority in Congress stands either in fear of Trump, or in sincere belief in his ways. **The result is the same.**

The third co-equal branch of government, **the Supreme Court,** has now tilted to the right in favor of Trumpism. It does not matter whether a Court which glories in 5 - 4 decisions, is constitutionally correct or not. The result is the same, and **shall become the enduring symbol of the disappearing checks and balances if Judge Kavanaugh** ever ascends to its bench.

As a judge and law professor, Judge Kavanaugh had penned his view of any U.S. president. In 2009, he stated in an article that **a chief executive was immune from civil or criminal investigation or prosecution** while occupying the White House. Too distracting from executive duties. Kavanaugh had therefore **put the Chief Executive above the law.**

That is not the position of the U.S. Constitution. Its Article II, Section 4 states: **"The President ... shall be removed from Office on impeachment for, and conviction of treason, bribery, or other high crimes and misdemeanors."** On that basis, Kavanaugh's former students at Yale University countered recently his belief in a totally immune president.

In a letter reported in the **New York Times** of July 20, 2018, they retorted: **"Judge Kavanaugh's nomination presents an emergency -for democratic life, for our safety and freedom, for the future of our country."**

Well, the not-so-surprising tenor of that letter **confirms Ratner's prophesy of 1953, predicting the emergence of an American dictator.** For infecting the judiciary, through the US Supreme Court of 5-4 decisions, with the position of a totally immunized president, makes a mockery of the **on-going investigations by Special Counsel, Robert Mueller** of Russian interference in the US elections of 2016.

The connectedness of these issues is the **essence of connecting the dots on today's American scene.** These are: **American governance, the rise of Trumpism, the erosion of checks and balances, and all the other aspects of American federalism** as anchored in the Rule of Law.

Let us propound those dots, beginning with the **oath of office:**

It includes the following words: **"... and will to the best of my ability, preserve, protect and defend the Constitution of the United States."** Such oath or affirmation by the President upon inauguration makes it incumbent upon such person to **serve the United States, not any other foreign power, and all Americans, not just those who voted for him (or her).**

But the incumbent President, **especially at the Helsinki Summit,** had by secreting himself alone with the Russian President, committed various legal violations: **No American official record of what transpired,** as required by the Official Records Act. Publicly, at the press conference that followed, **siding not with American intelligence services, but with assertions by Putin** that no Russian cyber-attack was perpetrated on the US.

In legal terms, that is the definition of treason: violation of allegiance to your sovereign (the American people) by adhering to their enemies. A breach of faith coming within the Constitutional scope of **"other high crimes and misdemeanors"** (Article II, Section 4). Impeachable offenses!!

Yet the presidential shock waves did not stop there. On July 19, the White House announced that **President Trump planned to invite President Putin to visit the White House in the fall.** The stunned reaction by **Dan Coats, the director of national intelligence was on public view.** He got the news, not from his President, but from a reporter who was interviewing him.

Coats' reaction to the news of that invitation, **"SAY THAT AGAIN?,"** shall forever live as the three words which frame **the mysterious retreat of America to the status** of a client-like State behind Russia.

Wondered Michelle Goldberg in the **New York Times** of July 17: "It was hard not to be staggered by the American President's slavish and toadying performance." But the Republican-controlled Senate, in the face of that American retreat, made more grievous by Trump's attacks on the European Union, NATO and the UN system, **stood as a paralyzed co-equal branch of government.**

Yes, the House speaker, Paul Ryan had said: **"We stand by our NATO allies and all those countries who are facing Russian aggression."** But the Republicans in Congress on the same day that Ryan spoke, also **blocked a series of measures put forward by Democrats, all anti-Putin resolutions.**

The Grand Old Party (GOP) which had been led by Lincoln, is no more, as it has been coopted by Mr. Trump. Strangely, the GOP, prior to the Trump coup, was the **champion of free trade, of immigration, of alliances confronting an expanding Soviet Union, and of universal institutions** - the UN, the World Bank, and the International Monetary Fund. These were structures negotiated between Roosevelt and Churchill as of 1942 -three years before the end of World War II.

That party is no more. The Trump Party now stands for: **high tariffs (a form of taxation); criminalizing asylum seekers; withdrawing from the UN Human Rights Council; withholding funds from UNESCO; attacking the World Trade Organization; threatening war against Venezuela; withdrawing from the 6-States Iran nuclear deal; blaming the dismemberment of the Ukraine on Obama.**

Moreover, Trump had praise for Putin's call for **surrendering American diplomats to Russia for interrogation;** and favored the expansion of the Mueller investigation into Russia's possible collusion with the Trump campaign **by including in it Putin operatives.**

"The Word 'Treason' Enters the Debate as the List of Trump Critics Grows," headlined the **New York Times** of July 18. The **Washington Post** of July 16, in a column by a noted former Republican, Max Boot, stated that **"accusing (Trump) of treason was once unthinkable. No longer... If anyone is the enemy of the people, it is Trump himself."**

Truthfulness is the underpinning of trust which binds the governed to the government. Again **"no longer"** under Trump who is reported to have **lied 3200 times in less than 2 years in office.** Falsehoods have been explained as **"alternative facts;"** and the aspiration for **"A More Perfect Union"** has been inverted into a movement by the American right towards **"the destruction of the Administrative State."**

Today in front of the White House, throngs of protesters banging on pots and pans, shouted **"Welcome Back Traitor."**

On Twitter, the word **"Traitor"** was used **800,000 times;** the word **"treason"** about **1.2 million times.**

65 years ago, I should have been more trusting in my professor, Sydney Ratner, who predicted the emergence of an American dictator.

Perspectives on Egypt, Islam and the Dark Era of Trump

THE UGLY FACES OF FOREIGN INTERVENTION IN INTERNAL AFFAIRS

Saturday, July 21, 2018

The **first face** is that **it is illegal.** Why? **Sovereignty is absolute.** That is unless two or more sovereignties agree to reciprocate exchanges. Like in granting diplomatic immunity to another country within national boundaries. Even such reciprocity is **limited to the premises of the foreign mission, the ambassador's residence, the diplomatic vehicle when engaged in official functions, and the diplomatic mailbag (pouch).**

The **second ugly face** of intervention in domestic affairs is that it **invites bad national feelings.** Sooner or later, such resentment might bring about retaliation and a **push-back amounting possibly to armed conflict.**

The **third ugly face** is that it makes a mockery of **cross-border cooperation which was born about 2000 years ago,** well before the birth of the UN. That early birth took place along the shores of the Italian north Mediterranean. When such cooperation is disturbed, the average citizen loses the fruits of the give and take.

And the **fourth ugly face of foreign intervention** is that the intervening government, though feeling good about its illegal interventions, would soon be emboldened to intervene in the private lives of its own citizens. For **illegal intervention abroad** is infectious internally, and soon boomerangs on the populace of the abusing government.

Having set forth a framework for the ills of intervention in domestic affairs, let us also recall the only exception to what is set forth above. That exception is what came to be known as of the 1950s as the **"international humanitarian intervention doctrine."** It is activated **only when the sovereign brings about havoc and mayhem to large groups of its population,** thus triggering an outside corrective mechanism to end the internal aggression.

Now beyond the above-stated theories and exceptions, we now need to cite examples drawn from the world scene of today. For good measure, we start with the **latest episode of Mr. Trump, while visiting the United Kingdom,** attacking the policy of the UK government as regards its exit from the European Union.

By doing so, the American President, who was a guest of Great Britain, personified the face of **"The Ugly American,"** immortalized in a novel. That novel signaled the **distance between being rich internally, and stupid externally.** Though a narrative, **"The Ugly American"** also evokes the natural hostility of any culture to be scorned by other cultures. In cultural terms, **poverty is not a sin. It is a temporary status.**

Trump, who by his own confessions, does not read much, had violated earlier this month in Great Britain more than one taboo (called red line). He whimsically spoke about what he doesn't know or is capable of grasping. He **embarrassed Theresa May, his hostess and Prime Minister.** He **ignited the wrath of the British populace in England and Scotland.** He **was scorned by the European Union and by NATO.** And he elevated even to greater heights, the blimp fashioned in his image: **an angry baby, floating with a cell phone over London. How could any of these results help the American people?!**

As I am of dual nationalities, **both Egyptian and American,** I turn my attention to various forms of American intervention in Egyptian domestic affairs. Let us start with the **recent hearings in US Congress regarding the American financial aid to Egypt since the signing of the Egypt/Israel peace treaty of 1979.**

The way US Senators addressed this matter on the floor of the Senate 8 days ago manifested, not only **ignorance about the framework of that issue.** But, more importantly, **an imperial tilt in the way they, in their Republican majority, disparaged the governance of 103 million Arabs who call themselves Egyptians.**

They should bear in mind that the **annual aid of $1.3 billion is not a** unilateral gift. **It is mostly spent in the U.S. on American products, mostly military equipment. It is an integral part of a treaty,** whose guarantor is the US itself. Disturbing that treaty, or any of its provisions, could be tantamount to disturbing peace in the Middle East. And how could either America or Israel benefit from that?

In that explosive context, the attacks on Egypt, through impugning the legitimacy of its Government, came **feigned concern for human rights in Egypt through the back door.** The question therefore naturally arises: **Have these senators objectively compared between the status of human rights in America and those in Egypt, even if they are entitled to do so?**

The U.S. Executive, through an annual State Department Human Rights Report on several countries, states the following in 2016 about Egypt: **"Domestic and international observers also concluded that government authorities professionally administered the parliamentary elections that took place October through December 2015 in accordance with the country's laws, while also expressing concern about restrictions on freedom of peaceful assembly, association, and expression and their negative effect on the political climate surrounding the elections."**

From the above, one could see **stark contradictions in the above assertions,** representing an erroneous value judgment on the internal affairs of another sovereign -Egypt. Aside from that, the **language of that official American concern embodies the very language set forth in the First Amendment of the U.S. Constitution.**

Egypt is constituted on the basis, not of the US Constitution, but of its own constitution of 2014. Its preamble states in Arabic reads: **"We women and men members of the Egyptian populace, are the masters of this sovereign country. This is our will, and this is the Constitution borne out of our revolution."** The language of that constituent document is the bulwark against all the ugly faces of foreign intervention in internal affairs.

But as a defense attorney, I need to go beyond the standard to attempt a comparison intended to show how foolish are these calls which generate this adversarial comparison. The **"holier than thou"** attitude propagated by today's reclusive and retreating Trumpist America **does not take into account the following facts:**

- Egypt is a country presently engaged in a brutalizing **campaign on three fronts: terrorism, reconstruction, and massive reallocation of** newly-found natural resources. During periods of transition, nations need to place the **rights of the general community above individual rights,** at least provisionally;

- In the same vein, **President Abraham Lincoln,** during the American Civil War in which 600,000 Americans perished, was **obliged to suspend the operation of sections of the US Constitution;**

- Egypt, which demographically comprises **one third of the entire Arab Nation, has no military forces occupying foreign territory.** By contrast, America, through what can be described as imperial security policy, has **troops of various sizes in 120 countries around the world;**

- Comparing the Egyptian regulations of public protest with that of the U.S. regulations, the **Egyptian equivalent is more liberal than its American equivalent.** The latter imposes police-enforced restrictions on permits for demonstrators in terms of **Time, Place, and Manner.** Witness the way the American movement of **"Occupy Wall Street"** was crushed brutally by the security forces in less than 2 hours;

- **America,** under its present tilt to the conservative right, whether religious or political, **is still trying to cope with its past of enslaving Afro-Americans.** The rise of Trumpism has been in part energized by the elections of a black American, Barack Obama, to the presidency twice from 2008 to 2016. By historical comparison with Egypt, the **white slaves of the Ottoman Empire, the Mamelouks, were able to advance to the rulership of Egypt until their military defeat by Napoleon in 1798, and Muhammad Ali in 1808;**

- On the international scene, **Egypt, a State of 7000 years, has never abrogated a treaty.** On the other hand, the present American administration sees in treaties shackles that could be broken liberally, even if they were security commitments to friends and allies. Note here that Egypt's nationalization in 1956 relative to the Suez Canal, **was not in terms of the Canal itself (a sovereign territory), but of the Company** which ran the Suez Canal;

- And let us remind those in America who see in the intervention in the internal affairs of others, a **"modus operandi"** -sometimes called **"divine destiny,"** that **Guantanamo shall always stand for a stain on the honor of the enterprise called "The USA."** No Rule of Law has been applied to 700 Muslims incarcerated as of 2002 without arraignment, charges, right to counsel, or the benefit of Habeas Corpus. Only one, Khalid Sheikh. Muhammad -was so tried.

Trump, while being a guest of the UK's Prime Minister, Theresa May, said to the British press that **Boris Johnson, a rival of the PM that he "would** make a great prime minister." An unthinkable intervention in the UK's internal affairs.

Here is an early example of Egypt's hostility toward foreign intervention. **Muhammad Ali, the great founder of modern Egypt was opposed to the construction of a Suez Canal in Egypt.** His famous opposition was expressed in the following words: **"I do not want a Bosporus in Egypt."** In reference to Turkey's problem with outside powers because of the channel separating between Asian and European Turkey.

This narrative is not intended to disparage the good which is still rendered by America in various ways around the world.

The main objective is to prove the folly of foreign interference in the internal affairs of other sovereign nations. A principle stressed by the UN Charter in Article 2 (para.7) as a means to fostering friendly relations among nations.

WHEN JOURNALISM BECOMES A TOOL FOR AMERICAN IMPERIALISM

Friday, August 3, 2018

Very ironic. The America of Trump is in full retreat globally, while its journalism becomes the tool for nefarious imperialism. The case in point: A full throated article in **The New York Times** of July 29, 2018 entitled **"The White House and the Strongman,"** by David Kirkpatrick. It is on Egypt where the writer was a correspondent for that paper whose motto is **"All The News That Is Fit To Print."**

So the news that is fit to print is now based on the **egregious claim that the Muslim Brotherhood, under Morsi, was illegally sacked by El-Sisi in July 2013.** On the fifth anniversary of Egypt's liberation from the fascist Islamic rule, resulting from an uprising by 35 million Egyptians on **June 30,** 2013, is **denigrated as a coup.** The Brotherhood, now officially declared in Egypt as a terrorist organization, is lionized by **The New York Times** as the victim of a brutal coup.

The writer claims that the presidency of Morsi (2012-2013) was a democratically-established order. Then he **contrasts it to the presidency of El-Sisi as a usurper putschist regime.** Such a contrast is the equivalent of saying that the **Nazi regime symbolized democracy,** which was overturned by the dictatorial regimes of England and France.

Fitzpatrick cites many sources whose voices support the **punishment of Egypt as a collapser of democratic rule in the Middle East.** Thus the Muslim Brotherhood has been lent a voice which defies not only the facts, but the very notion of sovereignty in Egypt, as in elsewhere. **That**

sovereignty flows from the people, and is immune from the imperialist impulses fully reflected in **The New York Times.**

What are the facts? The Brotherhood was given the incredible chance of **eligibility to compete for the presidency,** after the fall of Mubarak. That opportunity was **offered by the SCAF (Supreme Council of the Armed Forces),** the interim government (2011-2012) after the January 25 Revolution.

The armed forces, which held Egypt together from January 25, 2011 until the electoral victory of the Brotherhood, were the very **guarantors of that democratic transfer of power.**

Morsi, who was not the first choice by the Brotherhood for president, **won;** his opponent, **General Shafik, lost.** The margin of victory was 1.5% of the popular vote.

Now a **president of 103 million Egyptians (one-third of the Arab world)** was sworn in, no less than **4 times,** was chosen **before the 2013 Constitution was even drafted.** Speaking of putting the cart before the horse.

Thus began, not a regime for all Egyptians, but one bent on **using Egypt as a launching pad for a mythical Islamic Caliphate.** The Brotherhood's Supreme Guide said **"Hell with Egypt"** (Toz Fi Misr); the secular and Coptic voices were banished from the Constituent Assembly which drafted an Islamic constitution; the **burning of Coptic churches became common; the Shii community was terrorized; and the Pyramids, and the Sphinx** were called **"un-Islamic monuments of idolatry."** Tourism, (20% of Egypt's national revenue) evaporated

Between the completion of the drafting of the Islamic Constitution and the vote on it in a plebiscite, were **only 24 precious hours.** No real attempt was made to supervise that plebiscite, as **the judiciary was intimidated.** The Supreme Constitutional Court was besieged by Brotherhood thugs; and Morsi, whose mentors and manipulators were the **members of the Guidance Bureau, declared himself in November 2012,** to be above the law.

Hamas in Gaza was given a free reign in Sinai; Qatar and Turkey and Pakistan became models to be copied; Brotherhood's military were being organized as a parallel army; **Ethiopian, a Christian country, was threatened by war over its construction of a dam over a tributary of**

the **Nile within its territories; Al-Azhar was attacked** by male and female thugs; text books were revised to suit the Brotherhood's interpretation of **"Islam Uber Alles"** (Islam is the only true faith; all other creeds unworthy).

The **Brotherhoodization of Egypt for one full year (2012-2013) generated the corrective Revolution of June 30, 2013.** Once more the armed forces, through General El-Sisi, then Defense Minister, tried together with Egyptian liberal leaders to negotiate a new beginning with Morsi -a new Plebiscite. Even President Obama counseled Morsi **"History is waiting for you."** But to no avail.

From June 30 to July 3, 2013, the fate of a secular and inclusive Egypt hung in the balance. The **military leadership was keen on an inclusive Egypt, with the Brotherhood as a component.** But the Brotherhood clung to its fiction of **"Shariyah"** (legitimacy) -a mantra whose falsity was proven by the abuse of democracy for the sake of **"an Islamic Emirate"** in Egypt.

Fitzpatrick, who was an eye witness in Cairo to these events, now, in his present article in **The New York Times,** makes a false claim when he asserts that **"on July 3, 2013, General Sisi announced Mr. Morsi's removal."** The collective wisdom of the Egyptian leadership, responding to the massive popular demand for a secular Egypt, is now abbreviated by that author to a coup against a democratically-elected Brotherhood.

It is noteworthy that the Islamic constitution had no provision for a scripted method for the removal of an errant president. In that void, the popular will stepped in to fill that space.

Another strange switch in that **imperialist-like intervention in Egyptian internal affairs** by an American journalist: It behooves Fitzpatrick to **compare between how El-Sisi came to power twice (in 2014 and in 2018) to how Trump came to power in the US in 2017.** The Egyptian president came through an internationally-supervised elections on the basis of the secular Constitution of 2014. **Trump came to power through, the intervention of a foreign adversary, Russia, and is now calling the US Constitution "archaic."**

The definition of "archaic" is primitive, no longer in common use. *As to the definition of "democracy," it has so far never found a common definition. Even Kirkpatrick in his pro-Muslim Brotherhood prediction, has failed to provide us with the rationale of what he means by "The White House and the Strongman."*

DR. YASSIN EL-AYOUTY, ESQ.

MR. ATTORNEY GENERAL SESSIONS: WHY DID YOU DEPORT DUE PROCESS - THE PILLAR OF JUSTICE?

Friday, August 17, 2018

You, Mr. Sessions, are the premier law enforcer of these United States. **You have been vilified by President Trump publicly and repeatedly.** Though you are his appointee as Attorney General. You were the first US Senator to endorse that man for the presidency. **Though from all indications prior to the elections, Trump was proven unfit for that position.**

You, Jeff Sessions, have smilingly worn Trump's prop -a white hat declaring MAGA - **"Make American Great Again."** That mantra is patently false.

Yet, in Alabama, your home state, Mr. Sessions, **you were previously rejected for the position of judge.** This was no problem for Donald Trump, the former real estate so-called **"mogul"** whose **bankruptcy filings varied in number from 3 to 4.**

The man, Trump, for whom **"The Art of the Deal"** was written, giving him the false aura of a successful deal-maker, saw **in you, Jeff Sessions, a good deal.** He needed you as an early supporter, and you needed him for a cabinet job.

So in the position of the head of the Department of Justice (DOJ), what did you do over the **past 18 months of the turbulent presidency of Trump, to make "America Great Again?"** Why **"Again,"** when the U.S. has been great, including under the Obama presidency, until the Trump's presidency?

If I am, as per the prior paragraph, rather polemical, it is for a reason **-to impeach you, Mr. Attorney General, as a credible upholder of the law in America.** You probably have read the US Constitution. Its preamble begins by: **"We the people of the United States, in order to form a more perfect Union, establish Justice..."** But your Department of Justice, Mr. Sessions, has **abandoned that constitutional commitment. How?**

Through sabotaging the Rule of Law by **using the Department of Justice as an instrument to do away with judicial independence,** particularly in the area of immigration.

Case in point: The news of August 4, 2018, that: **"The Justice Department replaced a Philadelphia immigration judge (Steven Morley) who had asked for more legal information in a deportation case, inserting a new justice who quickly ordered the defendant (a Guatemalan) removed from the United States."**

Judge Morley was presiding over **the case of Reynaldo Castro-Tum, who came from Guatemala to the US as an unaccompanied minor** at the tender age of 17. Morley, in observation of due process, had asked for briefs to be filed on **whether the defendant, who failed to appear in court, had been properly notified of the hearing.**

That was Judge Morley's downfall. As law students in America, we have learnt in classes after classes in **"civil procedure,"** that **"service of process,"** meaning the proper notification to a party of the legal dispute of the obligation to appear in court at a certain time, as a vital requirement to satisfy **"due process."** It is even so **in Yemen** when I was retained by the World Bank in the year 2000 to **prepare a study on legal and judicial reform.**

In Yemen, I asked about the status of **"service of process."** I was told that in tribal areas there are no addresses, and there are no easy means of transportation to deliver papers in mountainous regions.

My recommendation to the Yemeni Department of Justice, **under former President Ali Abdullah Saleh,** was drawn from my childhood experience in rural and desert areas in eastern Egypt in the 1930's and 1940's: **Use bicycles or donkeys as means of transport,** and rely for address verification, on **the village elders.**

It worked, in Yemen, and was later reported in my **co-edited** book entitled **"Government Ethics and Law Enforcement (2000)."** Conclusion: Judge **Morley** of Philadelphia, in requesting more information before reaching a fair judgment, **was doing his** job through satisfying an essential aspect of **"justice for all,"** which is met through the application of due process.

That, for Sessions and his Department of Justice, was **not the way of making America great again.** To Sessions and Trump, law is an inconvenience that, like under all authoritarian regimes, should be dispensed with. Because it stands in the way of the emerging dictatorship in the United States of America.

And where is the observance of the preamble of the U.S. Constitution which includes **"... in order to ... establish justice, ensure domestic tranquility, provide for the common defense, promote the general welfare, and secure the Blessings of Liberty to ourselves, and our posterity ...?"**

And where, Mr. Attorney General Sessions, is the observance of another **"inconvenience"** -the 14th Amendment of the US Constitution? For, in part, it reads: **"... nor shall any state deprive any person of life, liberty, or property, without due process of law; nor deny to any person within its jurisdiction the equal protection of the laws."** The words **"any person"** make no distinction between resident and alien.

The contrived order of removal of defendant Reynaldo Castro-Tum, **is the crystallization of the deportation by the Sessions Department of Justice, of due process itself.** So Judge Morley had to be removed from his cases, and Assistant Chief **Immigration Judge Deepali Nadkami was dispatched to the Philadelphia Immigration Court.** To do what? To conduct a single hearing, resulting in the defendant's removal from the US **"without further inquiry."**

So this is the new order of the USA. That **new order stands for obstruction of the operation of due process,** through judicial independence, via respect for the Rule of Law and the separation of powers.

This is the genesis of Trump's repeated rants about the investigations into his campaign's possible collusion with Russia to promote him to the highest office in America. Trump's preferred attack on those investigations, from which Sessions had no choice but to recuse himself, is represented by Trump depicting them as **"witch hunt."**

Such non-recognition of a lawful process is in fact a **non-recognition of law itself.** As a body of enacted or customary rules recognized by a community as binding, **law is non-recognizable by the Trump administration in several ways.** Among these are:

- The conflation (fusing) of law and religion. The evidence: the **Muslim Travel Ban.** Unconstitutional under the First Amendment which states: **"Congress shall make no law respecting an establishment of religion, or prohibiting the free exercise thereof;"**

- The recent **declaration by Sessions of the New Religious Liberty.** An obfuscation of terms as it reflects **the evangelical approach to governance.** Here the Bible is regarded as a governance road map. **Precisely the sordid concepts advocated by ISIS and the Muslim Brotherhood;**

- The erosion of the Civil Rights Act of 1965 through **gradual restriction of the equality of races in America before the law.** This is reflected in the gerrymander whereby the voting blacks are either disenfranchised or burdened by distancing them from voting stations;

- **The packing of the Supreme Court by conservative justices.** Gorsuch, a Trump nominee, was confirmed as replacement of Scalia through changing of the Senate rules of super-majority needed for such confirmations. Obama's nominee, **Judge Mark Garland was denied even the courtesy of a Senate hearing;**

- Now another conservative ogre by the name of Brett Kavanaugh is nominated. His written record shows that he **advocates that no criminal or civil indictments or charges, nor can there be** any investigation instituted against a sitting president of the US. Exactly **tailored to delegitimize the Mueller** (special counsel) **investigation** of the possible obstruction of justice by Trump; and

- The attacks by Trump against the media as **"enemy of the people."** Such attacks have been decried even by the UN in early August. Reason: leading to possible violence due to muzzling (imposition of silence) of free expression.

The blow-back against such rogue siege against law and fairness in Trump's America is happening.

- In the case of replacing the Philadelphia immigration judge, a letter of protest was signed by 15 retired judges. They stated: **"As a democracy, we expect our judges to reach results based on what is just, even** where such results are not aligned with the desired outcomes of politicians."

- That July 30 letter condemns what it describes as **"interference with judicial independence."** It added: **"Important due process safeguards are required in deportation proceedings."** This is because the consequences can be life or death.
- The mid-term elections (November 2018) may result in the Democratic party ending the Republican party's majority in the House of Representatives. It is called the **"Blue Wave"** (Democratic majority). In essence, the Blue Wave if successful, would almost guarantee the drafting of impeachment articles against a President who is now considered by the liberal media as **"unwell."**
- A Democratic majority House of Representatives may plunge after this November in espousing a Trump impeachment.

Hope springs eternal. Deportation by the Justice Department of **"due process"** must have consequences. We could sense the panic of the American Firsters (meaning NYET to the **"Browning of America"**).

Supreme Court Justice Frankfurter addressed the issue of due process in a way that would shame Attorney General Sessions. The Honorable Justice declared that due process **"must be respected in periods of calm and in periods of trouble. It protects aliens as well as citizens."** America of today is going through a period of trouble, **epitomized by publicists like Ann Coulter.**

Characters like Trump, Sessions and Coulter try to concoct an affirmative story **-national security.** They are blind to a simple fact. **Credibility depends on proving accuracy.** No accuracy, no credibility.

The dictionary defines a "coulter" as an iron blade. But even iron blades could be blunted. But such blunting can be done through upholding the Rule of Law.

DR. YASSIN EL-AYOUTY, ESQ.

Perspectives on Egypt, Islam and the Dark Era of Trump

THE GENIUS OF THE PROPHET MUHAMMAD: FROM THE DESERT, LAYING THE FOUNDATION OF A MIGHTY MUSLIM NATION

Friday, August 31, 2018

This is not about Islam. It is about the art of nation-construction from zero nation in the 7th century to 1.7 Billions in the 21st century. It is the genius of Muhammad in constructing this mighty edifice with tools which our world of today sorely needs to employ.

It began with Muhammad, at the age of 40 (611 CE) advocating in Mecca that God is one. **That one-ness of God directly resonated with both the Jews and Christians in Arabia.** Triumphing over the many idols which the Arab tribes worshiped in Mecca during their pilgrimage season. A master ideological stroke which caused the Meccans to pursue, in bitter hostility, the new Prophet.

Yet, a cornerstone has been laid. The first adherent was a woman, Khdeejah, Muhammad's wife and employer; **the poor and meek in the Meccan lording tribe of Quraish, flocked to Islam.** It made them even as slaves equal to their masters. Another anathema to the proud tribal lords of the desert.

So potent weapons were employed: secrecy, selective conversion from idolatry to Islam. And immigration, first to Ethiopia, later to the Arabian city of Yathrib -a Jewish city northeast of Mecca.

The secrecy was a self-preservation stratagem. The conversion from multiple deities to one God was through persuasion: **"Why worship what** your own hands have created?" And why immigration to Ethiopia? That is where Christianity found in the Quranic description of Christ as **"the word of God"** a reflection of its own belief. Then the move to Yathrib was by invitation of the few converts to Islam. **It was their means of saving the troubled peace which characterized the forever war** between two tribal antagonists: **Al-Aus and Al-Khazraj.**

The move (immigration/Hijrah) from Mecca to Medina marked the beginnings of the Muslim **"State"** -in fact **"nation."** The date was September 20, 622 (and Muhammad was 51 years old). **Not surprisingly, it marked the beginning of the Muslim (Hejira) calendar -now at 1439 years.** Two pillars sustained the incipient nation: **The construction of a mosque, as a town hall and a school,** (where Muhammad is now buried), **and the communal sharing of property** between the immigrants (Al-Muhajeroon) and the Ansar (supporters), meaning the Yathrib Muslim population.

A bridge was thus constructed in Medina (Yathrib) across tribal chasms, the haves and the have-nots economically, and the Muslim-Jewish relationships memorialized in a pact of peace, though later it did not endure. **Tawheed** (the One-ness of God) permeating the two Semitic faiths) was ideologically sound, but communally an instigator of competition between Judaism and Islam.

Topping Muhammad's priorities was the equalizing between Arabs and non-Arabs (such as the Persians who were Yemen rulers); **between men and women in terms of licensing women's ownership of property,** and of enfranchising them as regards participation in Muhammad's councils. Women were even encouraged to quiz Muhammad publicly as regards his decisions. Their litmus test was to ask the Prophet: **"Is your decision based on personal opinion or an inspiration from God?"** If it was an opinion on which the participants in that **"Town hall in the Desert"** disagreed, Muhammad changed course.

In fact the first person who pledged allegiance to Muhammad was a woman **(Afra Bint Obeid Ibn Thaalabah).** The Quran, considered Muhammad's only miracle, made such allegiance (Baiaa) to Muhammad an allegiance to God himself. **"Surely, those who swear allegiance to you swear allegiance to God; the hand of God is over their hands."** The Quran, (Chapter 48/Verse 10).

What were the terms of that allegiance to Islam: No idolatry, as emphasis on the one-ness of God; **no theft; no adultery; not infanticide** (as the Arabs used to bury their infant daughters to avoid shaming them); **truthfulness; and no contravening the word of God (the Quran).** Piety, not ethnic or tribal roots, was the yardstick by which all humans were evaluated. **"Surely, the most honorable of you in the sight of God is the most pious of you."** (The Quran, Chapter 49, Verse 13).

Closely tied to the Muslim dogma as preached by Muhammad was **humanity as one universal cooperative.** It became a **cardinal call for friendly relations among all nations, across ethnicities, languages, and time zones.**

That revolutionary concept is today inscribed on a mural adorning a wall at the UN Headquarters in New York. It is a gift from Morocco which quotes from the Quran the following verses **"O mankind! We have created you from a male and a female, and made you nations and tribes, that you may know one another."** (Chapter 49, Verse 13).

The new nation was no longer held together by family lineage, but by a faith that regulated their lives flexibly, under the ethos of justice for all, Muslims and non-Muslims alike. The only difference between the two categories was that non-Muslim were made to pay a defense tax because of their exemption from defense services.

Calling them Zimmis is not an apartheid practice. Contrary to western orientalist depiction, **"zimma"** in Arabic means **"a security guarantee."** It is **also the sum total of all obligations to which a person commits. It is akin to a treaty obligation.** Its violation is not due to the faith, but due to the faithless practice of those who scorn human rights.

What bound this new nation together was an Islamic jurisprudence based on a tripod of principles and rules: **The Quran, non-changeable in text, but amenable to** interpretation (the science of Tafseer); the **Sunna of Muhammad, that is what the Prophet has said and done,** but also amenable to authentication since it was not written during the Prophet's life-time; and **"wisdom" (Hekmah), the resort to common sense in utilizing the other two bases for resolving a dispute or settling an issue.**

Within those parameters, the new community functioned, quarreled, reconciled, and spread outward. All within the **broad concept of Islam, meaning the submission to God's will.** While unity was stressed, communities were led by consensus (ijmaa) not throughout all Muslim regions, but within the community of scholars of each region. **Unity was in the ultimate purpose, not in sectoral decisions.**

The Quran exalted unity as **"harmony,"** taking into account the divergence of cultures, systems of governance, and changing circumstances. In praise of harmony the Quran stated: **"God is the One who united their hearts; had you (Muhammad) expended all the riches of the earth, you could not have united their hearts together."** (Chapter 8; Verse 63).

War, for the new nation, was restricted only to self-defense of territory (homeland) and faith. It is not exportable, nor is it waged beyond national borders. **And must be proportional.** A far far cry from the criminal ideology of jihadism which advocated the primacy of Islam and conversion to it by the sword - **"There is no compulsion in religion"** (The Quran, Chapter 2, Verse 256). Diplomacy to end wars and achieve peace was decreed. **"But if they incline to peace, then incline to it."** (The Quran, Chapter 8, Verse 61). **Prisoners of war are to be safely repatriated and exchanged, and an annual war-free month** (Muharram) was set aside.

Insurrection (Fitna) was regarded as a catastrophe, represented by the total breakdown of law and order. Unjust rulers should be removed provided that such efforts should not lead to ascertained mayhem. In all cases, injustice which violates the liberty and human rights of the community or the individual shall always be a violation of God's decrees.

The Quran calls the unjust **"an evildoer,"** who has no excuse whatsoever. **"On the Day (of Judgment) when the excuses of the evildoers shall avail them nothing; they shall have the curse and the evil abode."** (The Quran; Chapter 40; Verse 52).

When Muhammad died at the age of 63, the edifice of the Muslim Nation, having arisen from a Zero Nation in Arabia, evolved into a global Muslim entity existing in every corner of the earth.

Though divided and at times at war with one another and also within **(Syria, Yemen, and Libya),** it has kept the faith **as spread by its great founder. Muhammad.** The Prophet did not even name a successor; refused during his lifetime to have his sayings written, **and left no heir to claim a hereditary mantle.**

Today's pilgrimage of over 2 million to Mecca is a testimony of that enduring phenomenon which is still vastly misunderstood in many parts of the world. **Though Islamophobia has now morphed into anti-Islamism, the plain fact is that those aberrations are hurtful primarily to those who espouse them.** For they are the unwitting auxiliaries of groups like ISIS, Al-Qaeda and the like.

Muhammad died on June 8, 632 at the age of 63. His first successor as **"The First Enlightened Caliph,"** Abu-Bakr, gave the eulogy to a stunned Muslim community. In it, he pointed out the knob of the Prophet's enduring legacy. **"To the Believers, stay on the path of Justice."**

The pilgrimage to Mecca earlier this month numbered over 2 millions. **With a global waiting list estimated to stretch out for 583 years in the future.** Pillorying it by an ignoramus and an ethical thug like Rudy Giuliani proves his racism. For that pilgrimage instituted by Muhammad, as an optional manifestation of a faith of tolerance, **raises the ubiquitous flag of inclusiveness.**

The Prophet Muhammad was chased away from his birthplace, Mecca, by **vicious tribal campaigners who preferred to worship idols over the belief in the One God.** It was therefore axiomatic that his return victorious from Medina to Mecca, was initially thought to signal a blood path for his tormentors. Again Muhammad's genius asserted itself. He told the fearful Meccan throngs: **"From now on, you are released from your past!! (Al-Tolaqa)".**

That was the historic exercise by Muhammad's power of pardon. **No Nuremberg trials. No Tokyo trials. The victor of 1439 years ago did not write history, as it is the practice of our times. He caused history to be engraved about him.**

Thus, Abdel-Rahman Azzam, the first Secretary-General of the League of Arab States, titled his book about Muhammad: "The Hero of Heroes!!"

FROM A MAYOR AND A PROSECUTOR TO A HUCKSTER AND AN IMPOSTER: THE RISE AND FALL OF RUDOLPH GIULIANI

Friday, August 31, 2018

Gone are the days in 1998 when I was gleeful about him -the Honorable Mayor of New York City. Rudy Giuliani had agreed to write the prologue (foreword) to my book published in 2000. Its title was: **"Government Ethics and Law Enforcement."** With me as co-editors were two colleagues in the legal profession: **Kevin Ford, Esq., and Mark Davies, Esq.**

But in these chaotic times of Trump, Rudy has been appointed the President's personal lawyer, espousing anti-ethics to match his anti-law. The Giuliani of today feels no shame when he publicly says: **"The Truth Is Not the Truth."**

Yet as a former prosecutor, Giuliani should know that **the truth is a quality of being accurate or honest or sincere or loyal. It is conformity to fact or actuality. It is a statement proven to be or accepted as true. It is fidelity to an original or standard. It is veracity or verity.**

Mr. Giuliani should know that **"truth"** is the bedrock of an oath to **"tell the truth, and nothing but the truth, so Help Me God."** From there begins the law of evidence. Even the Muslim community of 1440 years ago adhered to that standard as their ABC in litigation. The Second Enlightened Caliph, Omar Ibn Al-Khattab decreed that **"The burden of evidence is shouldered by the plaintiff."**

Rudy: Can you still read? If yes, then check what the following masters have said. Charles Seymour declared: **"We seek the truth, and will endure the consequences."** And Thomas H. Huxley advised that **"veracity is the heart of morality."** And James Harvey Robinson referred to the term **"verity"** as applying to an enduring or repeatedly demonstrated truth. His very words were: **"beliefs that were accepted as eternal verities."**

So, Rudy, **your unconvincing narrative is an undisputed chican cry. For it is a deceptive subterfuge.** Playing with words -your **"truth is not truth"** is intended to convey that there is no accepted standard. **If so, then your own oath of office was nothing but fake.** So must has been Trump's oath upon inaugurating him as President of these United States in January 2017.

You, Sir, have affirmed in your prologue to my book on **"Government Ethics"** the following: **"Corruption and unethical behavior prevent any government from efficiently and effectively serving the needs of its citizens. In addition, corruption undermines respect for the rule of law and for the democratic process that are the very core of our system of government. Controlling this evil successfully is a constant challenge for any government."**

These are the first sentences you wrote for my book published by Praeger in the year 2000. It is a book which I saw fit to dedicate to **"the City of New York."** But that was the Giuliani whom I fully respected at that time.

And when my city was attacked by the criminal gang of Al-Qaeda, I saw fit to work on yet another book entitled **"Perspectives on 9/11,"** published in 2004 and dedicated to my beloved institution in Brooklyn -**"St. Francis College."**

I truly pity your fall from what you were to what you are now -a hot-air bag, a mouth piece for a declining presidency of a Liar-in-Chief, called Donald J. Trump. Your boss, by fact-checkers, has lied more than **four-thousand times,** since occupying the Oval Office.

The guidelines for both of you, Liar and Enabler, have been **"the destruction of the Administrative State."** A non-principle laid down by a fascist called **Steven Bannon,** who recently said in Europe: **"When they call you a racist, wear it with pride"** (or something to that effect). **What pride can any rational human being find in demeaning others** because of the color of their skin?

As a Bannonite, you Rudy attacked John Brennan, former Director of the CIA, now a professor at the venerable Fordham University School of Law. For **when Brennan said that the Muslim spectacle of Hajj to Mecca was a captivating scene,** you, Giuliani called for bringing charges against Brennan for endangering by that praise **"national security!!"**

Really, Rudy!! **Truthfully speaking, your and Trump's anti-Islamism is the very essence of threatening America's national security.** Your words, Rudy, are what the remnants of ISIS are waiting for. They are **the oxygen which is prolonging the life of jihadism beyond their shelf-life.**

And that is the Truth, so Help Me God!!

And why mix religion with politics, Mr. Lawyer Giuliani? **Religion is about faith, and politics are about power!!** Faith is in the heart; politics are in the mind. One is belief in the invisible; the other is an advocacy for the material. **The mix is combustible as we learnt from the Muslim Brotherhood and ISIS.**

You have plunged head-on mixing the Muslim pilgrimage with American national security. Only crazies can see any rationality in such a cocktail. Only you and Trump and Bannon Inc. can mix that cocktail during your **"Happy Hour."** Reason why Trump, on Monday, August 27 **urged the evangelical Christian leaders to break federal law and openly support him from the pulpit.**

Commented the New York Times of August 31, 2018 on that hallucination by saying: **"Truth, fantasy and deceit slosh together with Mr. Trump."** That was under the title: **"After Mr. Trump, the Deluge?"**

WE SHALL NEED MAGA AFTER THE EXIT OF PRESIDENT GAGA!!

Friday, September 7, 2018

This is in honor of John McCain -who **lived and died truthful to high principle.** The highest of these principles is love of country for which sacrificing is but a pay back for its having been there for him and millions others!!

With this as an introduction, I find in **MAGA (Make America Great Again)** an insult by Trump to all those who strove to construct the USA. The founding fathers recognized that the **Union needs constant improvement** -the periodic search for accommodating changing circumstances. So when Trump calls for MAGA, **he turns his back on the difference between evolution and destroying what we have.**

And for what purpose? To rebuild America in his own image. But what **image? His is never fixed. This president stands for an America which never was.** For that reason alone, **Donald J. Trump is no more than a Gaga,** a senile, doddering, which in French, means **"an old fool."**

Yet that fool, and those who stand by him, or in awe of him, has given us MAGA as a mantra which should be **our tool for repairing the damage inflicted by him on this great human experiment called America.**

Trump's sordid record begins with his being oblivious of what governing the US, a complex entity of 50 sovereignties (the 50 States) is all about. He has **demonstrated total ignorance of the separation of powers.** The US President, under our Constitution, is no Chairman of the Board. **Country** and company are two different entities: The former is the vehicle; the latter is a mere dependency governed and regulated by the former.

But President Gaga does not see it that way. "I can run the country and my company at the same time," he fulminated. And "I alone can fix it," he uttered at his rallies, **bamboozling his captive audience.** Those poor souls have been hoodwinked by **The Donald deliberate methods of deceit.** Trump, a bamboozler par excellence, has explained his ignorance of the US Constitution as, if I correctly recall, **"archaic; an inconvenience."**

To my mind, this can only mean that **"We the People of the United States...,"** words by which the Constitution begins, have now been abbreviated by President Gaga as **"We, Donald J. Trump."** Article II of the Constitution which provides for **"The executive power shall be vested in a President of the United States of America,"** seems to be interpreted by Donald the Narcissist **as a power overwhelming all others under the Constitution.**

- A president who regards the Department of Justice **as if it were created as a law firm whose task is to "protect"** him, is a president who believes that defending the U.S. should not be allowed unless it justifies his actions regardless of their dubious legality;

- **A president who uses his power of pardon as a backdoor exit** for those regarded as law breakers is himself a law breaker;

- A president whose call for an **"America First,"** yet applies it as **"America is for the whites only" is a president who abets racism and thus is an agent for civil strife.**

- A president who ignores George Washington's call for **"no entangling alliances"** is a president whose thought mechanism is **incapable of comprehending that that was not a call for no alliances.**

President Gaga has built walls around America, not only at the southern borders. **He has isolated this great country** from Canada to the north; Mexico to the south; Europe except for Russia to the east; and alienated the pacific region to the west, except for North Korea.

A president who believes American adversary, Russia, and **attacks the** credibility of 17 American intelligence agencies, is an executive who is courting impeachment.

A president who sees in the rise of the extreme right in Europe a **vindication of his own espousal of fascism** is an executive who has been unfaithful to his own oath of office. That oath is specified in Article II, Section I of the Constitution in these words: **"I do solemnly swear ... that I will faithfully execute the Office of President..."** In essence, **President Gaga,** by ignoring that he is leading a country based on the Rule of Law, **has destroyed his own legitimacy to occupy the Oval Office.**

As for this obsequious Congress, I shall leave that assessment to **David Leonhardt, the author of an op-ed column in the New York Times of September 3.** Disparaging the leaders of Congress who attended McCain's funeral services at Washington's National Cathedral, he said:

"They have refused to defend America's national security in the face of Russian attacks. They have refused to defend the rule of law against Trump's attacks. They have refused to defend the F.B.I., the Justice Department and the First Amendment. They have refused to defend the basic civil rights that Trump seeks to deny to dark-skinned American citizens, including the right to vote and the right to hold a passport."

That column closed by **"They were there for show, faced with a choice, they have rejected McCain's America for Trump's."**

Yes, we need MAGA to repair the daily damage, inflicted on it by Trump through his raving mania through which he sees himself as a great president. **A president who believes that one day, his utterances shall be regarded by history as being at par with Lincoln's Gettysburg address!!** Yet a great America shall assert itself again through reclaiming the values on which it was established 240 years ago.

Trump's exclusion from attendance at the McCain funeral services was a dignified response to Trump's autocratic governance. It was also a response to Trump's denial of McCain's heroism in the service of America. **A hero is a person noted for tests of courage or nobility of purpose.** None of these qualities has ever fit President Gaga.

His statement that McCain was considered a hero because he was captured **is so telling about the distance between Trump and the noble zone of sacrifice. Capturing a hero is the unhappy sequence of sacrifice for principle.** For all his 72 years of life, Donald Trump had experienced neither principle nor sacrifice.

So go on, Donald: In this dark period of American history stick to tweeting. **It is the only language by which birds can communicate with other creatures of feather.** That is until our real MAGA would cleanse the Office of the President from the stigma attached to it by President Gaga!!

Yet the most cruel joke of the Trump mal-administration is the **attempt to politicize the Supreme Court.** This dreary process began with **denying Judge Mark Garland, an Obama nominee, even the mere courtesy of a Senate hearing.** So when Justice Kennedy stepped down, the Trump ultra-right machine went into an over-drive by nominating Brett Kavanaugh.

Kavanaugh's record shows a **commitment to the controversial principle that a sitting US president cannot be investigated, or prosecuted or indicted.** In sum, a president is above the law, except through impeachment. But impeachment through the Senate is at present impossible due to the spineless Republican majority. **If confirmed, the Supreme Court of the US shall suffer a dangerous tilt to the Right which shall last for decades to come.**

This tampering with the Rule of Law in the US is by a President who wishes that the US public would tolerate his role-playing of a dictator. This charade shall reach its end in a humiliating collapse. Only then shall the three branches of government reclaim their soul in the system of checks and balances **-the essence of US democracy.**

SINCE 1882, THE RISE OF EGYPTIAN DEMOCRACY FOUND ITS MAIN PROTECTOR: THE EGYPTIAN ARMED FORCES

Friday, September 14, 2018

In Tahrir Square, in January 2011, the Egyptian Revolution I against Mubarak, was shielded by SCAF (The Supreme Council of the Armed Forces). And in June 2013, Revolution II against the Muslim Brotherhood was protected by the same armed forces. In the two uprisings, history has repeated itself in continuation of the events of 1882.

The armed forces, led by Ahmed Orabi, in support of the young Egyptian democracy of 1880, had performed the same role. Though overwhelmed by non-Egyptian factors, the oath of loyalty to Egypt administered to the officers by Sheikh Mohamed Abdo in May 1882 continued to operate for the past 136 years. It is the glue of fidelity to honor and country which still held in Tahrir for all these decades.

This blog is in celebration of that continuity which separates Egypt from a Syria, a Yemen, or a Libya, where chaos prevails, foreign interference is rampant, and bloodshed has tragically become the news of the day -every day.

Putting a date on that cohesion between civil and military in Egypt, I choose a dark date, an Egyptian Black September, namely September 14, 1882. Why? For against all odds, when the British occupation of Egypt began in July of that year, the head of state in Egypt, Khedewi Tewfik, accompanied the British army of occupation into Cairo on that Black September day.

What legitimacy could one attribute to that ruler reviewing in Abdeen Square, Cairo, a foreign army of occupation? A review which took place in front of Egypt's equivalent of the White House -namely, Abdeen Palace? Tewfik was then 30 years of age (he died in 1892 at the age of 40) fully deserving of the accusation by Orabi, then Egypt's War Minister, of "high treason."

Though the Orabi Revolution and Resistance faltered in 1882, the accolades bestowed on Orabi by his army and countrymen as "The Defender of the Land of Egypt." That honor was more than merited by the events of that time. Those events of the late 19th Century continue to reflect till today their larger meaning for an Egyptian rising democracy whose main protector is Egypt's armed forces.

The line from Orabi to Naguib and Nasser, to Sadat, to Tantawi, to El-Sisi remain unbroken, un-challenged, and permanently embedded in the psyche of that 7000-year old nation. Same nationalistic genes, same commitments, same inclination to keep on rising after every misstep.

A celebratory review of the events of 1880-1882 is in order, providing evidence of the deep roots which have historically bound a nation to its armed forces.

As foreign influence and interference in internal affairs in Egypt grew as of the 1840s, so has the resentment towards these phenomena by Egyptian society. Such nationalist fervor was spread by landowners, the educated classes and the armed forces. Following the inauguration of the Suez Canal in 1869 by Khedewi Ismail, Tewfik's father, the appetite of England and France for control of Egypt increased. Thus enhancing the national reaction in opposition, especially when it came to matters of representation, economy, or national defense.

With Egypt's first constitution of 1879, promulgated by Prime Minister Sherif Pasha towards the end of the reign of Khedewi Ismail in place, that document acquired a haloed status for all those who called Egypt their historic home. The terms Sherif Pasha, the Constitution and the House of representation stood, with a luminous circle around them, in the developing struggle for the very existence of an independent Egypt.

On the opposition side, stood Tewfik, foreign consuls, British designs over Egypt, and foreign lenders who managed to over-lend to an Egypt searching, at the time of Khedewi Ismail, to be as modern as Europe. The result was the establishment, for the first time in Egyptian political history of "The Nationalist Party" (Al-Hezb Al-Watani) in 1879 in Helwan, south of Cairo.

Crystallizing national demands, the first manifesto of The National Party was a true reflection of what the Orabi movement (the military) stood for. These included the total divestiture of the royal family of its land, the abolishment of directing the revenue from the Egyptian Rail Roads for foreign debt payment, and the capping of the interest on foreign debts at 4%.

To Khedewi Tewfik and his foreign backers, especially England, those demands were viewed as treason. The names of the party's membership were hotly sought after for banishment to the Sudan. Not only that these efforts failed. Another nationalist party was formed in Alexandria under the name of "Young Egypt" (Misr Al-Fatah).

With these developments, the tempo of confrontation between the Khedive, backed by an array of foreign powers and interests, and the Egyptian nationalists fronted by Orabi's armed forces was accelerating:

- In January 1881, the Officers Corp convened at Orabi's residence;
- There they issued a **petition to Khedive Tewfik calling for replacing the Turkish War Minister, Osman Rifqi, by an Egyptian;**
- Tewfik's decision was to **court martial Orabi and two of his senior lieutenants.** In response, the army attacked the military court, causing its members to flee, then **marched upon Abdeen Palace forcing Tewfik to replace the Turkish War Minister by an Orabi loyalist, Mahmoud Sami Al-Baroudi.**
- That was in February 1881. By May 1881, the armed forces and the leadership of the nationalist popular movement coalesced against the Palace and the various foreign actors.
- The **people and army alliance demanded the increase of the army** to 18,000, the fortification of the ports, **the establishment of a lower house of parliament,** and cabinet accountability before that parliament.

Such demands turned into an **outright rebellion against Tewfik:**

- The **Orabi army refused to heed any military orders by Tewfik,** including his orders to march on the Sudan to put down the Mehdi rebellion; ignored his orders to have the army dig up canals for fear of surrendering their weapons.

And when a European driving his car fatally killed an Egyptian soldier in Alexandria, resulting in a demonstration at Tewfik's Alexandria Palace (Ras El-Teen), **Tewfik ordered participating army officers to be exiled in the Sudan.** On September 9, 1881, Orabi marched his troops on Abdeen Palace.

Seemingly giving in to these army-people demands, **parliamentary elections were held, and a House of Representatives was inaugurated in December 1881.**

That was the tipping point for direct intervention by England and France:

- A joint Anglo-French memorandum was issued in January 1882 declaring **extreme displeasure at the emergence of a parliamentary system in Egypt;**
- It also dissembled fear for the future of Khedive Tewfik;
- The Anglo-French memorandum called, in the meantime, that the new-Egyptian Parliament **should not deal with the State's budget** (which included extortionist provisions for payments of debt and interest);

In defiance, a nationalist cabinet was formed, headed by Al-Baroudi, which included **Orabi as War Minister. A new Constitution was promulgated in February 1882, and the rights of Parliament to debate and decide on the budget was affirmed.** And in April 1882, a Turkish plot to assassinate Orabi and 40 other officers was unmasked. The Khedive, true to his colors, **refused to punish the accomplices.**

By May 1882, British and French naval vessels appeared at the port of Alexandria. But the French units later departed. And **on July 11, the British navy bombarded Alexandria.** And when the Egyptian army besieged the Khedewi Palace, **Tewfik called the British for rescue.**

The Egyptian drama of British occupation and the defeat of the Orabi army and the nationalist movement ended by the **British entry of Cairo on**

September 14, 1882 escorted by Tewfik who relished reviewing them at Abdeen Palace. Thus began an occupation which lasted for 72 years.

Historically, the Egyptian nationalist movement had the solid backing of the Armed Forces.

Today, September 14, I bow my head in prayer for Ahmed Orabi in whose village in the province of Sharkia I was born. There I was also taught that love of country and community is part of faith.

Perspectives on Egypt, Islam and the Dark Era of Trump

A SUNSGLOW OCCASION ENRICHING THE GLOBAL DEBATE ON IMMIGRATION

Friday, September 21, 2018

A raging debate on immigration denotes global interest. Such global interest has a sizeable legal perspective. And for an organization like SUNSGLOW, whose central mission since 1999 has been Global Training in the Rule of Law, it was obvious that it should contribute to that debate.

Hence the decision to assemble a high-level panel to deal with this topic under the title of **"Immigration As a Global Challenge."** Implementation took place at the SUNSGLOW historical venue, namely, **St. Francis College, Brooklyn, New York City,** whose President, **Dr. Miguel Martinez-Saenz,** is a SUNSGLOW Trustee.

On August 9, the College reserved for that event the Founders Hall Auditorium (from 6:00 to 8:00 pm) where **Vice President Jennifer Lancaster,** who is also Academic Dean, was deputized to welcome the panelists and the select audience.

This is perhaps the first time for the SUNSGLOW management to **report to our Board (Trustees, International Advisors, and Associates) through the wider medium of this blog posting.**

The panel consisted of **Carolina Maluje, Esq.** (Miami, Florida) as the first speaker. She was followed by **Dean Elizabeth F. Defeis,** Seton Hall University School of Law and Advisor to the Mission of the Holy See to the United Nations. The third speaker was SUNSGLOW Vice President, **Dr. Zahra Hend Shnayen.** Followed by me, as the last speaker.

The entire event was moderated by the Honorable Judge Elizabeth S. Stong, the U.S. Bankruptcy Court, Eastern District of New York, Brooklyn, New York City. Thanking her for her astute running of this event, I wrote: **"No one could have run our event as exquisitely as our distinguished judge and dear friend the Honorable Stong."**

And in thanking Dean Jennifer Lancaster of St. Francis College for her launching the panel, I wrote: **"If the Brooklyn Bridge is a St. Francis College symbol of connectedness, SUNSGLOW is one of your bridges to the UN and beyond. For it was during the tenure of my friend, the late Kofi Annan, UN Secretary-General, that a formal statement by him in 1999, declared: "SUNSGLOW is a UN Partner."**

Now to a selection of excerpts from what the panelists said on August 9.

Ms. Maluje reminded her audience of her immigrant background. She said:

"I also was attracted to immigration law because I come from a long line of immigrants. It seems that our family emigrates every generation, or so it appears. My father's family came from Syria (my grandparents) and my mother's family from Spain (my great grandparents). I know what it is to be an immigrant and see it firsthand. I adjusted under Reagan's law amnesty and I was fortunate to benefit from it, as well as my parents."

Then she delved into a depiction of the sorrowful portrayal of immigration laws during the present Trump administration. She said:

"Current changes during this new administration have been noticeable. Asylum law has taken a big blow in terms of protecting women from domestic violence and their relationships. Matter of A-B was a case that Attorney General Sessions referred to himself, and reversed protections for women in abusive relationships."

As to **Dean Defeis**, she addressed the outlook of **His Holiness Pope Francis** on today's suffering by the millions of immigrants in these words:

"Addressing immigration has become a centerpiece of the papacy of Pope Francis. In his first trip outside of Rome after his election as Pope in 2013, Francis chose to visit the Sicilian Island of Lampedusa, called by some, the "Ellis Island of Italy." At the time of his visit, more than 20,000 persons had died , fleeing hardship and persecution in hopes of a better life in Europe. As he spoke about those deaths, Pope Francis said it was "a thorn in my heart." The sad situation of so many migrants and refugees has been called by Pope Francis "a sign of the times."

The contrast between Canada's acceptance of its responsibilities towards today's immigration issues and that of the US was crystallized by Dr. Zahra Hend Shnayen:

"In 2016, there was an influx of refugees, due to the willingness of the Canadian administration to rescue those whose lives were in danger. In response, I joined other friends to form The Canadian Organization For The Integration of Newcomers. Through that organization, we were able to help those new Canadians in many ways, big and small. From helping them to cope with their past ordeal and present loneliness , to assisting them to become contributors to their new society. So we taught them how to look for employment; how to craft jewelry using local material; how to use the libraries."

She went on to cite the upward mobility of Canadian immigrants to top positions. These were her concluding words:

"Suffice it to note that several Canadian Prime Ministers were not Canadian born. These include Canada's second Prime Minister, Alexander Mackenzie."

Moving on to conclude the deliberations of that panel regarding immigration, I began by citing the **UN Global Compact on Immigration.** That instrument was announced on July 13, 2019. In this respect, I began by saying:

"On July 13, UN member States finalized the first agreement on international migration. Its title is "The Global Compact for Safe, Orderly and Regular Migration." It should come to nobody's surprise that the two countries which facilitated that Compact (meaning a Covenant arrived at by common consent) were Mexico and Switzerland."

On the legal context of that Compact, I informed the audience as follows:

Note that that Compact deals with whatever is not at the US/Mexico border. That border, in history, shall always stand for non-safe, extremely disorderly and the apex of irregularity. These are the results of the genocidal acts and acts of war, committed by the present American Administration. Ambassadors Camacho of Mexico and Ambassador Lauber of Switzerland, said to the world from the glass house of the UN the following:

- Article 10 of that Compact informs us that it is "the product of an unprecedented review of evidence and data gathered during an open, transparent and inclusive process... We learned that migration is a defining feature of our globalized world...;"
- The Compact rests on, among other things, the Universal Declaration of Human Rights, the International Covenant on Civil and Political Rights, the UN Convention against Transnational Organized Crime, the Slavery Convention.

The paralysis in American decision-making on immigration was the centerpiece of my statement. Here I said:

"Our dilemma in America is that we have a Congress whose Senate, with a Republican majority, does not act to pass a sane immigration law. And an Executive, who prides itself on saying that our Constitution is archaic. And a judiciary whose 5-4 decisions by the Supreme Court shall go on forever with a conservative tilt, if Brett Kavanugh is confirmed to the seat vacated by justice Kennedy."

So the flow of migrants, hundreds of whom have died from drowning in rickety boats overloaded by the pirates of the Mediterranean, and the flow of immigrants from Central America, whose lives have been put in danger by the US "zero tolerance" draconian policies, are twin companion flaws.

Thus we concluded that SUNSGLOW event regarding one of today's hottest issues dividing our world community. And it shall not be the last.

WHAT A BAD DAY FOR AMERICA AT THE UN!! AN AVALANCHE OF CONTRADICTIONS BY DONALD TRUMP AND OF LAUGHTER AT HIM

Friday, September 28, 2018

In his second annual appearance before the U.N. General Assembly, Donald Trump lived up to universal expectation. By making as little sense as possible **before the presidents and prime ministers of 193 member states.** An avalanche of contradictions, gushing out of the mouth of a man who doesn't like to read. Supplemented by much laughter at him.

So before an organization devoted to international cooperation for peace and prosperity, the **Donald gleefully announced:**
• **American withdrawal** from membership on the U.N. Human Rights Council;
• **Reduction of American contributions** to UN peace-keeping operations to 25% of the required budget;
• The readiness of America to use its **economic might to force other nations into submission** to American barriers created to the disadvantage of the freedom of trade (tariff, taxes.. etc.)
• **Accused China of violating the terms of its entry into the World Trade Organization,** while thanking it for its role in ameliorating the tensions between America and North Korea; and
• The **primacy of national sovereignty** which he favors over globalization intended to harmonize between cross-border relationship and national interest.

It was last year that Trump from the UN GA rostrum that **he threatened** to wipe **North Korea off the map.** But this year, his old threats turned to utter praise for the North Korea president. **Trump's floating hostility turned this year to Iran and Venezuela.** In defiance of plain truth, the unhinged American President states that the Iran nuclear deal was a embarrassment to the US and that **Venezuela needed a new leadership.**

Lying through his teeth, he insinuated that many countries supported his unilateral opting out of the six-party Iran nuclear deal. Not so by any means. The **International Atomic Energy Agency, through its inspectors, supported Iran's assertion of living up to the terms of that deal.** And France, Germany, the UK, **China and Russia** have manifested their incredulity about the American claims. Breaking international deals is not the kind of action to be lauded at the UN GA annual summit.

It was impossible to square the Trump's call for respect of national sovereignty and the emphasis on self defense, with his **declared threats against Venezuela and its leadership.** Trump had no regard for the right of Venezuela to choose **"socialism"** over capitalism. His disparaging remarks flew in the face of the UN Charter emphasis on non-intervention in internal affairs.

Trump's message was a blatant return to gunboat diplomacy through the advocacy of a **reborn Monroe doctrine (Monroeism)** under which South America had been regarded as an American protectorate. Obviously he did not take account the fact that the **president of this 73rd session of the General Assembly was a fine lady diplomat from Ecuador.**

More of Trump's contradictions before the world body:

•   **His false claim that Germany shall soon by over-dependent upon Russian national gas** for its energy needs. This is while the American President has, since inauguration, done his best to avoid criticizing Russia for anything, including its **alleged intervention in the 2016 American election.** Thus his untoward remarks about German dependency hit in 3 ways: German purported weakness; Russian politicization of its exports; and infringement of domestic affairs of two sovereign States.

- **Trump's call on States to pay for the cost of their own defense,** while proclaiming that America's might shall also serve the needs of its **"friends and allies."** No allusion to who are his or America's **"friends and allies,"** in view of his **"America First"** policy.
- Trump's implied **disparagement of the administration of his predecessors** through his claims that America has never before seen such rates of economic growth as compared to the pre-Trump era. He has ignored the historic fact that President Obama has, in 2008, inherited an economic mess which threatened even the car industry.

Trump's emphasis on going it alone overlooks the historic fact that America, since 1945 and without allies has not won any wars: not in Korea, not in Vietnam, not in Afghanistan. Denigrating NATO, the shield that had held western Europe safe from Soviet encroachment, has been Trump's signature European policy.

And his call for observance of the right of peoples to sovereignty and prosperity flies in the face of his dealing with the Palestinian people's plight under Israeli occupation, including his recognition of Jerusalem as the undivided capital of Israel.

His claims to respect of the Rule of aw could not be supported by **his own disregard for the US Constitution, nor by his denigration of the US Department of Justice, nor by his executive orders relating to the Muslim bans** regarding immigration to the US, nor of the first Amendment of the US Constitution in regard to the freedom of expression. For in a fascist vein, he has described the US media and even journalists as **"Enemy of the People."**

It was a bad day for America at the UN -a forum which was largely created by the US. The UN Charter compares in many ways to the principles and values enunciated by or implicit in the US Constitution.

The world laughed aloud at America, as represented by Trump. That occurred when he said: **"In less than two years, my administration has accomplished more than almost any administration in the history of my country."** Trump's nemesis, **Iran's President Hassan Rouhani seemed to have the last laugh** as he pointed out another contradiction: **"It is ironic that the United States government does not even conceal its plan for overthrowing the same government it invites to talk."**

Trump is nothing but a reality terminator. As the UN laughed at him, he confessed from the General Assembly rostrum that that **laughter was not the reaction which he expected.** But the following day, the reality terminator had a different interpretation. **"They were laughing with me."** Really? If so, why was there no applause?! Trump's brain seems to process realities as if to shield himself from reality.

In an op ed article in the New York Times of September 28, 2018, Susan Rice, former US Ambassador to the UN during the Obama presidency, said: "In these troubling times, up is down, black is white, and America stands alone, reckless ridiculed, among the nations of the world."

WHAT A SHAME!! THE U.S. SUPREME COURT IS NO LONGER "SUPREME"

Friday, October 5, 2018

Institutions, like individuals, could be fragile. Their fragility is dictated by several factors, chief among which is **how their function is perceived by those whom they are intended to serve.** The confirmation hearings of Judge Kavanaugh, nominated by President Trump to the Supreme Court, constitute a historic case on the **decline of public perception in the US of that co-equal branch of the American government.**

Article III of the U.S. Constitution provides in its Section I that **"The judicial power of the United States shall be vested in one Supreme Court."** Then it goes on to add an important condition -a sort of a character reference. **"The Judges, both of the supreme and inferior courts shall hold their offices during good behavior."**

The drama surrounding the **attempted rape accusations against Judge Kavanaugh** raises critical questions. The FBI fact-finding regarding his character did not prove culpability. It was a limited exercise in both duration and scope. Proving culpability requires investigating more than 4 persons. **Thus the Senate's Republican majority has been poised to ram that nomination through.** Could he as Justice Kavanaugh be impeached? And could Justice Clarence Thomas be impeached for Anita Hill accusations of 1991?

In theory, this is possible. In reality, it is nearly impossible. The damage to the perception of the Supreme Court as a neutral body judiciously deciding on cases and controversies (Article III, Section 2 of the Constitution) is already done. **A two dimensional damage: politicization, with Republican appointees, siding with Republican-inspired causes; and Democratic appointees, casting their opinions in an opposite direction.**

The Supreme Court of the future promises to be an arm of the Trump's Republican Party. Never mind for now, the moral reputational damage resulting from having seated not one, **but two justices suspected of being sexual predators.**

In that context, how can the US Supreme Court remain perceptionally **"supreme?"** This and other question marks about that 9-justices body hang over the grand edifice of that court. **Even prior to the Kavanaugh historic debate.** The truth is invariably hard to prove. This is exquisitely expressed in a book by Paul Bergman, entitled **"Trial Advocacy"** in a chapter on **"Truth and the Adversary System."**

On the issue of **"trial,"** Bergman says: **"Ironically, while you might instinctively agree that trial is a "search for truth," rarely can you prove "What really happened... Words have a limited power to convey real events."** Then he goes on to say: **"Some commentators may suggest that adversarial techniques obscure reality even further."**

Even the **Oxford Dictionary,** when it comes to defining **"truth,"** casts it in a muddy way. It says **"quality, state, of being true, or accurate or honest or sincere or loyal."** This fog is best expressed by the Arab sarcastic poem: **"After much exertion, he ended up defining the term "water" as "water."**

Of course, **the volcanic performance of Kavanaugh before the Senate's Judicial Committee should have prevented his nomination from confirmation.** Kavanaugh has dug up for all to see that **politics, not law,** as applicable to his case, **were his true calling.**

On Thursday, September 27, Kavanaugh demonstrated that there are **two of him in one skin.** Earlier that month, during the first round of confirmation hearings, there was Kavanaugh No.1 -a calm judicial demeanor. **"The Supreme Court, he said, must never be viewed as a partisan institution."** But on September 27, Kavanaugh No. 2, much like in the film **"Dr. Jekyll and Mr. Hyde,"** burst in the open, for the whole nation to see. **His diatribe stunned me (as it did millions) as an attorney and a member of the Bar of the Supreme Court.**

The real Kavanaugh was totally incoherent. **He was vicious, betraying a hidden belief in the conspiracy theory, the trade mark of Donald Trump who nominated him as a potential shield from possible impeachment.** Shouting his claims to innocence, Kavanaugh said: **"This whole two-week effort has been a calculated and orchestrated political hit."**

Then, as **if anger is a non-disputed evidence of innocence, he dug deeper in politicizing his case.** The charges levelled against him by his accuser, Dr. Christine Blasey Ford, were **"fueled with apparent pent-up anger about President Trump and the 2016 election, fear that has been unfairly stoked about my judicial record, revenge on behalf of the Clintons and millions of dollars in money from outside left-wing opposition groups."**

Would such a person be neutral in deciding a case which might come before the Supreme Court, **assessing the guilt or innocence of Trump complaining about his violation of the Presidential oath of Office?** That oath provides for **"to the best of my ability, preserve, protect and defend the Constitution of the United States?"** Judges are also humans with feelings. Even while they are wearing black robes.

And common sense dictates that **Kavanaugh the volcanic and Kavanaugh the judge are inseparable.** In the words of former President Harry Truman: **"If you haven't got common sense, you shouldn't get out of bed in the morning."**

Sadly, one should ask: **"Is the US Supreme Court for sale?"** If not, what prompts the Senate majority leader Mitch McConnell to say something to the effect of **"We shall plow forth with the Kavanaugh nomination?"**

September 27, 2018 and October 5 and 6, are dates that shall live in the annals of infamy. For they are pivot points for a **besmirched Supreme Court, a highly dysfunctional US Congress, and a President who has been called by many, including one of his former Cabinet members, "an idiot."** In today's American democracy, whose mainstays are **"The Rule of Law,"** and a robust system of **"checks and balances,"** those checks and balances do neither check nor balance.

The all-out war America has witnessed as of September 27, must have also terrified Chief Justice John G. Roberts, a devoted custodian of the court's prestige.

In 2016, the Chief Justice has concluded from a series of confirmation hearings, that those hearings were hobbled by rancorous partisanship: **"We don't work as Democrats or Republicans. And I think it's a very unfortunate impression the public might get from the confirmation process."**

Well, justice and fairness are largely about perception. They are not codified. There is a difference between "justice" and "law." Within that mix of perceptions, one factor looms large: President Trump is unhinged. A clown. And when you elect a clown, you get a circus!!

In an attempt to energize his supporters in West Virginia, **Trump the Clown, on September 29,** viciously mocked Senator Dianne Feinstein, Democrat of California and the ranking member of the Senate Judiciary Committee. Later, he mocked Kavanaugh's accuser, **Dr. Christine Blasey Ford. The President of the US, who is personally accused by 16 women of sexual offenses, naturally sided with his soul-mate, Kavanaugh.**

The President of the United States depicted Feinstein as confused before he turned on her party, saying: **"You see the meanness, the nastiness. They don't care who they hurt ... in order to get power and control."**

Words from a man whose whole life has been about self-aggrandizing. America of today is not the America intended to be by its great founders. The world laughed at Trump, the face of America, to his face at the UN on September 25.

Yet Trump and his aides insist that the world was laughing with him. Dream on!!

THE AMERICAN PRESIDENT IS "ANALFABETO" (IN SPANISH: "ILLITERATE")

Friday, November 9, 2018

Franklin Roosevelt articulated courage -the ability to withstand danger. **That was in the aftermath of Pearl Harbor (1941).** John Kennedy addressed **the commitment to country.** It was in his inaugural address (1961). Bush Jr. **roused the nation to seek out its 9/11 attackers** (2001). Judging by these lofty standards, it is not far fetched to **describe Trump as ANALFABETO.**

For Trump is **unable to read or write.** How do we know that? He consistently is marked by a lack of acquaintance with approved patterns of speaking or writing. So when he rounds up his lips, rocks on any podium right and left, grimaces to his wild supporters hinting at a non-recognizable smile, **his illiteracy gushes forward. Proving a very low IQ.**

About the effects of a hurricane on Puerto Rico, he blames the ineffectiveness of federal aid on the existence of **"Water - Big Water."** The same trait shows again at a recent rally in Montana by his base **(he has a fan club -not the presidential domain of All Americans).** So he praises Montana as **"the Big Sky."**

Trump's ignorance shows again when he struggles to foist the incredible hoax of his being a nuclear expert. **"My uncle, was an MIT scientist."** Then unabashedly added: **"I know about nuclear matters more than the Generals."** The tragedy of not knowing is not knowing what you don't know.

Our analfabeto president relies on imbecilic phrases -pleasing to the ear, faulty to reality. Campaigning for Republican victories in the mid-term elections, he attacks the Democrats as **"the Democratic Mobs,"** and salutes the Republican candidates as **"the Republican: Jobs."** Being the agent of combative divisiveness in America is his calling.

When Trump is pinned down by media questions about his sources, he yells back: **"Many people told me so."** And when he faces a follow-up question, his patent answer: **"You go find out."** Evasiveness is his nuclear option.

As to **"Fake News,"** he is the premier savant of fake news. **It is his sword and his armor.** Anticipating the impact of the Mueller investigations, if they are allowed to reach their conclusions, he sows the seeds of mistrust and disbelief. His way, really his entrapment, of getting off the legal hooks. So he repeats **"No obstruction; no collusion."**

Tagging any opponent of Trump by a Trumpian epithet has been elevated by this American President to **an industrial mass level.** He mocked Hillary Clinton as **"crooked Hillary;"** abused Jeb Bush as **"low energy Jeb;"** denounced John McCain as **"only a hero because he was captured;"** abused Stormy Daniels, his former lover as **"horse face."**

In a Nazi-style attempt to intimidate opponents, he and General Flynn, his convicted former national security advisor, whipped up their mobs into yelling **"Lock Her Up;"** her is **Hillary Clinton. Recruiting Russia as his ally in the elections of 2016,** he intones: **"Russia -Are you listening?"** Both Putin of Russia and Kim Jong-Un, of North Korea, are **"friends."** But Trudeau of Canada is an adversary whose country is **"ripping off America."**

This analfabeto looks upon America's security in terms, not of **"strength through alliances;"** but in terms of **"why are we still contributing funds towards NATO's defense of Europe?"** His superficial view of strategic alliances, such as those with South Korea and Japan is limited to **"how much it costs?"** Hence his present strained relationship with General Mattis and the Pentagon.

So is his near daily attacks on the now gone Attorney-General, **Jeff Sessions,** and his deputy, **Rod Rosenstein. "I don't have an Attorney-General,"** nor a **"Department of Justice."** His low regard for these institutions is due to **his stupid belief that they are his personal lawyers.** He rationalizes that their job is to protect him. **They owe a**

loyalty oath to him, not to the USA.

Among Trump's forward **"storm troops"** to his rallies are **agents who sell MAGA hats (Make America Great Again), for $25.** Others sell a book of the President's tweets for $35 each. The title is **"Just the Tweets;"** agents rehearse their pitches the night before these rallies. Trumpist volunteers wearing lime green T-shirts, declaring **"Voter Resistance,"** walk the crowds.

One supporter declares his faith in these terms: **"I'm not a Trump supporter out of anger or hate."** Then out of what? **"He's a really good performer. He directs that excitement to policies that are really good for us."** This analfabeto, otherwise known to his base as **"The Voice of Good,"** approaches the well rehearsed crowd, a paid agent announces: **"Ladies and gentlemen, please welcome the President."**

Trump, with clenched fists, declares, as he did recently in Iowa on October 9: **"The Democrat agenda is radical socialism and open borders."** The same theme has been used before. In Maryland, Trump declared: **"Republicans want to protect Medicare. Democrats want to raid Medicare to pay for their socialism."**

Sheer lies. The Democrats program is to expand **"Medicare for all."** But the well-practiced agents of **fascist Trump** never tire of informing their cohorts: **"If you don't send the Republicans back to the House and back to the Senate, it'll be tough on the president's soul!!"**

But the soul of this President seems to be fixed on the preparation for a sort of an eventual civil war. As a prelude, Trump glorifies street violence. And weaponizing the freedom of speech. Just go read **"The Plot to Destroy Democracy,"** a great book by **Malcolm Nance.**

Trump, since his non-merited elevation to the presidency, has amply demonstrated that he was totally unsuitable to lead. On Afghanistan, for example, he believes that his generals are weak. **"There's no victories,"** he lamented. **"You should be killing guys. You don't need a strategy to kill people."**

In response to the craziness of this analfabeto, **Rex Tillerson, then the Secretary of State,** blurted out his assessment at the end of a cabinet meeting. **"He's a fucking moron."** Trump had already left the meeting.

Under Trump, the unthinkable is happening to the US. A great country is becoming a failed State!! The main characteristic of a failed state **is the absence of process for decision-making and policy-coordination.** Epitomized by what Trump himself had said: **"I alone can fix it."** Trump claims that he is very smart. Not by any measure. This ANALFABETO had **personally gone bankrupt not once, not twice, but six times!!**

Trump is a perpetual congenital liar. Surpasses even Goebbles. Like all snake oil salesmen, Trump is masterful in delivering his lies. If one believes in his delivery, one would have been duped in buying false merchandise. He sells fear and divisiveness. And facts are his adversary.

In these mid-term elections, Trump's party (the Republican Party) lost in a big way to the Democrats. **Nearly 40 seats in the House of Representatives alone.** Trump's warning regarding **"a caravan"** from Central America about to invade the southern border, **turned into a big caravan of voters expressing their disgust with him.**

Trump's reaction: **"A victory,"** referring to the Senate which is still with a Republican slim majority. But, Mr. analfabeto, **you lost the House which shall reign you in -with subpoenas and demands for your tax returns.** Not to mention the outcome of the Mueller investigations.

The noose is tightening!!

TO ACHIEVE ORDERED LIBERTY, GOVERNANCE AND RELIGION HAVE TO BE KEPT APART

Friday, November 16, 2018

We begin with a quote from a great American jurist. Chief Justice Warren Burger of the Supreme Court (1969-1986) said: "Ever since people began living in tribes and villages, they have had to balance order with liberty. Individual freedom had to be weighed against the need for security for all."

Lofty words uttered by Burger in his capacity as Chairman of the Commission on the Bicentennial of the U.S. Constitution (1987). That Constitution has massively influenced the separation between governance and religion. Its First Amendment, the first of ten Amendments. In their collectivity, they are called "The Bill of Rights," which were ratified in December 1791.

Here follows what the First Amendment states:
"Congress shall make no law respecting an establishment of religion, or prohibiting the free exercise thereof; or abridging the freedom of speech, or of the press, or the rights of the people peaceably to assemble, and to petition the Government for a redress of grievance."

In the same vein, the UN Charter, as agreed in San Francisco in June 1945, reiterated the need for not taking religion as a criterion in human affairs. Its Article I, paragraph 3 reads as follows:
"To achieve international cooperation in solving international problems of an economic, social, cultural, or humanitarian character, and in promoting and encouraging respect for human rights and for fundamental freedoms

for all without distinction as to race, language, or religion."

The provisions above represent the summit of values to be observed by all societies and nations with one objective in mind: Keep faith in your heart, not on your sleeve. Don't brandish your religion as a global measure for approved human interaction. It does not work. Faith is not subject to negotiation or compromise. But man-made policies are concrete human products which are subject to alteration, negotiation, and accommodation.

That is where evangelism fails that global test. It claims some mythical superiority as regards to "human salvation." Salvation is for the hereafter not for the "now." The road to "the hereafter" is chosen by personal selection. But the road to "the now" is dictated by changing circumstances.

How is "evangelism" defined? Here is a general wording for it, not to denigrate it, but to keep it out of the global march towards international cooperation. Here is a reading of its omnibus meaning:
"Evangelic is teaching of the Gospel. Mainly in line of the Protestant school maintaining that the essence of the Gospel consists in the doctrine of salvation by faith. Also by good works and sacraments having no saving efficacy."

But evangelicals, otherwise knows as "the Christian Right" put God in the voting booth!! Their premier American spokesman is Ralph Reed of the Faith and Freedom Coalition. In September 2018, he boasted of the organizing power of the Christian Nationalist movement. That was at the Values Voters Summit where he wrongly predicted the failure of the Blue Wave (the capture by the Democrats of either or both the House and the Senate).

But his prediction was gone with the wind at the mid-term elections of Nov. 6. The Democrats, gaining nearly 40 new seats, have gained the House of Representatives. Reed's prophecy of "They (the Democrats) are going to be more shocked than they were the last time (2016)." Reed's prophetic utterance was as faulty as that of the Muslim Brotherhood in Egypt which claimed "legitimacy" in spite of the massive Egyptian crowds in June 2013 calling for it to disappear (IRHAL).

No amount of dollars spent by the Christian Nationalist movement in support of their choice for president, Trump, could avert the blue coup against the fascism of "America First" (America Uber Alles). It is estimated that movement, relying on an extensive network of conservative pastors, within the so-called "Family Research Council" had invested $18 million in

2018, up from $10 million in 2016, and $5 million in 2014.

The entire evangelical movement, which goes by various names including "Watchmen on the Wall," represents a regression from the Constitutional provision for separation between Church and State. Some of its by products are the walls represented by Muslim bans; but also by the barbed wire walls deployed at America's southern border against Central American asylum seekers.

At a rally in the State of Montana, Trump, the product of the concoction of political/evangelist/right, described that new wire wall as "the beautiful barbed wire." With military forces deployed at those borders to, ostensibly to block those migrants from "invading" the US, the cost is expected to reach $200 million. There is no specific budgetary allocation for that. But the out of control Commander In Chief (Trump) needed that foolish deployment as a political stunt.

In this lawless environment of the Trump era which is underpinned by evangelism, it is no surprise to hear J.C. Church, Watchmen on the Wall's national director to preach before November 6: "The No. 1 thing anybody can give you is the Supreme Christ. But the second greatest thing we can give this generation is the Supreme Court." Thus the evangelical needle is threaded to go from the voter, to Trump, to Congress, to the Supreme Court (as could be evidenced by the elevation of Kavanaugh to the 9th seat of the Supreme Court. What a difference between the Supreme Court of Burger and that of Roberts where 5 conservatives are aligned against 4 liberals. Kavanaugh has advocated the equivalency of "the President is above the law."

The degree of the popular rejection of the thesis of the evangelicals in the November mid-term elections could be measured by the lamentation of one of their leaders. Tami Fitzgerald, the executive director of the North Carolina Values Coalition told a pastors' meeting: "If we lose three seats to progressives, the whole Congress could be lost."

With this background of the marriage between faith and politics in view, it is no surprise to find the mindless President Trump, the creatures feature of that unconstitutional betrothal sulking in Paris at the 100th anniversary of World War I. Not only is he confronted by a hostile House of Representatives where articles of impeachment are already being considered. His elevation of "nationalism" over globalism has been forcefully rejected by this host, France's president Macron.

"Patriotism is one's love of country. Nationalism is hate of the other," said Macron with support of German Chancellor Merkel. To Trumpism, Macron and Merkel are the past. Putin and Kim Jong-Un are the future. The false dawn, as the Arabs say, that prods the human caravan to resume its trek, only to be enveloped later in total darkness.

So what do houses of worship do in the face of American law preventing them from campaigning for political causes? Otherwise they may lose their tax exemption status!! Leaders of the Christian nationalists are struggling to find a way out of this legal dilemma.

To their rescue, comes pastor Tami Fitzgerald. "I am telling you, you can talk about issues all day long as a pastor; you can tell people who you are going to vote for," She intoned. "But you must not publish that information in a church newsletter or state it from the pulpit."

Sheer chicanery -legal trickery, sophistry. Freedom of speech of the Constitution's First Amendment cannot overwhelm the injunction against "Congress shall make no law respecting an establishment of religion."

Evangelism, by its advocacy and operational intent, is establishing a political religious order -an enabler of a regressive political chaos, otherwise called "Trumpism!!"

Perspectives on Egypt, Islam and the Dark Era of Trump

ADOPTING A MUSLIM BROTHERHOOD REFRAIN: BRAINLESS TRUMP CALLS EL-SISI "A F... KILLER!!"

Friday, November 30, 2018

Really, Donald?! In October alone, you lied eleven-hundred times. By calling El-Sisi a killer, **you deserve a membership card in the Muslim Brotherhood!!** Congratulations!! You and Mohamed Morsi are soul mates - **habitual liars.** Both of you hold no belief in the values of your respective countries: America and Egypt.

Trump's falsehood calling El-Sisi a killer is now placed in two contexts: The **"truth"** context; and the **"leadership comparison"** context.

I am not a spokesman for the president of Egypt; have never met him; not paid by him; **but voted for him.** Trump has a megaphone -the bully pulpit of the White House. **El-Sisi has no lobby in the U.S.** Has no public relations firm in America. So let my voice, my blog, voice what I know **to be the bare facts.**

In the **"truth"** context, Donald Trump has lied to America at the rate of 30 to 40 lies daily. **That is a world record. Surpassing** even that of Hitler's propaganda minister, **Joseph Goebbels.** But with a difference: Goebbels used the big lies technique. His American clone, Trump, trades in **"retail."** Saturating the market. And that is the president of the U.S. who came to power, not through popular majority. But through an anachronism in the U.S. Constitution **-the Electoral College.**

By comparison, El-Sisi, to the best of my knowledge, has never lied to **the**

103 million Arabs who call themselves "Egyptians." A full one-third of the Arab nation. Does not make things up. Does neither exaggerate, nor conflate.

The Islamic adage bequeathed to 1.7 billion Muslims by Abu-Bakr, the First successor of the Prophet Muhammad says: **"Truth is a sacred trust. Lying is an abominable betrayal."**

El-Sisi was selected by Mohamed Morsi to the post of Defense Minister for his abiding by Islamic rules of conduct. There is no greater distance morally or ethically between Trump and El-Sisi!! **The former is a congenital liar; the latter is a habitual truth expounder.**

Now to the **"leadership comparison"** context. Trump rules by fear. In an interview as a presidential candidate, he said: **"Real power is -I don't even want to use the word -fear."** On the opposite side, stands El-Sisi as he assures Egypt to **fear neither the terrorist attacks in Sinai, nor the slow progress from a weak economy to an emerging economy,** now fuelled by the discovery of vast fields of natural gas.

On freedom of trade, stupid Trump claims without evidence, **that the outside world is ripping America off;** that the World Trade Organization is the **"worst"** ever international organization; **that Canada, Mexico, and China should be punished by high tariffs on steel and aluminum.**

Then look at El-Sisi: delivered a Second Suez Canal; bolstered trade with Africa, the Arab homeland, the European Union (including Greece and Cyprus). Stationed an aircraft carrier at the southern end of the Red Sea to **ensure freedom of navigation.**

On the use of the military, Trump presides over a country which is uncertain about the use of its armed forces. To stay in nearly 120 countries, or to retrench. If staying, the host countries, including South Korea, Japan, and Germany should, as Trump demands, **pay up the defense cost.** If leaving, Trump is shifting the rules of engagement with the Taliban. Namely: abandonment. **If Trump believes in what he says, then why does he, on November 10, scold President Macron of France for calling for the protection of Western Europe by building a European army?!** Trump who insults daily, ludicrously called Macron's suggestion an insult!!

But El-Sisi, a distinguished general and commander in chief, has no such problems. The only Egyptian forces abroad are those volunteered to the

UN Peace-keeping operations.

For Trump, treaties are to be shredded with abandon. He exited the Iran nuclear deal; the Paris Accord on climate change; the Trans Pacific Partnership, and the North American Free Trade Association (NAFTA).

By contrast, Egypt has never abandoned an international agreement. Never!! Even in regard to the Suez Canal treaty. Nasser, in 1956, did not nationalize the Canal (it is sovereign territory not subject to nationalization). **He nationalized the Suez Canal Company. All shareholders were fully compensated.**

By his utterances and executive orders, **Trump is an avowed racist.** El-Sisi presides over a country in which the color of skin varies from white to brown, to black. All equal under the law. Dark color is even celebrated in Egyptian songs: **"Asmar Ya Samarah!!"**

By contrast, Trump's father was a member of the Ku Klux Klan. And he and his Donald, have denied Afro-Americans renting any of their apartments in Queens, New York.

Compare this to Egypt, a country which prides itself for **its membership in the African Union (the AU).** But Trump has called those countries **"shithole countries."** In the mold of a confirmed liar, he denied saying it. One of his lap dogs, **Senator Lindsey Graham mocked that denial to Trump's face. "You said it, Mr. President."**

They say that **inside each bully is a coward. Fear is the bully's weapon.** Trump, in desperate search for matters to frighten American citizens, has found in his tool kit: **immigration. "The caravan from Central America is about to invade our southern borders. Middle Easterners are among them. Tough fearsome men."**

Trump has shirked his duty to serve in the military. But suddenly he became America's savior from **"the brown people's invasion."** That caravan is no more than a bunch of poor refugees fleeing their countries in search for a better life.

Trump's foolish claims were rebutted by his predecessor. Obama, referring to Trump's deploying US military to **"confront the caravan,"** described that deployment as **"a political stunt."** Trump called on the military to respond to any stone throwing by **"rifle fire." A war crime.** Again to Obama in the opposition: **"Our military deserves better."**

As to Egypt, **thousands of Syrians and Iraqis have been peacefully integrated within** Egyptian society. And the danger to America did not come from **"Middle Easterners."** But from American white misfits with assault rifles, condoned by mixing fictitious fear with the amity between the Republican party and the National Rifle Association.

On women and youth, the difference between Trump and El-Sisi could not be more stark.

Trump, on video, is recorded gloating over his inclination to grab women by their genitals. **"When you are a celebrity, they let you do it."** In Moscow, **the Russians have videoed him in the company of prostitutes in his hotel room.** And youth for Trump, are mere props with Trump's hats in rallies screaming for the blood of his adversary.

El-Sisi, by contrast, is a pious person, a family man, with one-third of his Cabinet made up of able women. And when it comes to youth, just study **El-Sisi's regular jamborees with youth.** Being inspired by the ethos of public service for country and community. Their motto is **"Long Live Egypt"** (Tahiya Misr). Not the dark motivator induced by Trump (**"America First"**). Meaning: America for the whites only. There is no **"Egypt First"** in the Egyptian public discourse.

When it comes to the judiciary, **Trump's goal is to extend his sticky fingers of control to the Supreme Court.** Thus translating **"a More Perfect Union"** into **"control of the three branches of government."** What a relief that Trump's Republican Party has **lost the House of Representatives in the mid-term elections.**

The battle for confirming Judge Kavanaugh for the Supreme Court was won for one obvious but faulty reason: **"The President cannot be prosecuted."** An affront to the Constitution, though now condoned by an Acting Attorney-General. But is **expected to be soon overwhelmed by the results of the investigation by the Special Counsel, Robert Mueller,** in the Trump campaign's alleged collusion with Russia in its cyber attack on America.

By contrast, the Egyptian Constitution of 2014, is fully observed as it states in Article 184 that **"interference in matters of justice is a crime with no statute of limitation (SOL)."**

Chief of Staff, General John Kelly, has found that Oval Office business and **decision making was haphazard, chaotic.** In his book, on Trump in the White House, Woodward quotes Kelly saying: **"The President's unhinged."** And **"The President just really doesn't understand anything."**

Does calling El-Sisi an **"F... killer"** merit devoting this entire blog posting to it as a rebuttal? **Yes, if you take the propaganda of the Muslim Brotherhood into account!!**

That epithet comes straight from the idiotic propaganda resulting from the failure of the Brotherhood's **attempt to convert Egypt from a secular State into an Islamic emirate.**

Let us here recall that the Brotherhood responded to the 30 June 2013 Egyptian Revolution by trying to **hold the country hostage.**

After the dismissal of **Morsi as a failing ideological president,** the Brotherhood's goons besieged Cairo by **occupying two central public squares: Rabaa and El-Nahda. For 6 weeks,** that siege went on, challenging the security forces to clear those rebellious enclaves.

More than 800 persons, including police officers, were killed. Since its inception in 1928, the Brotherhood's ideology included self-victimization **"in the name of God."** Its call for **"dying in the name of God is our fervent hope"** is a pre-destination intent.

El-Sisi killed nobody. The Islamists died needlessly in that confrontation. In legal practice, we call this **"suicide by the police,"** through the **"assumption of risk."**

Trump's adoption of the Brotherhood's hopeless call for a fresh rebellion brands that brainless man a Quixotic figure. **Trump, though showing outward amity to El-Sisi, is a brainless fool for whom friendship is only a way of self-ingratiation.**

The 19th century **French philosopher, Ernest Renan** provided an apt definition of **"a nation." A nation is a soul,** a spiritual principle. **In the age of Trump, principles are mere soap bubbles floating in the air.** An air-filled cavity.

As is well known, Trump is known to be obsequious toward Putin of Russia. In the language of intelligence, Trump's role in this regard is known as that of **"the useful idiot."**

By contrast, the President of Egypt is nobody's useful idiot.

An American friend of mine has reminded me of something regarding the history of America's presidents of whom Trump is Number 45. He wrote: **"We have had a lot of dumb presidents. But I am not sure any of them (prior to Trump) have thought themselves brilliant!!"**

THE RULE OF LAW VS. THE RULE OF TRUMP!!

Friday, December 7, 2018

By nearly all accounts, this is a dark period in American history. **By choices made by a real estate deal maker, called Donald Trump, America stands alone in a world of diversity.** The deal maker has proved to be a deal breaker. From the sanity of prior administrations, we are now **in a cold war with China, compliant with the whims of Russia, in an attack mode towards Canada and Mexico.**

Gone with the wind **"Make America Great Again."** Why? It was only an empty and destructive slogan. Its primary evisceration has been due to the fact that **the Rule of Law has been confronted at every corner by the Rule of Trump.** An America, under that unhinged man is threatened by being disemboweled of its true vibrancy -a Rules-based government.

Trump's wreaking ball was programmed to **hit people's trust in the Constitution and laws as a first target.** His early mentor, Steve Bannon opined that **"the destruction of the Administrative State"** is priority No. One. When they softened that term, the Trumpists began to refer to **"the deep State"** interlaced with conspiracies. **The court system, as a by-product of the Constitution became an inviting target.**

Upon his inauguration as President in January 2017, Trump has violated his Oath of Office. Under the Constitution, he has sworn that he will **"to the best of my ability, preserve, protect and defend the Constitution of the United States."** (Article II, Section I). However prior to that inauguration, Trump has **publicly called on Russia to interfere in the 2016 elections** to tip the scales against Hillary Clinton.

That call was never rescinded; in fact it was **followed up by praise for Putin,** one on one meeting with Putin, and by **indicting Michael Flynn, his first national security advisor,** by Special Counsel Robert Mueller on a variety of charges relating to connections to both Russia and Turkey.

The unlawful attempts by Trump to sabotage the independence of both the Department of Justice and the FBI backfired in two directions: The President failed to get FBI Director James Comey either to pledge loyalty to him personally, or to go easy on investigating **"a good man"** (Flynn), eventuated in the dismissal of Comey.

After publicly asserting that that dismissal was the result of **"that Russia thing"** (to quote Trump), **the unthinking President** put that action at the wrong door: **Comey's handling of the Hillary Clinton's run for the presidency** -Comey's unfortunate divulging immediately prior to the 2016 elections that Hillary was under investigations (because of an innocuous finding in the emails of a former aide **-Huma Abedin.**

These patterns of illegal violations under the Rule of Trump could not be separated from his championing of the **"Birther Movement."** That phony non-issue was **hurled at the legitimacy of Trump's predecessor - President Obama.** That issue's central claim was that Obama was not born in the US, but in Kenya. It was contrived to cast Trump's predecessor as not a **"person (who was not) a natural born citizen"** (Article I, Section I of the Constitution).

When Trump was confronted by **"the long form"** of Obama's birth certificate from Hawaii, he hid in his usual rabbit hole. Claiming that **"many people told me that,"** or **"documents can be forged,"** Trump's wreaking ball was targeting the trust of the populace in the legitimacy of its constitutional system.

That fraud by Trump, which had all the hallmarks of a dishonest trickery (the crafty underhanded ingenuity) **had one aim: Deception as a means of shaking the pillars of faith of the American people in their system of governance.** For the production of an **"interloper"** occupying the White House was one of the many instruments in Trump's tool-box **to induce suspicion in the electoral system.**

Those Trump shenanigans paved the way to the hallucinating claims under the Rule of Trump of **"fake news."** That mantra became a crafty **Trump mischievous activity -an industry.** The press and the media were now declared by the Trump's Oval Office **"enemy of the people."**

"Fake news" were Trump's response to the Constitutional call in its first Amendment to **"no law ... abridging the freedom of the press."** Only a fake president like **Trump could not comprehend that the press is for the governed not the government.** His fear of the truth forces him to look upon **reality as a worthless imitation passed off as genuine.**

Under the Rule of Trump, the curtailment of another Constitutional right to **"the freedom of speech"** is a presidential prerogative. For he, being an alien to any vehicle or voice of documented news, such as CNN, **catapults him in the dictatorial zone of Nixonian cover-ups.** No surprise. Trump's aspiration to the demise of democracy makes him aspire **to reinvent America in the mold of North Korea.**

Trump's concept of **"my base"** rejects the notion that a president has only one base as large as the entire American population. He was not elected to take care of 49 million people who support him, but of 340 million co-citizens. **His abstention from condemnation of neo-Nazism, anti-Semitism, and racism has provided a redundancy of evidence of his being unfit to be president.**

The ban on Muslims, representing an unconstitutional joining of religion and the State, **was rejected by the US judiciary.** So in true form to **his soul-mate, Goebbels of the Nazi era,** another language had to be used to **cover his religious fascism.** Thus the term of **"Middle Easterners"** became a dog-whistle to his base that national security was at peril because of Muslims (i.e. Middle Easterners).

But isn't the Muslim region one of the primary locations for Trump, his family, and his organization to make more money? Yes, it is. But Trump, from the get-go, **has regarded the Supreme Executive as above the law.** So what if the Constitution, in Article II, Section I provides that **"The President ... shall not receive within (his tenure) any other Emolument...?!"**

Trump has made it public that the law is an impediment; that **"I can run the country and my company at the same time;"** and that **higher rents from foreigners as tenants at his hotels or clubs cannot be regarded as "emoluments."** Nor can the use of the **White House (which is the people's house)** as a sales area, like Macy's in New York City, for his daughter, Ivanka's clothes and jewelry. All of this is forbidden under the emoluments clause.

Like her father, Ivanka became a Senior Advisor to the president, and a salesperson at the same time. **Is Ivanka a presidential staffer whose security clearance is limited by the law, or is she an admittee to meetings where only those with high security clearance are enabled to be participants?** In Bob Woodward's book on Trump, "Fear," the issue of defining Ivanka was the subject of a **"shout-out."** It was **between Bannon and Ivanka** who defied Bannon by shouting **"I shall never be a staffer."**

Total vagueness!! The very environment in which the Trump's presidency lives its daily life. Such as: **Is the Department of Justice intended as personal lawyers for the Presidency? No!!** But this is what Trump fancied Eric Holder, Obama's attorney general to be. In the fashion of medieval kings, Trump had told Obama that he **admired how Holder had protected him. Obama's response is reported to have been that the position of an attorney-general is to protect the people.**

These are alien thoughts to Trump. His life parameters have always been, not external, but internal. **And law to Trump is an externality -an imposition on the whims of a crafty potentate.** This was reflected in many ways, including his firing of Jeff Sessions as attorney general. For appropriately recusing himself from the Mueller investigation of Russia meddling in the 2016 American elections and beyond, **Sessions has been viewed by Trump as a traitor.**

For a replacement, crazy Trump picked up an Acting Attorney General, Whitaker, (now gone). His main qualification was that he had publicly advocated that the **Mueller probe was an over-reach, thus illegitimate.**

That appointment was violative of the law. It does not comport with the Constitution's Appointments clause. Nor does it accord with the 1998 Federal Vacancies Reform Act.

Clashing with Trump on the meaning of judicial independence, **Chief Justice John Roberts of the US Supreme Court struck back.** Trump had attacked a judge who had ruled against his asylum policy. The President called that federal judge **"an Obama judge."** In a dignified rebuttal, Roberts said on November 21: **"We do not have Obama judges or Trump judges, Bush judges or Clinton judges. That independent judiciary is something we should all be thankful for."**

And Trump was forced to provide written answers to Mueller's questions. **"Those were easy questions,"** Trump intoned. **"I did not need lawyers to help me answer them." Those were words worthy of the captain of a sinking regime.

A quiet military resistance to the impudence of Trump as Commander in Chief cannot be missed. **Its latest manifestations is the rebuke targeting Trump by retired Admiral William McRaven.** As the chancellor of the huge University of Texas system, that American hero characterized in Trump's attack on the news media in a graphic way. Trump's description of the media as the **"enemy of the people"** was **"the greatest threat to American democracy."**

As President, Trump knows only one form of sacrifice. Instead of **"one for all,"** it is **"all for Trump."** In the 2018 mid-term elections, Trump was not on the ballot. But at his rallies, he declaimed: **"A vote for (name of candidate) is a vote for me."**

He **lost the House of Representatives in spite of the gerrymandering and vote suppression.** But being of a psychopathic personality, Trump claimed **"a near perfect victory."** To his delusional mind, **law is a dark cloud. It does not exist if you don't look at it!!**

In the final analysis, the Rule of Trump is expected to be overwhelmed by the Rule of Law. For the latter is in the DNA of this country. The former is a foreign transplant which shall be rejected by the American body politic!!

The avalanche of indictments and guilty pleas by top aides of Trump tells us that the dawn is about to vanquish the Trump dark era.

DR. YASSIN EL-AYOUTY, ESQ.

Perspectives on Egypt, Islam and the Dark Era of Trump

BELOW THE MASON-DIXON LINE THERE IS ANOTHER AMERICA WITH A MIND OF ITS OWN

Friday, December 21, 2018

Call it what you may. Trump Land has a mind of its own. That is where 49 million Americans live. This is the other America which **"the progressives"** choose not to see. But they are there. **Living under two flags:** The Stars and Stripes (for the USA), and the Confederate flag for the region below the Mason-Dixon line.

That other America refuses to be ignored. It has its own ethos, its own version of history, its **own heroes, including General Robert E. Lee and Donald Trump.** This is the so-called **"Base"** which fills Trump's lungs with lots of oxygen. Yes, their highest level of education is probably a high school certificate. But they are very vocal.

Where is the mind of that **"other America?"** What is their symbiotic relationship with **Donald Trump -America's mad emperor?** Why are they sticking with him? Why does he exult in their presence? Especially when they are wearing his hat proclaiming **MAGA (Make America Great Again)** -A kind of swastika, not in a symbol, but in letters.

Here is what they think, what they passionately believe in, what propels them to say **"Trump is the greatest American President,"** even as they lose jobs. Their sincerity is **pathetic -but cannot be overlooked.**

"Build The Wall!!" They yell. Without a wall on the southern border, they feel unsafe. When you ask them: **"Would Mexico pay for it?"** They do not stutter as they respond: **"It may."** What are their statistics on the benefit of calling for the wall? Ninety-percent has been the reduction in the number of **"those invading us from the south."** How about the central Americans fleeing north for fear of their lives? **"That is their problem. We have to keep Americans and our jobs safe from them."**

When you point out the devastation of climate change, such as Hurricane Harvey which decimated parts of the South, including Texas, they shrug it off. They mouth off what Trump has been proclaiming: **"It is a hoax." "Not man-made."** The Bible, to them, has replaced scientific studies regarding storms and hurricanes. **Devastation is a heavenly reminder to them to build it again. A symbol of death and resurrection.**

Is coal good or bad? To the other America, it is good. Good for jobs, good for energy, good for America. How about its effects on the environment, on health, on the landscape? Negligible, they say. **"When Hillary attacked coal, she attacked our livelihood, our way of life."** To them, smoke stacks are signs of progress, of America the manufacturer, America is bountiful.

"Are these your views also about oil exploration and refining?" No hesitation as they respond gleefully **"yes." "Otherwise,"** they add argumentatively, **"go back to America of old-America of horse and buggy."** They show off with the miles and miles of oil installations. To them, **when they smell oil, they smell money.** The same coveted odor.

How about God? **"Do you believe in God?"** -you ask? They look at you as if you were stark crazy. **"Jesus Is Alive,"** they respond, with their hands pointing at big signs **making that proclamation at the entrance to most of their towns. Revival singing is their connection to the Almighty,** and the words in their holy books are taken literally. Like in the case of Muslim Brotherhood which, since its inception in 1928 in Egypt, has tried to spread the belief that **"The Quran Is Our Constitution."**

Abortion in Trump Land is a violation of both the will of God, and of personal liberty. They regard life as beginning at conception. Roe v. Wade, as a case granting the right to abortion as **"a constitutional right,"** was wrongly decided. Reversing it by the same high court is a course correction. **"If you don't want children, give them to someone who can raise them,"** they insist. Yes we agree to the **death penalty for adults,** they point out, but not to fetuses which have no say until they are born.

"What do you think of Trump's support for people marching with swastikas on arm bands?" This is the right of those marching. The right to freedom of expression. They keep **"the leftists from the North out of our streets."** Without those defenders of our autonomy, **Government as an evil intruder,** would run our lives. The States are the decider, not Washington.

"Are you a racist when espousing that virulent type of nationalism?" No, is their quick answer. We are proud white Americans. And we shall defend the Trump call for **"America First"** at all costs. Even when it means that **"America is for Whites only."** Why? **"Because we believe that the Whites are supporting the non-Whites, by their tax dollars.**

And what do you think of removing the statues of southern generals, like Robert E. Lee, from your public squares? Indignantly they respond: **"This is atrocious. Those generals have fought for our freedom. They lived and died for us. This is our history. Don't obliterate our history. If you don't like our statues or our flag of the Confederacy, stay out of our midst. This is our part of the United States. Don't call what happens during the Lincoln presidency 'the civil war.' Call it by its real name: 'The War Between the States.'"**

Conclusion: The United States is at present, a divided country. The civil ware of old is now fought as **"a cultural civil war."** The demonstrators for **"the Blue Wave,"** (democrats winning in the midterm elections of November 6, 2018) are called **"the grand children of Nancy Pelosi"** (the former democratic House Speaker and the next, as of January 2019.)

Regardless of the outcome of the midterm elections which won for the Democrats 40 additional seats, **"the other America"** is not likely to fade away. The Trump's efforts at dividing this nation threatens to be lasting. **"Toward a More Perfect Union"** looks today to be a pie in the sky.

For the Republican party has now been coopted by Trump. Alas!! Hate, chaos, isolation from the world are the big signs of America of today. "Power Is Fear" -to quote Trump!! The other America with tattoos over its arms has espoused it.

DR. YASSIN EL-AYOUTY, ESQ.

ABOUT THE AUTHOR

Dr. Yassin El-Ayouty, Esq. is an attorney and professor of law and politics, residing in New York. He has a has a Ph.D. from New York University in international law and organization (1966); J.D.from Cardozo School of Law(1994). U.S. Fulbright Scholar (1952-1954); Recipient of N.Y.U. Founders Day Award, and Cardozo Faculty Award for Best Legal Writing. Member of American Bars and Federation of Arab Bars. Practising litigation in America and abroad. Served the UN for 32 years, including "Spokesman" during Algeria's independence war. Assisted Rafael Lemkin on genocide convention. And co-founded the UN Institute for Training and Research (1965). Directed Africa Division, UN Political Affairs. Advisor to Forbes Magazine for ten years. Established SUNSGLOW-Global Training in the Rule of Law in 1998. Adjunct Professor at Cairo Law. Distinguished Visiting Professor, Nova Law Center, Florida (1996-2002). Taught at Cardozo and Fordham Law (1996-2015). Presently at St.Francis College; Emeritus Professor at Stony Brook University, New York. Member of Al-Azhar's Council of Muslim Elders; Legal Advisor for UN Security Council affairs, Permanent Mission of the State of Kuwait, U.N. Author and blogger.

www.ingramcontent.com/pod-product-compliance
Lightning Source LLC
Chambersburg PA
CBHW021352210526
45463CB00001B/74